THE TRIAL OF PETER MANUEL

By the same author:
THE TRIAL OF JEANNIE DONALD

THE TRIAL OF
PETER MANUEL

The Man who Talked too much

by
JOHN GRAY WILSON

London
SECKER & WARBURG
1959

Printed in England by
Western Printing Services Ltd, Bristol
and first published 1959
by
Martin Secker & Warburg Ltd
7 John Street, London
W.C.1

To
N. W.

CONTENTS

CHAPTER   *page*

1. The Crimes—1956   11
2. The Crimes—1957–1958   23
3. The Indictment   34
4. The Trial—First and Second Days   45
5. The Trial—Third Day   63
6. The Trial—Fourth Day   77
7. The Trial—Fifth and Sixth Days   90
8. The Trial—Medical Evidence   106
9. The Trial—Inspector McNeill   111
10. "Manuel, QC"   128
11. The Crown Case Closed   139
12. The Defence Case   153
13. Manuel's Story   170
14. The Speeches   190
15. The Charge and Verdict   201
16. The Appeal   215
17. Some Problems   223
    Postscript   239

5

MAP OF DISTRICT

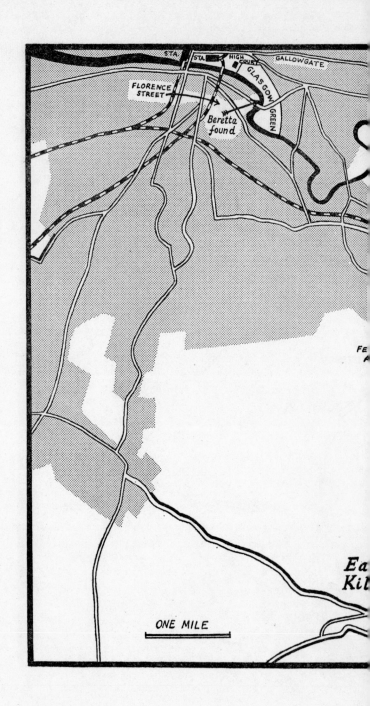

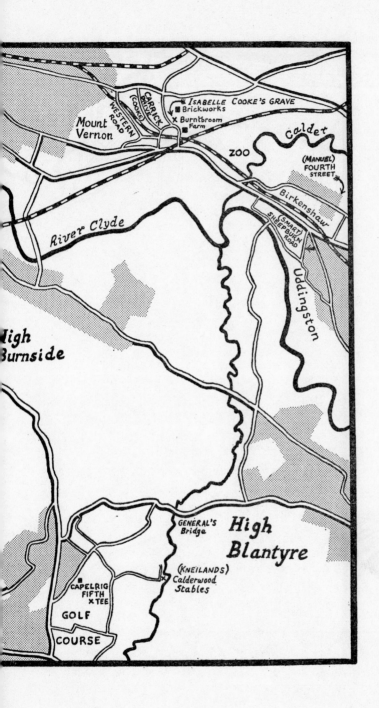

CHAPTER 1

THE CRIMES—1956

THIS is the story of a man who could not keep his mouth shut. It is the story of a patient police investigation which lasted over two years. It is the story of a trial unique in our criminal annals, a trial that brought face to face, one questioning from the dock and the other answering from a wheel chair, two men each accusing the other of the same three murders, two men with hate in their eyes.

To the east and south-east of Glasgow lies an expanse of Lowland Scotland whose natural features are pleasant enough —green fields, trees and hedges covering a gently undulating country through which run the River Clyde and a number of smaller streams. Parts of it are still pleasant enough, but it is always difficult to avoid the consciousness of industry, even where industry itself is invisible. At the back of one's mind there is the feeling that just round the next corner, or behind that clump of old trees, lies a coal-mine with its heaped spoil, or a brickworks, or a factory of some kind, for all these have been mixing with and swallowing up the farms.

The old villages too have been inexorably changing their character over many years. The first immigrants from the city built substantial grey stone villas. Their successors preferred red sandstone. There followed the inevitable rash of brick and roughcast bungalows, in row upon row of undistinguished and almost indistinguishable similarity, a similarity that is stressed rather than minimised by the variations from house to house, a similarity that seems to extend finally even to the trees that

11

stand in the gardens. Last come the council houses. The more recent of them, in appearance and more particularly in their siting, show a considerable improvement over their pre-decessors, public and private.

Not a very inspiring landscape? Frankly, no. And the people who live there are very much like the rest of us—most of them. But take a rectangle just over four miles from east to west and six from north to south, place it a little east of Glasgow and you have the scene of eight murders, all committed within two years. One man stood trial for them all—Peter Thomas Anthony Manuel.

This criminological paradise is easily reached from Glasgow. An appropriate starting point is the High Court, where the trial took place. This stands on the north bank of the Clyde, at the corner of Clyde Street and Saltmarket, opposite Glasgow Green. On the other bank of the river lies the notorious district of the Gorbals, now being demolished and rebuilt. We shall have to visit the Gorbals later. A quarter of a mile north by Saltmarket is Glasgow Cross, from which two streets run east-ward. The one to the north at first bears the sinister name of Gallowgate, then becomes Tollcross Road.

As the road leaves the city boundary, the countryside seems to open out and, about a mile further on, the bungalows of Mount Vernon appear on the slopes of higher ground on the north of the road. No 5 Carrick Drive, which lies on the far side of the railway, was the home of Isabelle Cooke, who was mur-dered on 28th December 1957. Her body was found buried in a newly-ploughed field on the adjacent farm of Burntbroom in the early hours of 16th January 1958.

Although we are beyond the boundaries of the city of Glas-gow, the Corporation's tramway system continues for a mile and a half past Mount Vernon to Calderpark Zoo. A minor road (B 7001) turns off to the left about a hundred yards after the terminus and in another half-mile we reach a group of council houses which extends for some distance along the north side of the road. This is Birkenshaw. At the extreme east end is No 32 Fourth Street, where Peter Manuel lived with his parents.

Look south from the road. Half a mile away, on the banks of the Clyde, you can see the town of Uddingston, on the main road a mile to the east of where we left it. The road which runs down to the south at the west end of the town is Sheepburn Road; and the first house on the left of Sheepburn Road is No 38. Mr and Mrs Peter James Smart and their eleven-year-old son Michael were murdered there on 1st January 1958.

A road running south from the main road, half-way between Uddingston and Calderpark Zoo, takes us to High Blantyre, where we turn right, along A 776, to East Kilbride, about eight miles from Uddingston. This developing satellite town of Glasgow has a layout of straight or gently curving main roads, with housing areas set well back from them, and there is a maze of roundabouts with pedestrian subways and overbridges, which forms a marked contrast with the unplanned pleasantness of the old village. Once there was a golf course, which lay to the east of the town, but this is rapidly being effaced by bulldozers and still more housing areas. On 2nd January 1956, Anne Kneilands was murdered in a narrow strip of trees which stood near the fifth tee.

This is the most southerly point of our tour and we can return to Glasgow by A 749. Before we reach the city, however, we pass High Burnside, some four and a half miles from the golf course. In July 1956 Mr and Mrs William Watt and their daughter Vivienne moved into a new house at 5 Fennsbank Avenue there. Two months later, while Mr Watt was away on a fishing holiday, Mrs Watt and Vivienne and Mrs Watt's sister, Mrs Brown, were murdered in that house.

Five miles more brings us back to the starting point of the tour—the High Court buildings. Twenty-six miles, no more, through this very ordinary urban and suburban landscape has been enough to show just how compact the area is—less compact, admittedly, than the square mile in Glasgow associated with the names of Madeleine Smith, Mrs McLachlan, Dr Pritchard and Oscar Slater: but, after all, the five murders for which these four were tried occurred over a period of fifty-one years. The eight murders for which Manuel was tried all fell within two years.

The story begins in East Kilbride on 4th January 1956. On the afternoon of that day George Gribbon, a forty-year-old labourer, was walking, as he regularly did, on the golf course. About three o'clock he went into the trees near the fifth tee to look for lost golf balls. There, lying in a hollow, was the body of a girl, her clothing disarranged and her head split open.

Gribbon paused only long enough to make sure that she was dead. He then went to some men working on one of the new roads in the district and asked them to telephone for the police. They did not seem interested—perhaps they thought the whole thing was a joke. Ordinary people find it hard to believe that they can be affected by crime and still harder to realise that they may be in on the beginning of a sensational murder case. So Gribbon had to telephone for the police himself.

Sergeant William Woods of the Lanarkshire County Constabulary soon arrived and the hunt was up. It did not take long to identify the dead girl as Anne Kneilands, a seventeen-year-old girl who had been living with her parents and a brother and sister in converted stables on the Calderwood estate, about a mile and a half away. Her father had reported her as missing on the previous day. On Friday 30th December she had been to a dance at the East Kilbride Town Hall with her sister Alice. They met two young men, Jim Harrow and Andrew Murnin, Andrew Murnin being Anne's partner. He arranged to meet her at six o'clock on Monday, 2nd January, at Capelrig Farm, a bus terminus near her home. Anne kept that appointment but Murnin did not. He went to a party and met some friends. Ungentlemanly conduct, perhaps, but things like that are apt to happen in Scotland at the New Year, especially with young men on leave from the services. The sense of time is easily blunted.

About 6.20 Anne called on the Simpsons, family friends who lived at the farm. According to witnesses, she was at the bus stop in time to catch the bus that left at 6.10, but she did not get on to it. Apparently, however, she told the Simpsons she had missed the bus. In any case, she was probably very disinclined to wait for thirty minutes in the cold of a January evening in the hope or expectation that Murnin would appear. She may have thought that, if he did arrive late, it would do him good to wait for her. At any rate she stayed with Mrs Simpson for only a quarter of an hour and left in good time to catch the 6.40 bus, which she got on alone.

Unusually for her, she had not told the Simpsons where she was going. But she told the conductress, whom she knew, that she was going to East Kilbride to meet a friend. Perhaps by this time she had concluded that Murnin had made a mistake about the place where they were to meet. She got off the bus at the Willow Café, a modern building near a corner where the new town meets the old. About 7.10, the driver of a bus running on the return journey to Capelrig saw Anne, whom he knew, at the Post Office at East Kilbride and had the impression that she was one of a dozen people who joined him there. What happened to her between that time (if she did in fact join the second bus) and her death is still officially a mystery.

A young attractive girl had been murdered. There were signs of a struggle and the marks of running feet on the ground, suggesting an attempt to escape. Her clothing was disarranged. One stocking and her knickers were missing. All seemed to indicate a sex crime, although medical examination disclosed no signs of any sexual interference. There was no arrest. Here were all the ingredients of a newsworthy story and the newspapers made the most of it, with stories and with photographs of any persons who seemed to be concerned. It is curious that most press photographs of the victim make her look small and dark, but in fact she was tall (five feet ten inches) and blonde.

One photograph which appeared in the press on 14th January showed Peter Manuel, one of the people the police had interviewed. If he had been seen with Anne Kneilands on the night of her murder, or indeed at any time, if he had even been in East Kilbride on the critical night, surely the police would have been told. But the picture brought no response.

Days, weeks, months passed. Appeals were made for four girls who had been seen talking to Anne at the café where she left the bus. It was reported that she had been seen talking to a young man in a low-slung car and also that she had been to a dance in Blantyre between ten o'clock and midnight with a tall, well-built man.

At the end of the month, seven Glasgow business men offered rewards amounting to £900 for information which would lead to the discovery of the murderer of either Anne Kneilands or Anne Steele, a fifty-five-year-old woman who was found battered to death in her flat in Dennistoun, Glasgow, on 11th January.

But no arrest was made and public interest as represented by the press died down. But the public interest represented by the police and the criminal authorities remained alive.

Within one week in September of the same year, three houses in Lanarkshire were broken into. Mr and Mrs Henry Platt and their son Geoffrey lived in a house at Bothwell, which is just outside the area of our main story. On 12th September they left for a fortnight's caravanning holiday in the Lake District. Three days later the police were called to the empty house, where a window had been broken.

Inside there was a scene of considerable disorder. A deed box, whose place was in Mr Platt's wardrobe, had been forced open and laid on a settee in the lounge. Some of its contents were stacked beside it, others were strewn about the floor. An empty soup tin and some soup were in a small pan in the kitchen. More soup was scattered about the floor and some was in a jug beside the bed in an upstairs bedroom. There was dirt, apparently from someone's boots, on the bedcover. There were holes in a quilt and a blanket, and the mattress had a slit, about seven or eight inches long, which looked as though it had been made by a pair of scissors. A pair was in fact lying on the floor near the bed.

Back in the kitchen there was another empty tin. The pears which it had contained were lying on the carpet; the juice had been drunk. Whoever had entered had apparently not felt the need for solid food. He or she was content with liquid refreshment of a perfectly innocent nature.

The police eventually got in touch with the family at Coniston on 18th September and they returned home. Here they found that a number of articles were missing, including a stopwatch or chronograph, some tools, an electric razor and a watch. More valuable articles, however, had been left untouched. The razor was of an experimental type produced by Phillips at their Hamilton factory. It was not on sale to the public but factory employees could buy them. One had been bought for Geoffrey Platt, the sixteen-year-old son of the house.

Again there was no arrest. The scene switches to High Burnside, first at No 18 Fennsbank Avenue, a house occupied by two sisters called Martin. They too had chosen the month of September for their holiday and on Saturday 15th September (the day on which the Platt burglary was discovered) they left for Wester Ross. Before they left, they carefully examined the fastenings of the windows and doors. Burglar catches were in place on the windows and the front door was secured, according to them, by no fewer than three locks—a Yale lock, an ordinary mortice lock and a "special lock". This does not agree with the evidence of Constable Steele, the first police officer on the scene. He did not mention any "special lock" and seems to have found the mortice lock unsecured. Perhaps the ladies exaggerated their security measures.

In any case their holiday was interrupted when the police called them back on Monday 17th September. Mrs Helen McNab, a neighbour with whom they left their keys during their absence, looked round the outside of the house on Saturday afternoon and found all in order. About 2.20 p.m. on Monday, Mrs Agnes Brown was walking in Fennsbank Avenue and stopped to chat with a friend. She let her visual attention wander and noticed that one of the glass panels in the front door had been broken. Sensibly she reported this at once to police officers who were busily engaged about sixty yards away at No 5.

Constable Steele was sent to carry out the preliminary investigations. He got the keys from Mrs McNab and went to the house, which he was able to enter by simply turning the key in the Yale lock.

Further investigation was left to the CID, who found inside the house disorder rather like that in the Platts' house—an open tin of soup, its contents spilled on the floor; an open tin

B

of spaghetti; orange peel and pips scattered about. Rooms had
been ransacked and their contents strewn in other rooms. There
were dirty footmarks at one end of the settee as though someone with dirty boots had been reclining at full length, and there
was a small burn mark on the carpet as if that person had
stretched out a lazy hand to stub a cigarette. Dirty footmarks
appeared also on one of the beds upstairs.

Some articles, not the most valuable, were later found to be
missing—four pairs of nylon stockings, a few shillings and two
gold rings. The rings were to be the subject of heated argument
at the trial and it cannot be said that their fate is at all clear.

As well as the glass panel in the front door, a window at the
back of the house had been broken. The inference drawn by
the CID was that the intruder had failed to get in by the window because of the burglar catch and had entered by the front
door, putting his hand through the broken panel and simply
turning the Yale handle inside.

The same method of entering had been used at No 5 Fennsbank Avenue, where police officers were already investigating
a more serious crime. The householder, William Watt, a new-
comer to the district who owned a large bakery business in
Glasgow, was enjoying a fortnight's fishing holiday at Lochgilphead, Argyll. But he had not left the house empty, for his
invalid wife and his sixteen-year-old daughter Vivienne stayed
behind. Mrs Margaret Brown, Mrs Watt's sister, was staying
with them.

On that Monday, 17th September 1956, Mrs Collison, the
daily help, arrived as usual about 8.45 a.m. Usually the back
door was unlocked when she arrived, as Vivienne, who was a
student at Skerry's College, had to leave before Mrs Collison
came. But on this morning it was locked. Mrs Collison looked
through the windows. They were still curtained, but by opening
them a little (burglar catches again) she could move the curtains
enough to see into Vivienne's bedroom. The girl seemed to be
sound asleep under a blanket. Knocking on the window failed
to rouse her.

Mrs Collison went to the front door and saw that a glass
panel had been broken. She looked through and saw that all

the interior doors, except that of the kitchenette, were open. A call through the broken panel to Mrs Watt brought no reply.

As she stood there, Mrs Valente appeared from next door. Then the postman, Peter Collier, arrived. He put his hand through the broken panel and turned the Yale handle. The door opened.

Mrs Collison and the postman went into the silent house. In the front bedroom Mrs Watt and Mrs Brown lay dead in bed, one bleeding from the nose and the other from the mouth, the bedclothes pulled tidily up to their necks.

Mrs Valente ran off as soon as Mrs Collison reported what she had seen. The postman asked where the telephone was and Mrs Collison told him. While he telephoned for the police, she went into the back bedroom. Vivienne lay in bed, the clothes pulled up over her head as Mrs Collison had already seen them through the window. What she had not then seen was a pillow saturated with blood.

Suddenly the silence was broken by three or four loud snores and Mrs Collison ran out to ask Collier to phone for an ambulance. He said they had better wait for the police, who arrived in twenty or thirty minutes. By that time Vivienne Watt was dead, shot through the head, like her mother and her aunt, at very close range.

The front room at first showed no signs of disorder. In Vivienne's room, however, clothing, some of it torn, and buttons and ribbons were strewn over the floor and furniture. A bedside lamp had been broken and the pieces scattered about. On the carpet there were a cigarette end, a spent match and the mark of a burn.

When the bedclothes were removed for examination of the bodies, it was found that Mrs Brown's pyjama trousers had been ripped from the waist-band down the right leg, presumably by the killer. Mrs Watt's nightdress had a small tear, but little significance could be attached to this, as it might have been caused by normal wear. Both bodies were lying in a natural position, as if they had been shot while sleeping and never moved.

Vivienne's room showed a very different picture. She was lying in an uncomfortable and unnatural position, one in which the medical experts thought she could probably not have slept. She was wearing only a pyjama jacket and a cardigan, both being buttonless. Her pyjama trousers, ripped and also without their buttons, were lying on top of the bed. Buttons lay about the floor. Again the inference was that the damage to her garments and the removal of the trousers had been forcibly done by her assailant. This was borne out by bruising on her body and thighs.

One minor sartorial mystery was never cleared up. Among the garments lying on the floor was a brassiere, torn in front and with the shoulder straps adrift, but its fastening intact, again as if it had been torn from her body. Had she been wearing it in bed?

Medical examination of all three women showed no signs of sexual interference. Vivienne was a virgin. The two older women had apparently died instantaneously about 6 a.m. or earlier, Vivienne about 9.30. But all could have been shot about the same time.

Mr Watt was told of the murders shortly before noon near Lochgilphead, where he was fishing. At first he did not seem to understand what had happened, then he collapsed weeping into a chair. A friend accompanied him in his car to Alexandria, Dunbartonshire, a few miles south of Loch Lomond, where he was met by officers of the Lanarkshire police. They took him to Rutherglen police station and a few days later he identified the three bodies in the Glasgow city mortuary.

Four murders, three housebreakings in nine months; the same disorderly vandalism, the same footmarks from a burglar who liked his ease in the Platts' and the Martins' houses; the same means of entry in the Martins' and the Watts' houses and, though this may be of little importance, the same use in each house of the carpet as an ashtray; the same interference with women's clothing without actual sexual interference in the Watt and the Kneilands murders. It is a curious chain that links these crimes together.

A further link, this time between the Watt murders and the Platt housebreaking, was to be discovered shortly before

Christmas 1957—more than a year later. You will remember that the damage done in the Platt house had included holes in the bedclothes and a slit in the mattress. Mrs Platt, like a good housewife, sewed up the slit and thought no more about it. About September 1957, she or her husband felt a hard lump in the mattress and, on reopening the seam, found a watch which had been missing since the invasion of their house. Another hard lump was felt just before Christmas. This was a bullet from a .38 revolver. Ballistic examination proved that it had been fired from the gun which had been used in the Watt murders.

The brutal murder of three defenceless sleeping women brought new terror to the neighbourhood and grist to the mills of the press. William Watt was several times interviewed by the police, the interviews lasting up to ninety minutes. He was also interviewed by the press, to whom he uttered threats of vengeance and promises of reward.

Superintendent Hendry of the Lanarkshire CID (now retired) also made several statements, but he always refused to comment on a series of reports that detectives had visited "a small hotel in the West of Scotland" for inquiries and had, on separate visits, removed an alarm clock and bedding for examination.

The usual rumours circulated. One, discounted as "100 per cent imagination" by a police spokesman, came from four boys who told the police that a scarfaced man had fired shots at them in a wood near the Watts' house and then thrown a knife. Oddly enough, a scarfaced man was in fact associated with the gun used in these murders.

Of the many suggestions made to help the police, perhaps the most interesting came from an anonymous Glasgow ratepayer, that they should employ one Peter Hurkes, a Dutch "detective with an X-ray mind", who described himself as a professional practitioner of telepathy and of psychology. It was said that he baffled criminals, police and himself. Perhaps the police felt themselves sufficiently baffled without any international assistance.

Then with a shock the public read of William Watt's arrest

on 27th September 1956. Always willing to assume the worst, they concluded that one chapter of the investigation was closed and that the Lochgilphead alibi had been broken. As we shall see from the evidence at the trial there was perhaps some justification for the latter conclusion.

But the police and the Crown Office were not satisfied and the patient search for evidence went on. The police appealed for information from anyone who might have been on Renfrew Ferry between 2 and 6 a.m. on 17th September. A great many people responded. Searches were made for a gun in the Crinan Canal near Lochgilphead and at Carmunnock, which lies on the route which bypasses Glasgow between Renfrew Ferry and High Burnside.

Eventually, after sixty-seven days in Barlinnie Prison, Watt was released on 3rd December. This created an even greater sensation. But no one else took his place.

This was a thoroughly unsatisfactory state of affairs, both for the public and for Watt himself. He had been arrested and then released without standing trial. Suspicion was bound to hang about him like a cloud until the actual murderer was found, tried and convicted. Until then there was of necessity in the public mind an uneasy feeling that his release was due only to a lack of convincing evidence.

But no arrest was made for over a year, a year in which public anxiety was unallayed and folk slept uneasily of nights.

CHAPTER 2

THE CRIMES 1957–1958

AFTER the Watt murders, things were reasonably quiet in Lanarkshire from the criminal point of view. There was a slight increase in crime but nothing really sensational. As it happened, Peter Manuel was in Barlinnie Prison from 2nd October 1956 until 30th November 1957. The jury at his trial, however, were not allowed to know this.

On Christmas Day, 1957, there occurred, unnoticed, the prelude to the next act of the drama. This was a minor case of housebreaking at 66 Wester Road, Mount Vernon, the home of the Reverend Alexander Macrae Houston. He and his wife left home about noon to spend the day with friends. On their return they found both doors open and a window broken. A camera, a new pair of men's gloves (a Christmas present from friends who lived not far off in Carrick Drive) and £2 from a missionary collecting box were missing.

Three days later Mr and Mrs William Cooke left their house at 5 Carrick Drive about 4 o'clock. Mr Cooke's mother and his eldest child, Isabelle, a seventeen-year-old schoolgirl, were in the house. Isabelle left about 7.15 to meet a classmate, Douglas Bryden, and go with him to a dance in Uddingston. Douglas lived in Strathaven, which is some eleven miles on the other side of Uddingston, so it was arranged that Isabelle should meet him at the bus stop in Uddingston. She did not do so and Douglas waited in vain for forty-five minutes on a dark and windy night.

The south end of Carrick Drive, where No 5 is situated, is a cul-de-sac, but there is a footpath which runs south across the

Shettleston–Bothwell railway line on to London Road, along which run the Uddingston buses. This walk takes about seven minutes.

About 7.30, Mrs Gardiner, whose house in Hamilton Road lay near the path, heard a single loud shout, as if of someone in fright, coming from the direction of the path. It was not a male voice. Her dog began to bark and she could not hear any other cries, if other cries there were.

Mr and Mrs Cooke returned home about 8 o'clock, after Isabelle left. They knew of her plans and had no reason to worry about her absence. About 11.45 they went to bed, perhaps a little worried by this time. After half an hour, there was no sign of her and their worry increased. This was, remember, a Saturday night in Scotland and there would be no late dancing. They got up and dressed, then went out to look for her, walking slowly up and down the path several times without result. Then Mr Cooke drove his car slowly along the road in case she was walking home.

All was useless and the Cookes returned to bed about 3.30. Perhaps they slept, perhaps they did not. There was one straw of hope at which they clutched. Isabelle might have missed all transport home and decided to spend the night with friends. The Cookes' telephone was out of order, no incoming calls being received, so that she had no way of letting her parents know.

In the morning Mr Cooke visited some friends with whom she might have stayed, again without result. About 10 o'clock he reported her disappearance to the police, who at once began a search, while Mr Cooke continued with swelling anxiety to make further inquiries of his friends.

On the same day, Sunday 29th December, the police found a cosmetic pouchette under a railway bridge in Mount Vernon Avenue. The Cookes recognised it as Isabelle's, but of the girl herself there was no sign.

The search continued. On the following Sunday, the Reverend Mr Houston, who had suffered his trivial loss on Christmas Day, appealed from the pulpit for volunteers to help the police and several hundred searchers scoured the district. Garments and undergarments, and even individual buttons, were found, but Isabelle's disappearance remained a mystery, in spite of the usual false reports that she had been seen in different towns in Scotland and England. Rivers were dragged. The fire brigade dammed and pumped out water from the North Calder Water, about a mile and a half away from her home. Railway goods yards in many parts of Scotland were searched, as the police at one time had a theory that her body might have been dropped over a bridge into a passing wagon. It hardly seems likely, however, that such an unusual piece of freight would have remained unnoticed for long by even the most unobservant railwayman.

There was no sign of Isabelle. Of all those bereaved by this series of crimes, surely the Cookes had the hardest lot to bear. They must have known that she was dead. She had been happy at home with her family. She was not the kind of girl to run away from home. But, however certainly their reason pointed to the truth, they must have been tortured beyond endurance by the illogical hope that one day she would run in, her mass of dark hair dancing with her, as she had often done in the past.

But before assured knowledge brought its bitter relief, murder had struck again in this little area.

Sheepburn Road is at the west end of Uddingston, where Isabelle had been going to dance with Douglas Bryden, about two and a half miles south-east of Mount Vernon. The bungalow which the Smart family had built for themselves about 1954 is more open to view than most of the stone houses which form the greater part of the road, for its garden lacks the trees that hide the older houses from the eye. In June 1958, after the trial of Manuel for the murder of the family, it stood gaunt and empty, the curtains drawn, with a vase of dead flowers standing desolate between the pane and one chintz curtain, looking blankly on to the luxuriant growth of what had once been a trim lawn and flower beds.

This, however, is to anticipate. In 1957 Peter James Smart was manager of the office of W. & J. R. Watson, Ltd., civil engineering contractors, in London Road, Glasgow. He was a self-made man, who had worked up to a responsible position at the age of forty-five from a humble start. He enjoyed a good salary and had the use of one of the firm's cars, which he kept in his own garage behind the house.

Mr Smart received his usual monthly pay cheque of £187 15s. 11d. on Tuesday 31st December 1957. He took it to the Parkhead Cross branch of the Commercial Bank of Scotland and drew out £35, £15 of which was due by him to the office. He repaid £10 of his debt in new Commercial Bank £1 notes, which are of a blue colour, and it is reasonable to suppose that the notes which he kept were also new.

As usual in Scotland, 31st December marked the opening of a holiday and Mr Smart was not due to return to work until Monday 6th January 1958. Mr and Mrs Jackman, who lived opposite, called on the Smarts between 8 and 8.30 on Tuesday evening. At this time, the Smarts had not made up their minds how to spend the holiday, husband and wife having different ideas. It was almost settled, however, that they would visit Mr Smart's parents near Jedburgh; another plan was to go to the Dumbuck Hotel, Dumbarton, the proprietor of which, William McManus, was a friend. In the end, however, they were destined to go to neither.

Their failure to arrive in Jedburgh caused no real surprise, as the weather was hard and Mr Smart was known to dislike driving on bad roads.

On that Tuesday evening, too, the Smarts had not decided whether or not to welcome the New Year in traditional style. They had had a late night the night before and thought of going to bed early. The Jackmans went out visiting and returned home with friends about 2 a.m. At that time a light was showing in one of the Smarts' front rooms and another in the kitchenette. The front room light was out by 2.30, when the Jackmans said good-night to their friends, and at that time the kitchenette light also went out, leaving the front of the house in darkness.

Between 9.30 and 10 a.m. on 1st January, Mr Jackman saw that the garage doors were open and the garage empty. The next day, he went across in a friendly way to shut the garage doors and saw that the curtains in the windows of the two bedrooms at the back of the house were drawn. In front, the curtains of the dining-room, to the right of the front door, were drawn, those of the lounge to the left open. The same observation was made by the postman when he delivered a letter on 2nd January.

On Friday 3rd January, David Pirrett, an eleven-year-old friend of young Michael Smart, walked past the house about 2 p.m. with his mother. He too noticed that the dining-room curtains were drawn and those of the lounge open. Later that day, however, Mrs Leonard, a close friend of the family, remarked that the lounge curtains were drawn and the window open. This struck her as unusual, as Mrs Smart was always very careful, when she went away, to close the windows and leave the curtains open. About 7.30 p.m., her husband saw a light through the closed curtains of the dining-room and assumed that the Smarts had returned home.

The same conclusion was drawn by Mr Jackman and the postman on the next day, Saturday 4th January, when they both noticed that the dining-room curtains, which until then had been closed, were open. Mrs Duncan, the Smarts' next-door neighbour, who collected from their front doorstep newspapers which had not been pushed under the door, agreed that the dining-room curtains were closed on Friday and open on Saturday. She also noticed that the lounge windows, which had been open on Friday, were closed on Saturday. It is hard to avoid the inference that someone, authorised or not, was in the house on Friday evening. But we do not know who that person was.

About 8.50 a.m. on 2nd January 1958, Mr Smart's car was seen standing empty in Florence Street, in the Gorbals district of Glasgow, with children playing about it. Its presence was reported to the police that evening and they tried to get in touch with Mr Smart and his employers. They had no success until Monday 6th January, when the office opened after the holiday.

As Mr Smart had not returned to work, a foreman joiner was sent out to Uddingston to make inquiries. He found milk and newspapers outside the front door and no signs of life. As the local police, to whom he applied for information, could not help him, he made some unsuccessful attempts to trace Mr Smart himself. He then went back to Sheepburn Road.

By this time, a police sergeant and a constable were on the

scene. The front door was securely locked but they were able to get in by pushing against the back door, the lock of which was defective. On the floor behind the front door there were letters and postcards bearing postmarks from 31st December to 3rd January, a newspaper dated 2nd January (Scottish newspapers are not published on 1st January), a child's comic dated 3rd January and a copy of the *Radio Times* for the week 5th to 11th January 1958. These had apparently been pushed below the door, as there was no letterbox.

In one bedroom Mr and Mrs Smart were dead in bed, shot through the head at close range. There was a lot of blood about but no sign of disorder in the bedclothes. In the other bedroom young Michael also lay in bed, shot through the head at close range, without any disturbance of the bedclothes. All had been dead for some days.

Various articles were lying in the kitchenette, but these were all such as might have been expected. The only thing which calls for specific mention is an opened tin of salmon.

The only money in the house was two coins, a two-shilling piece and a sixpence which were on the mantelpiece in the parents' room.

For over a week there was no arrest, although the police were busily prosecuting their inquiries. A close search was made for the gun which had been used. Rivers were dragged and the surrounding fields gone over inch by inch. Mine detectors were brought into use but proved no more successful than the old-fashioned methods. The fears that had affected the Burnside area in September 1956, when the Watt family was found shot, became terror in Uddingston. Women and children were rarely seen out after dark. One local ironmonger reported to the press on Friday that in the week after the discovery of the murders he had sold no fewer than six dozen door chains, for which normally there was little demand, and that his stock of door bolts had gone completely.

On Tuesday 7th January the Glasgow CID were called in to assist their Lanarkshire colleagues, Detective-Superintendent Alexander Brown and Detective-Inspector Thomas Goodall being detailed for the investigations. Superintendent Brown had been instructed to assist in the search for Isabelle Cooke as early as 1st January but it had been decided that, after familiarising himself with the district, he should merely await further developments.

Tuesday 14th January 1958 marks an important stage in the investigation. The newspapers of that date reported that Superintendent Murdo Mackenzie of the Lanarkshire County Constabulary had said that a man was arrested at the weekend in connection with the Smart murders and that inquiries were being made in Liverpool. In fact what happened on 14th January was rather more sensational.

The investigations on which the police had been engaged included an interview with the manager of the Parkhead Cross branch of the Commercial Bank, where Mr Smart had drawn £35 on 31st December. They heard of this transaction and, from other sources, learned that a young man with a notorious criminal record, who had apparently been very short of money just before the New Year, had been spending freely on 1st January. A warrant was obtained from the Sheriff to search for money, banknotes and keys believed to have been stolen from the Smart house. The premises to be searched were 32 Fourth Street, Birkenshaw, the home of Samuel Manuel, Peter Manuel's father.

It was not the first visit paid to that house by the police during the period of this narrative. In January 1956, Chief Superintendent James Hendry of the Lanarkshire CID called several times to question Peter Manuel, a labourer who had been seen at East Kilbride on 4th January 1956 with scratches on his face, as to his whereabouts on 2nd and 3rd January. On 12th January 1956, a warrant was obtained to take his clothing from the house for examination. We may assume that the experts found no significant evidence linking him with the murder of Anne Kneilands, as no evidence on the subject was led at the trial. In September 1956, after the Watt murders, the house was searched on a warrant for a gun. This was "on information received". If we may believe Manuel (not perhaps the easiest of tasks), this search was a desultory one and the police failed to find a gun which was there.

The search of 14th January 1958, however, was anything but desultory. About 6.45 a.m., an impressive number of police officers arrived at the door—Superintendent Brown and Inspector Goodall of Glasgow and, from the Lanarkshire force, Chief Inspector Muncie, Detective-Inspector McNeill, Inspector Scott, Detective-Sergeant Weir, a policewoman sergeant and two constables, nine in all.

When they arrived, Samuel Manuel was leaving for work. He was told of the purpose of the visit and shown the warrant. On being advised to turn back to the house he did so, although with some reluctance, explaining that he had to get to work.

The six senior officers entered the house along with the indignant Samuel Manuel. Mrs Manuel was up and about and Peter's brother James was getting ready to go to work. Peter Manuel himself was still asleep in a bedchair. Samuel Manuel demanded to be allowed to read the warrant and when he had done so, according to the police evidence, "had some very bitter remarks to make". The subject-matter of the remarks was not brought out but is perhaps not beyond all conjecture. Then Peter woke up and, in his turn, asked to see the warrant and was allowed to do so. Superintendent Brown then cautioned the parents and Peter and read the warrant aloud to them.

At this stage Peter Manuel told his mother to "phone Jimmy Bell the reporter, and Dowdall". (Lawrence Dowdall is one of the most able criminal solicitors in Glasgow and he figured as a very important witness at the trial.) It appears that Peter Manuel was behaving in rather a truculent manner. Superintendent Brown told him to get dressed, as he was being taken to Bellshill police station for an identification parade. At this stage, the search had not begun.

This deficiency was made good after Peter Manuel left in a police car. The money, banknotes and keys covered by the warrant were not found, but the police discovered a new pair of gloves and a camera, similar to those which had been missing from the Reverend Mr Houston's house. They were taken to Mount Vernon for identification. When the officer returned, Samuel Manuel was invited to give an explanation. He said that he had bought the camera two years earlier at "the barrows"—Glasgow's second-hand market, which figures in a great many explanations of this kind—and that the gloves had been a Christmas present, he thought from the United States. He was charged with the theft of the articles by housebreaking or, alternatively, with resetting (receiving) them. In his turn he was removed to the police station.

Other articles removed from the house included a National Assistance form in the name of Peter Manuel, bearing on it the name "Mr McKay" and a telephone number which the Glasgow officers recognised as that of a club known as the Gordon Club; a bankbook in the name of Peter Manuel showing a credit balance of 2s 2d; his driving licence; all his clothes; and a champagne bottle.

From that day matters marched dramatically forward. Peter Manuel was charged with the Smart murders that night and appeared in chambers before the JP Court in Hamilton the next day. On the same day Samuel Manuel appeared before the Sheriff at Airdrie charged with housebreaking at 66 Wester Road, Mount Vernon, and was ordered to be detained until Friday.

On Friday 16th January it was announced in the press that Isabelle Cooke's body had been found. The news was broken to her parents by Mr Houston.

On Saturday the press reported that investigations into the Watt and Kneilands murders were being reopened.

On the same day Peter Manuel again appeared before the JP Court, now charged with four murders (that of Isabelle Cooke having been added), and was remitted to the Sheriff Court.

On Tuesday 21st January the Durham County Police announced that they had interviewed a man in connection with the murder of Sydney Dunn, a Newcastle-on-Tyne taxidriver, who had been found shot near his taxi on the moors at Edmondbyers, County Durham, on 8th December 1957.

On Wednesday 29th January Peter Manuel was charged with the murder of Sydney Dunn.

The papers of Friday 31st January reported that new leads

had been obtained in the Burnside and East Kilbride murders
(Watt and Kneilands).

On the following Wednesday it was announced that the
search for the weapon used in the Anne Kneilands case had
been called off, as the river which was being dragged had been
swollen by rain. The police were acting on the theory that "an
iron bar may have been thrown into the river from the General's
Bridge by her attacker". An appeal was also made by the police
for information about the finding of the girl's handbag "between East Kilbride and High Blantyre". The General's Bridge
lies on this road. We shall learn later just how the police were
able to narrow the scope of their search.

For some time, a short stretch of the River Clyde near the
High Court buildings in Glasgow had been searched for two
guns, that used in the Smart murders and that used over a year
earlier in the Watt case. Electro-magnets of ever-increasing size
had been used without result. On Friday 7th February a diver,
David Bell, was employed to search and found a Webley
revolver within thirty minutes of first going down. This was the
first time that a diver had been so employed in Scotland. It
was a considerable feat, as the water was so dirty that the
search had to be made by touch.

The following Thursday the same diver found a Beretta
automatic. The Webley was ballistically identified as that used
in the Watt murders and the Beretta as that used on the Smarts.
Again we shall learn how the police were able to direct the
diver's efforts so exactly.

By Saturday 15th February, just over a month after his arrest,
Peter Manuel had been charged with nine murders—the three
Smarts, Isabelle Cooke, Sydney Dunn, and now Anne Kneilands and the three women at High Burnside. A curious statement was reported in the *Glasgow Herald* of Monday 17th
February as having been made by Mr John Ferns, Manuel's
solicitor: "According to information which I have received, I
have reason to believe that my client has been charged with
the murders of the Watt family and of Anne Kneilands." This
seems to be carrying professional caution almost too far.

From this time press comment died away. On 4th April

Manuel appeared in the Sheriff Court in Glasgow to answer to the indictment served on him at the instance of the Lord Advocate. His solicitors did not content themselves with the usual simple plea of "not guilty", but in addition lodged a document containing a note of special defences. The nature of these was not disclosed until the trial opened.

The proceedings in the Sheriff Court were purely formal and Sheriff H. S. Wilson continued the case until 14th April for trial before Lord Cameron and a jury.

As it happened, however, the trial was not to take place on that date.

c

CHAPTER 3

THE INDICTMENT

THE lull before the storms and tempests of the trial gives us a good chance to consider quietly the actual charges against Peter Manuel and the questions which the jury had to answer at the end of the day.

In all, the indictment which had been served on 27th March contained eight charges—four of capital murder (involving eight persons), three of theft by housebreaking and one of simple theft. Put shortly they were as follows:—

(1) the capital murder of Anne Kneilands on 2nd January 1956 by striking her repeatedly on the head with a piece of iron or similar instrument and robbing her of a watch, a pair of earrings, a French coin, a belt and a handbag;

(2) breaking into the Platts' house at Bothwell between 12th and 15th September 1956 and (a) stealing an electric razor, some tools and certain other articles and (b) maliciously damaging a mattress by firing a loaded firearm into it;

(3) breaking into the Martins' house at High Burnside between 15th and 17th September 1956 and stealing two rings, four pairs of nylon stockings and six shillings;

(4) breaking into the Watts' house at High Burnside on 17th September 1956 and the capital murder by shooting of Mrs Watt, Mrs Brown and Vivienne Watt;

34

(5) breaking into the Rev. Alexander Houston's house at Mount Vernon on 25th December 1957 and stealing a camera, a pair of gloves, a sock and £2;

(6) the capital murder of Isabelle Cooke on 28th December 1957, tearing off her clothing and tying a brassiere round her neck and a headscarf round her face and mouth, and robbing her of a pair of shoes, a brush, a fan, a stole, a pouchette of cosmetics and a handbag;

(7) breaking into the Smarts' house at Uddingston on 1st January 1958 and the capital murder by shooting of Mr and Mrs Smart and Michael: also robbing Mr Smart of £30 and a number of keys and Mrs Smart of a pair of gloves, a purse and eighteen shillings; and

(8) the theft on 1st January 1958 of Mr Smart's motor-car.

The murder of Sydney Dunn was not included, as this took place in England and the Scottish Courts had no jurisdiction.

The phrase "capital murder" is new enough to deserve some explanation. Before the Homicide Act, 1957, all murders (though not all killings) were capital and the only sentence which could follow conviction was death. By the Act, however, a distinction was drawn between capital murders and other murders, only the former of which carried the death sentence. Two classes of capital murder are illustrated in the indictment against Manuel, namely murder done in the course or furtherance of theft (the Anne Kneilands and Isabelle Cooke charges, and also possibly those relating to Mr and Mrs Smart) and murder by shooting (the Watt and Smart cases). The Crown could expect no difficulty in proving that the Watts and the Smarts met their deaths by shooting. Therefore, if they proved further that Manuel was the person who fired the shots, conviction of capital murder would follow. In the other two murder cases, it was necessary for the Crown to prove more than Manuel's responsibility for the deaths. They had to prove that the killing was done "in the course or furtherance of theft". In other words, if the object of the assault in each case had been theft or the overcoming of resistance to theft, and death had resulted from that assault, then the crime was capital murder. On the other hand, if the object of the assault had been something else—for example rape—and the theft had taken place incidentally to, or more likely after, the assault and death, then the crime was murder, but not capital murder.

As Lord Cameron remarked when he charged the jury, there does not seem to be much logic in that distinction. It nevertheless is a distinction drawn by Parliament and capital murder is, as the advocate-depute said at the trial, the creature of Parliament. It was ascribing too much cynicism to him to quote him, as some papers did, as saying that capital murder was a feature of Parliament. Or perhaps it was merely wishful thinking.

One other form of capital murder may also be mentioned. If, before conviction of any murder, an accused person has been previously convicted of another murder, both having been committed in Great Britain, the second murder, no matter what its intention or method, is a capital murder. Note that the first conviction must be before the second conviction, and not necessarily before the second murder. This might have been of importance had the jury convicted of murder in the Anne Kneilands and Isabelle Cooke cases alone, negativing theft in each case.

The multiplicity of charges in a single indictment may appear, to the English reader at least, to require some explanation. There is a marked difference between English and Scots practice in this respect. In England the rule is that each murder charge stands alone on a single indictment, and the accused is tried for only one murder at a time, whereas in Scotland it has been perfectly proper, and indeed in some cases necessary, from time immemorial to combine several different charges in one indictment. At first sight, therefore, it would seem that English law guards more jealously against the possibility of an accused person being prejudiced in his defence to one charge by evidence relating to another charge altogether.

The matter, however, is not quite so simple. In 1915 George Joseph Smith was charged with the murder of Bessie Constance Annie Mundy by drowning her in a bath. During the trial evidence was admitted, quite properly by English law, to show that on subsequent occasions Smith had bigamously married Alice Burnham and Margaret Lofty and had murdered them in the same way. The object, of course, was to strengthen an otherwise weak case by showing that Smith had adopted a system of murder. More recently, there was the case of Timothy John Evans, who was tried only for the murder of his infant child. There was, however, another indictment charging him with the murder of his wife. Evidence was admitted relating to both charges.

In Scotland, if an accused person thinks that multiplication of charges in a single indictment will prejudice him in his defence, he may apply to the Court for separation of charges. If the motion is granted, the only evidence which may be led is that relating to the particular charge which is being tried at the time. Probably the most celebrated example of this procedure is the trial of Burke and his paramour McDougall in 1828 (Hare, whose name is infamously inseparable from that of Burke, was not tried: he chose the easier way out of turning King's evidence). Here the indictment contained three charges of murder, one implicating both Burke and McDougall, the other two only Burke. The Court ordered that the charges should be tried separately and the Lord Advocate elected, as he was entitled to do, to proceed on the one charge in which both accused were involved.

The motion is, however, more often refused than granted. And it will inevitably be refused if there appears to be some connection in time, place or character between the different charges. Thus, Dr Pritchard failed in an attempt to have the charges of poisoning his mother-in-law and his wife tried separately.

No motion was made on behalf of Manuel to have the charges separately tried. The only charge which could possibly have been tried by itself was the first, the murder of Anne Kneilands. The Platt and Martin housebreakings were closely connected with the Watt murders and these three charges would inevitably have been taken together. Similarly, as we can see, the Houston housebreaking and the murders of Isabelle Cooke and the Smart family, together with the theft of the car, were linked, at least in point of time. The most that could have been hoped for was separation into three groups. Even here there was the difficulty that a certain pattern could be discerned in the Kneilands murder, the Watt murders and the Cooke murder. In each case there had been interference, more or less gross, with women's clothing, without any sexual interference. The final speech for the Crown stressed this link and this makes it in the highest degree probable that any such motion would have been strenuously opposed. On the whole it is very unlikely that a motion for separation would have succeeded.

Multiplication of charges in some cases is designed for the protection of the accused against surprise. When he is on trial it is incompetent for the Crown to lead evidence tending to show that he has been guilty of any offence other than those which appear in the indictment. He cannot be faced suddenly with a suggestion that he is guilty of other crimes. Thus, in Dr Pritchard's trial, the Solicitor-General proposed to ask Mary McLeod, who had been a servant of the accused, whether he had given her anything to procure a miscarriage, but the question was disallowed. Similarly, in the trial of A. J. Monson for murder in 1893 (the Ardlamont case), evidence tending to show that a signature had been forged was disallowed, although it formed a matter of some importance to the Crown case.

This strict rule of Scots law explains why some charges, trifling in themselves, appeared in the indictment against Peter Manuel in the august company of four murder charges. It is inconceivable, for example, that malicious damage to a mattress (head (b) of the second charge) would have been brought before the High Court of Justiciary at all had it not been for the intimate connection between that and the Watt murders. So also the theft by housebreaking from Mr Houston of a camera and a pair of gloves would have been unimportant but for the fact that the camera and gloves were found in Manuel's house and evidence had to be led about them.

This digression into some differences between English and Scots practice in relation to the indictment makes it appropriate to deal here with the "special defences" to which I have already referred, although this involves anticipating their disclosure to the public, which did not take place until the trial opened on 12th May.

Generally speaking, it is sufficient for an accused person to plead "not guilty". In some cases, however, he puts forward a positive defence. He is then bound to give special notice in writing before the trial itself. The most common forms of such defences are self-defence, where the accused blames the alleged victim of assault or murder for having first attacked him; alibi, where he avers that, at the time the crime was committed, he was in a specified place; and insanity, where he claims that he was not responsible for his actings at the time. There is also, tucked away in the text-books, the special defence of impeachment, where the accused blames some other named person for the crime with which he is himself charged, but this is rarely used. It had not been used in a murder case since the trial of Mrs Jessie McLachlan in 1862.

Impeachment, as a defence, has some major difficulties. For one thing, it usually involves attacking someone who has already come under police investigation which has resulted in no proceedings being taken. In other words, the accused is trying to prove something which the authorities, with their enormously greater resources, have probably decided is impossible. On the other hand, the burden of proof on him in these circumstances is less than that which lies on the Crown. He need not prove his case beyond reasonable doubt. It is enough to show that, on a balance of probabilities, the person named by him is guilty. Indeed, it is enough for him if the matter is left in such doubt that the jury cannot see where the truth lies, for in such a case the Crown cannot be said to have proved the guilt of the accused beyond reasonable doubt. And that is a task which the Crown must perform before any Court or jury can convict on any criminal charge.

Peter Manuel used two special defences, impeachment and alibi. For the Martin housebreaking he blamed Charles Tallis, a prisoner in Peterhead Prison, and Mrs Mary Bowes, both Crown witnesses. For the Watt murders he blamed William Watt, who of course had already come under suspicion and been detained in prison for sixty-seven days. Manuel also pleaded an alibi for the Smart murders, claiming that, between the hours of 1 and 10 a.m., between which times the murders were believed to have been committed, he was at home in the company of his parents, his brother and sister and one Ronald Faubert of the United States Army. This last named witness, who did not appear at the trial, was less independent than might appear, for he also was a relative. The alibi was weakened by the fact that Manuel's house was only about half a mile from the Smarts' house, so that during the heavy somnolence that affects so many Scottish households in the early hours of the morning of 1st January it would have been quite an easy matter for anyone to slip out and commit a murder or two—half an hour was ample time for such a simple job.

In this matter of special defences, there is to be noted a further difference between Scots and English procedure, which may be illustrated by a reference to the case, already mentioned, of Timothy John Evans. He, you will remember, was tried for the murder of his child, but evidence was admitted relating to the murder of his wife, with which he was not charged at that trial, although an indictment waited in case of acquittal on the first charge. His defence substantially was that the murderer was another resident in the same house, John Reginald Halliday Christie. No written notice was necessary for this defence. It is true that the prosecution were not taken by surprise, as in one of the contradictory statements which Evans made to the police, he had already blamed Christie. They therefore had full warning of what was likely to happen and this was made quite clear by the emphasis with which Christie, when he entered the witness-box, was presented to the jury as a man whose military and police record entitled him to considerable respect.

But the prosecution *might*, in another case, have been taken by surprise if an accused (in England) blamed someone else without giving notice. In this respect, the law of Scotland seems to be more anxious to avoid embarrassing the prosecution than is that of England and this may seem inconsistent with its anxiety to protect the accused in other ways. In fact, however, the object of the Scottish procedure as a whole is the consistent one of ensuring, as far as possible, that the issue is set sharply in focus from the beginning. The necessity of doing this by formal written pleadings is perhaps emphasised by the fact that Scottish criminal procedure, unlike English, does not provide for an opening speech for the prosecution at the beginning of the trial. All that happens is that the indictment and any special defences are read to the jury and the evidence is then led. If the indictment is exceptionally complicated, a summary of it may be prepared and read to the jury, in order once more to focus their attention on the essential questions.

It is high time we returned to the case of Manuel. The indictment, as we have seen, contained eight charges, four of capital murder, three of theft by housebreaking and one of theft. In one murder charge and one housebreaking charge the accused blamed or impeached other persons, and in another murder charge he pleaded an alibi. The trial was ordained to take place on 14th April 1958.

On Wednesday 9th April, however, Mr W. R. Grieve, QC, second in the team of three who were instructed for the defence, appeared in the High Court of Justiciary in Edinburgh before the Lord Justice-General (Clyde), Lord Russell and Lord Wheatley to speak to a petition presented on behalf of the accused for a postponement. The ground was that further investigation had to be made and that the accused would suffer prejudice if postponement were not granted. Counsel assured the Court that the special defence had not been put forward without information which seemed to justify it, but that further evidence had still to be sought. Tantalisingly for the press and the public, no hint of the nature of the special defence was yet allowed to leak out. Mere references by counsel to "head (b)", while intelligible enough to the Judges with their copies before them, were difficult for the most ingenious reporter to clothe in dramatic garb.

The advocate-depute did not strenuously oppose the motion, but pointed out that considerable inconvenience would be caused to many people—jurors, witnesses and others—if the trial did not proceed.

In the circumstances the Court granted a postponement and

the new date was fixed as 12th May. Another difficulty arose. By statute, if an accused person is not brought to trial *and the trial concluded* within 110 days of his committal to prison, he is automatically free, and free from prosecution in the future on that charge, unless the Court sees fit to extend the time where the delay is due to some cause not involving fault on the part of the prosecutor. The 110 days would run out for Manuel on 13th May—the day after that now fixed for the opening of the trial. In these circumstances the Court extended the period of custody pending the outcome of the trial until 30th June.

It may seem strange, in view of the state of public feeling in Lanarkshire, that no attempt was made by the defence to have the trial transferred to Edinburgh. This course is not infrequently adopted where it is thought that prejudice may result to the accused from being tried in front of a local jury. It was adopted in three famous Glasgow murder trials, those of Madeleine Smith, Dr Pritchard and Oscar Slater.

In Manuel's case, I understand that the question was informally discussed between Mr Leslie and the Lord Advocate but it was decided that present-day methods of publicity would make such a change of venue of little practical value. The defence decided to take their chance in Glasgow—provided that the net for the jury list was cast as widely as possible in a geographical sense.

Removal to Edinburgh may involve some disadvantage to the defence. Cases on circuit are invariably prosecuted by the junior counsel who is, for the time, advocate-depute on the circuit. The law officers, traditionally, do not go on circuit. But they appear regularly to prosecute, at least in important cases, in the High Court in Edinburgh. Madeleine Smith, as befitted one of her sex and background, had the personal attention of both the Lord Advocate and the Solicitor-General; Dr Pritchard was prosecuted by the Solicitor-General; and Oscar Slater by the Lord Advocate.

The tradition that law officers do not go on circuit seems without foundation. There does not appear to be any valid reason why, in a case involving the public interest as much as the Manuel case, the rule should not admit of an exception. To say this is not to question the ability of Mr Gordon Gillies, the advocate-depute who conducted the prosecution. But many members of the public felt, and the feeling is not a new one, that their interests would be better protected by a law officer and this feeling is one it would be perfectly legitimate to consider.

Further, an incident which occurred on the third day of the trial gave warning of a danger involved. Mr Gillies, as is usual, had invited a young junior to assist him in the conduct of the case. This was Mr Ronald Sutherland, who had been called to the bar only in 1956. His duties normally would have been limited to backstage work, with perhaps the examination of one or two comparatively unimportant witnesses. On the third day, however, Mr Gillies was overcome by a giddy turn just as he was about to enter the courtroom and Mr Sutherland had to take over the conduct of the Crown case for the whole of that morning. The first two witnesses were very important—Charles Tallis and Mrs Mary Bowes, the two involved in Manuel's special defence of impeachment on the third charge. As it happened, he played his part very well; but it is unfair to an inexperienced junior to place such a burden on his shoulders without warning and, had he not proved equal to the task, one can easily see how the interests of justice might have been perverted.

In order to minimise the risk, another advocate-depute, Mr Victor Skae, was summoned from Edinburgh. He was, however, at the time responsible for another circuit and could not have been completely familiar with the case. In the event his presence proved unnecessary and he sat as an observer in court for the rest of the day, Mr Gillies having recovered for the afternoon session.

Had the prosecution been conducted by one of the law officers, with the advocate-depute acting as his junior, as in Edinburgh, the same danger would not have been involved. Had the law officer been taken ill, he would have had as his substitute an experienced junior in the person of the advocate-depute.

The prosecution was in fact left in the hands of the advocate-depute, Mr Gordon Gillies, assisted by Mr Sutherland.

The conduct of the defence had originally been entrusted to Mr Harald Leslie, QC, and Mr Malcolm Morison. Both had undertaken this arduous task gratuitously, in accordance with ancient Scottish practice, going back to a statute of 1424. I understand, however, that fees were eventually forthcoming, and this is gratifying to record. But it is worth emphasising that fees were not looked for, as every person accused of murder in Scotland, no matter how poor, is entitled to have the services of a senior member of the bar. Each year, the Faculty of Advocates nominates a panel of juniors to defend poor persons in criminal cases in the High Court, either in Edinburgh or on circuit. All seniors, however, including the Dean of Faculty, are liable for service in murder cases, a service which is freely and ungrudgingly given, and this point was to be made quite clear in the course of the trial.

In the course of preparing for the trial, an unusual if not unique situation arose. Counsel, of course, paid several visits to Barlinnie Prison, where Manuel was detained, in order to plan the defence. In the course of these discussions, Manuel made it quite clear that he insisted on blaming William Watt for the murders of his wife, daughter and sister-in-law. This was highly embarrassing for Mr Leslie, who had earlier been instructed to appear on behalf of Watt when he seemed, in the eyes of the Crown, the villain of the piece. In the circumstances, his first reaction was to refuse to appear for Manuel. He had been prepared to defend Watt; now he was being instructed to prosecute him. After consultation with the Dean of Faculty, however, it was decided that the proper course was to bring in a second senior counsel, Mr W. R. Grieve, QC, who would make himself primarily responsible for the conduct of the case in so far as it related to the Watt murders.

CHAPTER 4

THE TRIAL—
FIRST AND SECOND DAYS

THE approaching trial had aroused more public interest than any other in living memory in Scotland and special arrangements were made to regulate admission to the court. Spacious as the North Court in Glasgow is, it could obviously not hold a fraction of those who were likely to want to attend. After priority had been given to witnesses who wished to remain after giving their evidence, to the press and to persons professionally and officially interested in one way or another, the public accommodation had to be limited to a mere sixty.

After several false starts, a queue began to form for those sixty places about 8.20 on the night of Sunday 11th May. Heading the queue was William Perryman, Dalriada Crescent, Motherwell—the street in which lived the impeached Mrs Mary Bowes. A sixteen-year-old boy joined about 11 p.m. but he was sent home by the police as being too young. Unfortunately they did not do so until 8.30 a.m., so that he lost a night in bed for nothing. When the number waiting reached sixty, latecomers were turned away.

About 10.10 a.m., the patient sixty were admitted to the public gallery. As they looked down, they saw facing them the Judge's bench and, below it, a semicircular table with chairs round it, covered with papers but still reasonably tidy. The chairs were empty, except for that on the straight side, just under the bench, where the clerk of court sat busy with his last-minute duties. To their right were the three seats for the jury of fifteen, according to Scottish practice, but these too were still empty. To the left, facing the jury-box across the table, was the witness-box, with four steps leading up to it. Two padded benches behind the glass back of the witness-box were for the accommodation of Glasgow magistrates and the sheriffs.

In the centre of the court, facing the bench, was the railed dock, still empty, where Manuel was to sit, and behind that, stretching to the back of the court under the gallery, the seats reserved for the press, for witnesses whose evidence had been given and for the other spectators with priority. At the moment it was mainly occupied by the press and by members of the public who had been summoned to form the panel from which the jury was to be balloted.

All round the well of the court were stacked the usual grisly stock in trade of a murder trial—bloodstained bedding and clothing, guns, a cardboard box which was later to be opened and reveal a girl's shattered skull, and a collection of pieces of rusty iron which would have been normal enough on a junk heap but took on a sinister appearance from their context.

Shortly before 10.30, the bustle that had been going on in the well of the court grew to a climax and died away. Manuel, a short powerfully built man, with thick glossy black hair, neatly dressed in a blazer and slate-grey trousers, was escorted up the stairs from the cells below and took his place in the dock between two policemen, sitting one on each side, white gloved hands holding their truncheons quietly across their knees. Counsel entered to take their places round the table, the advocate-depute and his assistant to the Judge's right next the witness-box and the defence on the left next the jury. Papers were shuffled for a while and then a fanfare of trumpets brought the court to silence.

Preceded by the macer in his black gown Lord Cameron, the trial Judge, and his colleague Lord Migdale, who was to preside over trials in the South Court, entered accompanied by the Rev. Robert Morris, whose dark robes contrasted vividly with the white and scarlet of the Judges. All stood as Mr Morris prayed. Then, with the departure of Lord Migdale and Mr Morris, Lord Cameron was alone on the bench with the shorthand writer to conduct his first murder trial since his appointment in 1955.

The clerk rose in his place under the bench and opened the legal proceedings with the time-honoured words: "Call the diet, Her Majesty's Advocate against Peter Thomas Anthony Manuel." Manuel rose in his place, stared blankly and calmly at the Judge and sat down. From his place at the table Mr Leslie rose and stated in his rich Orcadian voice that his client adhered to his plea of "not guilty" and also to the special defences already intimated.

There was to be a further delay to the trial. Mr Leslie produced a copy of the *News of the World* of the previous day and drew his Lordship's attention to an article on the trial with which there was prominently associated a photograph of the accused.

"In my humble submission," he said, "this is an impropriety. It is most important that fairness to the accused, and indeed to the Crown, should be maintained throughout; and a likeness appearing may well influence identification, which must take place after a lapse of time. Perhaps if I mention this matter it may be sufficient to prevent such a practice continuing."

Lord Cameron said that he would consider what action, if any, should be taken and pointed out to the members of the press present how important it was that nothing should be done or said, by way of press publication, that would prejudice in any way a fair trial. When the Court resumed after lunch, he intimated that he had decided to report the matter to the Lord Advocate for his consideration to take any action he thought fit.

It seems remarkable that it should not have been realised that such a publication was, to say the least, ill-advised. In the Heath case, after the murder of Mrs Margery Gardner, Scotland Yard, in spite of the protests of the press, had firmly requested that no photograph of Heath should be published and the press had, with reluctance, complied. The reason for the request was to avoid any suggestion by defending counsel at the trial that witnesses identifying Heath had been influenced by a press photograph. In Heath's case, two strong arguments were in opposition. The reply of the press was that Heath was still at liberty and they feared that, if he were not soon apprehended, there would be other victims. As we now know, these fears were justified a fortnight later when Doreen Marshall was murdered. But that argument of public safety was not open in the Manuel case, for Peter Manuel was safely in Barlinnie Prison when the photograph was published, and publication could serve no useful or legitimate purpose.

After this preliminary incident a jury of nine men and six women was empanelled.

One name was objected to. At one stage, Manuel's advisers had suggested an all-male jury but their client had refused, on the ground that he was entitled to be tried by a jury balloted at random. Further, he claimed, "I have a way with the ladies."

The clerk of the court then read the indictment and the special defences. This was the first time that the press or public had been allowed any inkling of these defences and as their meaning was realised a gasp ran round the crowded courtroom. Newspapers of that afternoon and the next day used their biggest type for the headlines—"'Shot Family' Charge in Special Defence": "Manuel Names Wm. Watt": "Bakery Chief Accused of 3 Killings by 8-Murder Charge Man—MANUEL SHOCKS LAWYERS."

Such a sensational opening was bound to be followed by apparent anticlimax. The care that is needed to prove beyond all reasonable doubt charges of the gravity of those which Manuel faced necessarily involves a great deal of evidence the bearing of which is not readily obvious. As the trial proceeded, members of the fortunate sixty in the public gallery, deprived of their night's sleep, began to doze off but were wakened by the police on duty.

After a constable had given formal evidence of preparing two plans, one of the East Kilbride area and the other of the Mount Vernon area, evidence was led by Mr Gillies about the disappearance of Anne Kneilands and the discovery of her body. The first witnesses were her parents and her sister Alice. As the substance of their evidence appears in the first chapter. I need not repeat it here. As was only natural, both Mrs Kneilands and her daughter had a hard struggle to maintain their composure, Alice in particular being very distressed and at times almost inaudible.

They were followed in the witness-box by Andrew Murnin, who somewhat ashamedly explained why he had not kept his appointment with Anne on the evening of 2nd January. In cross-examination by Mr Leslie, he said that there were about a hundred people at the dance where he had met Anne and that she had danced with quite a number of men whom he did not know.

The Court then heard of Anne's visit to Mrs Simpson and her last known journey to East Kilbride.

Interest livened with the next witness, sixty-eight-year-old Hugh Marshall. Some time after 8.30 p.m. on 2nd January he was out with his dogs. He stood by a fence in Maxwellton Avenue (not far from the golf course) while the dogs ran about in a field. Suddenly from the direction of the golf course there was a yell. "It was a scream or yell—a voice crying 'Oh, oh.' Then I heard it again."

The witness raised his arm as if to ward off a blow and said "It was just as if somebody was hitting you and you cried 'Oh.'"

After George Gribbon had given his evidence about the finding of Anne Kneilands' body, Sergeant (now Inspector) William Woods of the Lanarkshire Constabulary gave a detailed description, with reference to photographs, of the body and its surroundings. To reach the trees where it lay, he had to cross a deep ditch and a two-strand barbed-wire fence. This word "ditch", incidentally, as Manuel was to remark much later in the trial, did not do justice to an excavation some 8 feet deep and 23 feet wide at the top, with sloping sides.

The body was lying in a small hollow, in a prone position, the right arm across the face and the left arm stretching down to the hips. It was invisible from more than a few yards away. The girl's skull had been badly battered. Her clothing was ruffled up, as if she had been dragged along the ground. Her left stocking was missing (this was a mistake on the witness's part, but one of no importance), as were her shoes. There were no underpants or knickers and no hat.

D

Some distance away the police found a coat belt and a wrist watch. At this part there was an area of flattened grass heavily saturated with blood and brain material—much more so than the place where the body was found. It appeared that the girl had been killed there and her body removed after death to the hollow for concealment.

On the following day a search discovered a pair of shoes, one in the mud and soil on the west side of the ditch and the other on the east embankment, nearer the trees. From the position of the shoes, which were embedded in the ground, and the length of stride indicated by footmarks, the witness concluded that the shoes had been sucked from her feet by the mud as she ran across the ditch.

Small scrapes and abrasions on the girl's body he associated with her having crashed into or stumbled over the barbed-wire fence.

About 340 yards away he found the girl's missing headscarf, an earring and a French coin (these were among the articles which Manuel was accused of stealing, to make this charge one of capital murder).

Mr Grieve's cross-examination was directed to throwing doubt on the accuracy of the inspector's memory by testing it against the photographs. Thus, he had said that the girl's left stocking was missing; but photographs of the body showed a line running down the left leg, which looked like the seam of a stocking. Photographs of the frosty ground on which the body lay showed no marks indicative of running. This, it may be remarked, was not very conclusive of anything if the girl had been killed at some distance and her body moved after death. Any signs of running would have stopped at the point where she was killed. Finally he agreed that his association of the scratches and abrasions with the barbed-wire fence were speculation. This was unduly modest; it would not have been unreasonable to describe that association as legitimate inference.

In reply to Lord Cameron, the witness said that the shoes were found 20 yards apart, one being 110 yards from the heavy saturation of blood where Anne Kneilands had presumably been killed. In that 110 yards there were no signs of anyone having run barefoot. And on that inconclusive note the witness left the witness-box.

A local doctor, Dr David Mullen, spoke briefly to the injuries which the girl had received.

So far—and the trial had by now entered the afternoon of the first day—it was pretty clearly established that Anne Kneilands had been brutally murdered. It might be taken that the crime had been committed shortly after 8.30 p.m. on 2nd January 1956. But so far there had been no mention of Manuel.

That was now to be remedied by the Crown's first attempt—admittedly not very strong—to link the accused with the murder. Constable Marr had been instructed to interview the witness Gribbon, who had discovered the body, on 2nd January. On his way, he met and talked with a man, who was one of a squad of Gas Board workmen waiting at the roadside for transport home. Asked who that man was, the constable raised his arm and pointed at Manuel in the dock. His attention had been attracted by severe scratches on Manuel's nose and right cheek, which appeared to be recent.

Another constable, James Jardine, was on duty near the Calderwood housing scheme, where Manuel's squad was working, on the following Monday, 9th January. A complaint was made to him and he went to investigate an alleged theft from a hut on the site. He saw the foreman Corrins and also Manuel, who had scratches on both sides of his face which seemed to be "two or three days old".

Richard Corrins, the foreman, said that Manuel's face had been free from scratches when work stopped at noon on Saturday 31st December 1955 for the New Year's holiday. When they started work again on Wednesday 4th January, he noticed marks on Manuel's face, which he described as "cuts". Manuel explained that he had got them in a fight (this was quite a possible explanation in view of the way in which some Scots celebrate the birth of the New Year).

Asked in cross-examination, "Where did Manuel live?" Corrins answered "In Birkenshaw, about eight and a half or nine miles away."

Another Gas Board workman, John Lennan, corroborated

the evidence about scratches on Manuel's face after the New Year holiday. Asked "What sort of scratches were they? Were they the sort inflicted with a razor or a fist?", he replied, "It seemed to me they were inflicted with finger nails."

And that, for the time being, was that, so far as related to the murder of Anne Kneilands, with the exception of a short passage in the evidence of the next witness, Detective-Sergeant James Skewies of the Lanarkshire CID, who spoke to having taken photographs of her body and of the area in which it was found.

The rest of the sergeant's evidence related to the Watt murders and the housebreaking at No 18 Fennsbank Avenue. As this was not followed up until the main body of the police evidence was reached in the second week of the trial, we can omit further reference to Sergeant Skewies at this point.

Working patiently through the indictment, the advocate-depute turned to the second charge, that of theft by housebreaking at the Platts' house in Bothwell and malicious damage to a mattress. The first witness was the householder, Henry James Platt, who told how he and his wife and son left on 12th September 1956 for their interrupted caravan tour of the Lake District and how, on their return home, they found the house in disorder. In March of the following year, they moved from Bothwell to Dalserf, taking their furnishings with them.

One night just before Christmas 1957, his wife showed him a bullet which she had found in the mattress which had been slit and repaired. He looked at it with some curiosity but neither he nor his wife paid much attention to it and it was put into a drawer.

"We were like most people," he said, "slightly sceptical that anything would happen to us. In a half-hearted sort of way we associated it with the holes in the bedclothes, but it seemed so fantastic that we put it out of our minds at the time—until we heard that the police were after a .38 revolver, and the penny dropped, and we took it to the police."

The witness then spoke of the articles which were missing from the house, and in particular the electric razor, which he had got from a friend to give to his son. He agreed that it could be described as "factory soiled".

In cross-examination by Mr Leslie, he told again how his wife had found the bullet. He knew it was a .38 bullet because, as he said drily, "I measured the width myself." Its presence was a mystery. "None of your family," Mr Leslie asked with a smile, "had been using the bedroom as a gun range anyway?" The witness assented.

Later he agreed that the most valuable things in the house had not been stolen. He had the impression that "there had been a disturbance and the laddie, whoever it was, had rushed away quickly."

After Mrs Platt had given evidence, Geoffrey Peter Platt identified the razor as the one his father had given him. A slight dent in the shield over the cutter was exactly like the one on his razor. When the police showed him a razor early in 1958, he was able to tell them that there had been a small chip on one of the capacitators inside the one he had lost. He then took the case off the razor in the police hands and found the same chip. He offered to show what he meant and, when Mr Gillies agreed, produced a screwdriver from his pocket, opened the razor again and pointed out the chip he had referred to.

The only difference between his razor and the one shown him in court was that the latter had the initials "T.L." scratched on the case. These initials do not correspond with the name of any person mentioned in connection with the razor, either by prosecution or defence.

Geoffrey's evidence of identification was extraordinarily convincing and the next two witnesses, from Phillips' factory at Hamilton, put the matter virtually beyond doubt when they said that the razor in court was one of a batch of only 50 which had been produced experimentally and were not on sale to the public, although they could be obtained by factory employees. One of them, the witness Mrs Clarke, had bought one for Mr Platt to give to his son.

Finally, on this first day, Miss Margaret Martin told how she and her sister left for their September holiday in Wester Ross but were recalled on Monday 17th September. Three days later (her estimate of time was used by Manuel at the end of the trial to make an important point) she was asked by the police to make an inventory of missing articles. These included two gold rings. Although they had many visits from reporters, they had told them as little as possible. It certainly seems, from Miss Martin's evidence, that no mention of any gold rings could have been made in the press until the evening papers of 21st September, or the morning papers of the 22nd. But, in fact, they were referred to at least two days earlier, though this does not appear in the evidence.

At this point, a few minutes after 5 o'clock, the court adjourned until the next day and the jury went off for the first of many nights of isolation from their families and friends.

The second day began with the evidence of three more witnesses about the Martin case—Mrs McNab, with whom the keys of the house had been left, Mrs Brown, who first noticed and reported the interference with the front door, and Constable Steele, who carried out the first preliminary investigation. None of this was very exciting.

The remaining evidence of the day, however, made up for that. First Mrs Collison, the Watts' daily help, described the Watt household as she knew it. Mr and Mrs Watt seemed an affectionate husband and wife. "I never saw an angry word from the first day I went there until the last day. They always seemed to get on together." Similarly Mr Watt and his daughter always seemed on good terms.

The family moved to High Burnside only on 13th July 1956. In August Mrs Watt and Vivienne went on holiday, leaving Mr Watt at home. They came back one Sunday about the beginning of September and on the next Sunday Mr Watt left for his holiday. The murders took place a week after that.

Mrs Collison then described how she found the house locked on the morning of Monday 17th September when she arrived as usual about 8.45 a.m. "I didn't know what had happened. I thought 'Whatever has happened? Has Mr Watt come home? Has anyone been in? Has there been a row and have they all gone away?' "

After telling the Court how she and the postman entered the

house and found two dead and one dying woman, she identified various articles of clothing as Vivienne's.

Mr Grieve rose to cross-examine. First he asked a few questions about the position of the bodies as shown on the police photographs. Then he switched to the relations between Mr Watt and his family. Sometimes, said the witness, she did not see Mr Watt for a week at a time. He was seldom in the house when she arrived in the mornings.

"Can we take it that you saw very little of Mr and Mrs Watt together in each other's company, either at Cumbernauld Road or at High Burnside?"—"Well, if Mrs Watt felt like going out, Mr Watt would take her. They seldom went out in the mornings—only sometimes on business if Mrs Watt felt well enough."

"Did you ever see them going out together pleasure-bound in the mornings?"—"A few times."

"Apart from the occasions when Mr and Mrs Watt went out together in the morning, what other opportunity did you have of seeing them together?"—"The only time I saw them together was when Mr Watt was in the house."

Mrs Collison went on to say that Mr Watt went away alone from time to time, though not very frequently, on fishing or shooting trips. Mr Grieve then switched to the thoughts that had passed through Mrs Collison's mind when she could not get in on the Monday morning.

"You said that you had wondered what had happened inside the house. You went on to say, if I heard you correctly, 'I wondered had Mr Watt come home.' Why did that cross your mind?"—"I thought someone had been in and probably a row had started or something and they had all went away out the house." The witness paused and went on: "I did not know what to think. A thing I had never seen was a row in Mr Watt's house."

Another switch of subject. Mr Grieve brought out that Mr Watt came up to the witness' house the next night to ask if she knew the whereabouts of the keys of the bureau in the dining-room.

"Did he say why he wanted the keys?"—"Yes, he said he wanted the society books."

"What did he mean by that?"—"Insurances."

After a few more questions, Mr Grieve asked: "Did you speak to Mr Watt about the crime?"—"I asked him if he thought it was robbery, and he said 'No; a little piece of jewellery had been taken; Mrs Watt's watch had been taken.' I said 'Who do you think it was?' and he said 'If it was who I think it was I know them.' Mr Watt did not indicate who he thought it was."

Peter Collier, the postman who opened the door, corroborated Mrs Collison about the scene inside the house and Dr Arthur Nelson of Rutherglen spoke to his preliminary medical examination about 9.30 a.m.

After a neighbour, Frank Gilfillan, had spoken to hearing music from the Watts' house in the early hours of 17th September (not an unusual thing), Deanna Maria Valente, of 6 Fennsbank Avenue, next door to the Watts, gave a picture of her friend Vivienne's last night alive. They had been friendly at Skerry's College before the Watts came to live next door.

On Sunday evening, she and Vivienne went into Glasgow and walked around window-shopping for a little. They had a meal in a café and bought some rolls from one of Mr Watt's bakeries. They got back to Fennsbank Avenue shortly after 9.30 and went first into the witness' house and then into the Watts', where they found Mrs Watt and Mrs Brown. After listening to gramophone records, they all had tea and sandwiches, then the two girls went into Vivienne's bedroom. Neither smoked in the room.

Between 10 and 10.30 the telephone rang. Mrs Watt answered and later called Vivienne, who went out and came back saying she had spoken to her father. "I'm mad because father did not give me money this week, but he's promised to double it when he gets back."

About 11.40, Deanna left, saying good-night to Mrs Brown and Mrs Watt, who was looking well, "better than I remember seeing her". Vivienne stood at the door until Deanna reached her own house. She seemed perfectly cheerful and said "I'll see you tomorrow." Then Deanna went to bed, but did not sleep for some time, as the radio in the Watts' house was playing. Vivienne had a favourite programme—the "Top Ten".

Nothing of importance was elicited by Mr Grieve in his cross-examination or by Lord Cameron.

The next witness was Mrs Valente, Deanna's mother, to whom Mrs Collison had appealed for help when she could not get into the house. The advocate-depute asked her "Is there a safe of any sort in your house?"—"No, none at all."

"Is your husband, so far as you know, in the habit of keeping large sums of money at home?"—"No."

"How does he manage his money affairs? Has he a bank account"—"He keeps it in his work, whatever it is."

"Does he have any large sums of money in the house at Fennsbank Avenue?"—"Oh, no."

The purpose of this evidence was to discredit in advance one of the stories which Manuel had told about the Watt murders.

Two telephone officials gave evidence that a call was received at the exchange about 1.26 a.m. on Monday 17th September from the Watts' house asking for an alarm call to be made at 7 a.m. At 7 a.m. the number was called three times without answer. This served to narrow the time for the murders to between these two points.

Superintendent Andrew McClure of the Lanarkshire Constabulary spoke to the condition of the Watts' house when he made an investigation starting about 9.20 on the Monday morning. So far as he could see, Vivienne was dead by that time, but her body was still warm. As the rest of his evidence has been summarised in the first chapter, it can be passed over.

From the respectable middle-class atmosphere of Fennsbank Avenue, the trial made its first descent into the Glasgow underworld with James Tinney O'Neil, known as "Scout" O'Neil. One Saturday just over a week before the Watt murders, he said he met Manuel at the corner of Macfarlane Street and Gallowgate in Glasgow. They went into a public-house, where they talked about "commonday things, anything at all—different things". Later they went to a football match and after the match returned to the public-house. Manuel asked him if he could get him a gun from one Peter (or Dick) Hamilton for a hold-up in

Liverpool. He then left the public-house in a taxi and O'Neil stayed on for a little. Later he went to Hamilton, who said he would see what he could do about it. It was arranged that all three should meet the next morning.

The meeting took place in the street, Manuel and Hamilton went into a close and, said O'Neil modestly, "I just turned my back."

Four or five minutes later Manuel came out of the close alone and O'Neil had a further opportunity of illustrating his quiet tact.

"Did you ask him whether he got the gun or not?"—"No."

"Were you not interested in the transaction?"—"To a certain extent, but I didn't force the issue. I left it to Manuel to tell me."

"Did he tell you?"—"No."

"Do you know whether he got the gun or not?"—"I can't tell you."

After further pressing by the advocate-depute, O'Neil said that when Manuel came out of the close he slapped his hands on his jacket pockets.

"What did you take from that?"—"It was hard to say."

"Did you take it to mean that he had got it or that he had not got it?"—"I took it that he had got it."

The advocate-depute's sigh of relief is almost audible on the printed page.

In cross-examination O'Neil was as hard to pin down.

"Were you short of money at the time?"—"Possibly."

"When you met Manuel had you any money to spend?"—"The first time, yes."

"You were trying to get money from various people, were you not?"—"No."

"Were you in the habit of getting guns for people?"—"I don't think so."

"Will you answer the question yes or no?"—"No."

"Did you know Hamilton was a man who was in the way of getting guns for people?"—"No."

"Do you say that you have told a consistent story about these matters?"—"That's my story here."

Lord Cameron had no better success.

"What is your employment?"—"I am unemployed just now."

"I did not ask you that. What is your employment?"—"General employment."

"What do you live on?"—"On the assistance board. I am sick."

James Tinney O'Neil is the scarfaced man whom I have promised to associate with the gun used in the Watt case.

Peter Hamilton followed. He remembered O'Neil asking him for a gun in a public-house on a Saturday night just before the Watt murders. Manuel was with him (this does not agree with O'Neil, and there are several points where these two worthies do not coincide). Hamilton was not quite sure which spoke first about the gun.

On the following (Sunday) morning, Hamilton met Manuel and O'Neil accidentally. Manuel asked "Have you got the gun?" The witness took both to his house, where he had a gun. It had been in his possession quite a number of years. He got it from an "RAF fellow" called Henry Campbell. The witness took Manuel "ben the room" and Manuel asked again for the gun. He said it was to send to London. Hamilton gave the gun and seven or eight bullets, wrapped in a piece of rag, and Manuel handed him in return a £5 note.

"Was there any discussion about the price to be paid for the gun?"—"No price was mentioned."

"Were you not interested in what price you would get for it?"—"No, no."

"Why did you accept the £5?"—"Well, would you not have took it?"

Lord Cameron rebuked the witness. "You are being asked questions about a gun which, according to you, was to be used for a criminal hold-up. Kindly answer the questions."—"He was looking for a gun and I gave it him."

"How did you come to get £5?"—"Well, he just gave it me."

Later, Hamilton said that he had gone to Bothwell police station and then to Glasgow police headquarters to identify a gun. Shown one in court, he said it was not the gun he had picked out at police headquarters but one which he had been shown later at the Sheriff Court. It was like the one he had, the only difference being that the ring at the butt was missing.

In cross-examination, Hamilton said that he was a bookmaker's clerk, which Mr Grieve translated, with the witness' agreement, as "bookie's runner". He earned his living by taking street bets.

"If you had not been offered any money for the gun by Manuel, would you have handed the gun over?"—"Yes."

"Were you prepared to give it away?"—"Yes."

"Had you done this thing before?"—"No."

"Why did O'Neil come to you?"—"He knew I had a gun. He approached me quite a number of years ago. But he only asked me. He said he was in a wee bit of trouble and asked me: 'Do you think you could get me a gun?'"

"What did you say on that occasion?"—"I said no."

"What was the purpose of getting this gun from the man Campbell who was in the RAF?"—"I happened to meet him in the Bridgegate and he was selling it."

"And why did you buy it?"—"Well, I was in a wee bit of trouble myself."

"And how much did you pay for it?"—"I couldn't tell—£2 to £3, I am not sure."

"So you were quite accustomed to buying guns being sold for money?"—"That was the first."

Henry Michael Campbell was the next witness. In January 1951, he had been stationed with the RAF at Finningley, near Doncaster. While he was there he came into possession of a revolver.

"I got a job brushing up about the officers' quarters. I went into the officers' quarters and found the revolver and took it."

Lord Cameron—"You mean you stole it?"—"Yes, sir."

The revolver was in a leather holster. Campbell took it home with him when he went on leave, along with twenty or thirty rounds of ammunition in a cloth bag. He overstayed his weekend leave by fourteen days and decided to sell the gun to get back to camp. He went to the Bridgegate and there met Peter Hamilton.

"Why did you go there?"—"Because they said it was easy to sell things there."

"Had you been told that?"—"I just more or less knew. Hamilton told me he would give me the money for the gun. That would let me return to my unit."

"How much did he give you?"—"I just can't remember the price. It was something like 30s."

The witness examined a gun in court and agreed that it was like the one he had sold Hamilton, except that it lacked a ring at the butt.

In cross-examination he said that he had never heard of any inquiry held at the camp about the missing gun.

Joseph Liddell, the next witness, said he had met Manuel in the appropriately named Crook Inn, Uddingston, on the Friday evening before the Watts were killed. They had a general conversation about their work with the county council and, quite casually, Manuel pulled a revolver from his waistband and showed it to him. He had been, he said, helping a second-hand dealer to clear a house belonging to two old ladies, when he saw the gun hanging in a holster in the attic. His intention was to take it into Glasgow to sell it to "some poor bastard who would blow his brains out."

The gun he saw in Manuel's hand did not have a ring in the butt.

The day's evidence ended with the macabre history of the cow that died.

The Sunday before the Watts were killed, John Lafferty had been drinking with Manuel in the Woodend Hotel, Mossend, for five hours, both being, no doubt, for the purposes of the Scottish licensing laws, *bona fide* travellers. The advocate-depute asked "Was there anything he said which particularly struck you?"—"He told me he had shot a cow through the head."

"Did he indicate what district it was?"—"I took it that it was the district adjacent to his house."

"What was the result, did he say, of shooting the cow in the head?"—"It just died, that's all. . . . He said he had put a gun against the cow's head and pulled the trigger."

"What part of the head?"—"The nostril."

In cross-examination Mr Leslie asked, "Did you believe the story about the cow?"—"No, I could not imagine a cow standing and letting anyone walk up and shoot it."

"You knew Manuel?"—"Yes."

"Was he given to being a bit fanciful?"—"Yes."

In spite of Lafferty's doubts, there was some corroboration. A farmer near Manuel's house said that on the morning of 16th September (the day before the Watt murders), he found that one of his heifers was missing. It was lying in a field.

"What sort of state was it in?"—"It was quite normal, except it was dead."

Apart from a little blood coming from its nose, there was no sign to indicate the cause of death and, in accordance with the regulations, he notified the police. A veterinary surgeon examined the corpse and tested it for anthrax but the result was negative. He made no other examination with a view to establishing positively the cause of death.

CHAPTER 5

THE TRIAL
—THIRD DAY

O<small>N</small> Wednesday 14th May the trial began about an hour late because of the indisposition of the advocate-depute, to which I have already referred.

First to give evidence was Charles Tallis, prisoner at Peterhead Prison and a housebreaker by profession (though this was not brought out to the jury), who was accused by Manuel in one of his special defences of being guilty of the housebreaking at the Martins' house. In the year 1956, he said, he was quite friendly with Manuel and they went for a few drinks together.

Mr Sutherland then asked, "During your conversations with Manuel was there ever any talk about guns?"—"Yes."

"Who mentioned the subject?"—"Peter Manuel."

"And what did he say?"—"About the month of June he told me he had a gun and some bullets that would not fit the gun. The bullets were not the same and they fell through the magazine. He asked me what I thought should be done to make the bullets fit."

"Did he ever show you the gun?"—"No."

"Did you ever tell him what he could do to get the bullets through?"—"I told him the gun could be bushed."

This evidence seems quite irrelevant except to paint Manuel as a gunman. The month of June 1956 was before Manuel had bought the gun used in the Watt murders. In any case that was a revolver and did not have a magazine. The gun used in the Smart murders, on the other hand, was an automatic with a magazine which was defective because of a broken spring. But Manuel obtained this gun only towards the end of 1957.

Tallis then went on to give his account of what he did during the weekend of 15th–17th September 1956. On Saturday 15th September, Mrs Bowes' son Allan was married. Tallis was at the ceremony about 2 o'clock and also at the reception, which went on until 11 p.m. He then went back to Mrs Bowes' house in a hired car. Also in the house were the newly married couple and the bride's mother. Allan and his bride and his mother-in-law (surely an unusual honeymoon party) left together between 1 and 2 a.m., leaving Tallis and Mrs Bowes, who were sleeping together, in the house. Mrs Bowes' other son, James, might also have been there.

On the next day, Sunday, Tallis borrowed Allan's car to visit his sister in hospital and on his return went to the Woodend Hotel, Mossend, for a drink. This was the hotel where, that same day, two other *bona fide* travellers, Manuel and John Lafferty, were discussing the dead cow. He took two half-bottles of whisky back with him to Mrs Bowes' house, where he arrived about 6 o'clock. Later he went with Mrs Bowes, Allan and his wife and her mother to the Royal Hotel, Lesmahagow, where they stayed until 11 p.m., when they returned to Mrs Bowes' house for supper. Allan and his wife (we do not hear of his mother-in-law on this occasion) left about 1 o'clock. Neither Tallis nor Mrs Bowes left the house again that night. He had never been inside 18 Fennsbank Avenue, or indeed at Burnside, in his life.

Next day, Monday 17th September, he went to Manuel's house about 1.45 p.m. They went to the Crook Inn, Uddingston, for a drink. Over their drink they discussed the Suez Canal crisis and the Middle East.

Soon Manuel plucked the sleeve of Tallis' coat and said "Drink up and come outside. I want to talk to you." They left the public-house and went to Birkenshaw, where Manuel's mother was working in the garden. Tallis stayed outside with her while Manuel went in, saying "I've left something on the bed, ma. I'll just be a few minutes."

When he came out, he and Tallis went to get a bus for Glasgow. As they were crossing a children's recreation ground, Manuel pulled two rings from his pocket and said "These are the two hottest rings you ever saw in your life."

Tallis' answer was interesting. "I don't understand you. I have seen hundreds of hot rings. I don't see how those are hotter than any others."

Manuel said nothing but put the rings back in his pocket.

One of the rings had two red stones at the side and a centre stone of a clear or green colour and the other had either three or five clear stones. They looked old-fashioned—"You wouldn't think anyone would be expected to buy these rings," added this connoisseur. He was unable to give a fuller description, as he "only got a brief swatch at them."

That evening he went to a cinema with Manuel and later to a public-house in Glasgow. While he was there he read in a newspaper of the Watt murders and the Martin housebreaking.

"I put the thing in front of him. I said 'You have told me they were two hot rings. What have you done with them? Have you still got them?' He said 'No.'"

"Did he tell you what he had done with them?"—"He said 'I put them in a stank below the Central Bridge when you were looking in a shop window.' I said 'No wonder you say these are the hottest rings.'" (A "stank" is the grating in a street gutter, so there may be two old-fashioned rings still to be found by anyone who cares to explore the Glasgow sewage system.)

After a translation of the word "hot" as "stolen" and a denial that he had ever seen William Watt in his life—"And I have never seen Peter Manuel with him either"—Tallis' evidence-in-chief ended and Mr Leslie rose to cross-examine.

"You were asked if you were quite friendly with Peter Manuel and you said 'Yes.' Are you quite friendly with Peter Manuel?"—"I was."

"Yes, you *were*." Mr Leslie paused, then shot his next question. "You're pretty knowledgeable about guns?"—"No, no. I am knowledgeable about fitting. I am an engineer to trade."

In spite of all Mr Leslie could do, Tallis continued to deny

E

any knowledge of guns. He had never held a revolver in his hands, nor even a bullet. His advice about bushing the gun came from his general engineering knowledge (in September 1956 he had been employed as a toolmaker and toolsetter).

Mr Leslie then tried to make Tallis admit that he had been at least in the Burnside district at some time in his life, but the witness would not even make this concession. Then, after a retelling of the story about the hot rings, the questioning switched to the special defence involving Tallis. Again he denied any knowledge of Fennsbank Avenue. He also denied ever having had an electric razor in his life (this was, of course, not connected with the Misses Martin, but with the Platts—its relevance appears later).

"Have you ever met Mr Watt?"—"I have never met the man in my life or spoken to him or seen him even."

"Never arranged to get a gun for him?"—"No. I have never made any arrangements about any gun."

"Never got a gun back from him?"—"I have never handled a revolver in my life. The only time I have handled a gun was in the RAF and then it was a rifle."

"Did you not speak to Manuel on 17th September about rings which were in your possession?"—"No. He was the man that showed me the rings."

"Had Mary Bowes any rings at that time?"—"Yes, she always had rings."

"Had she any desire to sell them?"—"Oh, no."

"Shortly before 16th September did you say to Manuel that you were going to wreck a house in Burnside?"—"No."

"Are you sure?"—"Positive."

"Did you ask him if he would help?"—"What reason had I to go and burst up anybody's house? I have no cribs with anybody."

"Was any mention made between you and Manuel of the rings coming out of the Watt house?"—"No. He never mentioned anything about rings after that. I never mentioned them again until the police came to me."

"Did you want a gun early in September 1956?"—"I never

wanted a gun in my life. I would not take twenty guns if I saw them."

"Did you not ask Manuel to get you a gun?"—"I never asked anybody for a gun."

Tallis was then shown the gun which had been identified by O'Neil, Hamilton and Campbell. He said that according to the maker's name it was a Webley but that he had never heard of a Webley revolver, and continued to protest that he had never owned a gun at any time. He had never seen the gun, never been shown it by the police.

"I suppose you say you were never given a gun at any time in Mary Bowes' house?"—"No."

"Did you ever mention to Manuel that you were to be paid a sum of money by somebody for wrecking a house?"—"No. I don't think I could be induced to do anything like that."

"In the Double-Six public-house in Broomielaw in September 1956, were you and Manuel together?"—"Yes."

"Did you tell Manuel on that occasion that you and Mary Bowes had broken into the house at 18 Fennsbank Avenue?" —"No, Mary Bowes never broke into a house in her life."

"Listen to the question. Did you, when together with Manuel in the Double-Six public-house on 17th September 1956, tell him that you and Mary Bowes had broken into No 18 Fennsbank Avenue?"—"No."

"Did you not say that you had been disturbed by a car coming from No 19?"—"It is the first I have heard of it."

"And that you had to resume what you were doing after the car had gone?"—"No."

"Do you remember a reference to the headlamps of a car?" —"I was never at Burnside to see a car."

"Whose footprints are in the garden?"—"I don't know anything about them."

"Were they not caused when you were disturbed by the car?" —"That is a lot of rubbish. I know nothing about it."

"Did you tell Manuel about the Lesmahagow trip?"—"Yes. I could not be sure if I told him who went with us."

"Did you also mention nylon stockings coming from 18 Fennsbank Avenue?"—"No."

"Did Manuel ask you what you knew about the Watt business?"—"No. He never asked me anything."

"Did you say, from your point of view, the less known the better?"—"No. You couldn't have shut him up about it with a gun—if I had had one."

"Did you know whose car was used in connection with the Watt murders?"—"No. I know nothing about the Watt murders, nothing at all."

"What do you know about Mr Watt?"—"I know nothing at all. I have never been with the man at any time in my life and I do not even know him."

"Immediately after the Watt murders, did you have a gun to dispose of?"—"No, I never had a gun in the first place to dispose of."

"Did you try to get rid of it at the Manuel house?"—"No, I have never had a gun. I distinctly told you I have never had a gun at any moment in my life."

"What about the bullets?"—"That was an entirely different matter. I was talking from the point of view of an engineer and he was asking me about fitting the bullets."

And that was the end of Mr Leslie's cross-examination. He was attempting to involve Tallis not only in the Martin housebreaking, but also in the Platt case and the Watt murders—not necessarily as the murderer but at least in a subordinate capacity. We shall see the point of the cross-examination when we hear Manuel's account of what happened—or rather his account of what Tallis said happened. But there was very little change to be got from Tallis.

Tallis was followed by Mrs Bowes, his mistress and the person accused along with him. She virtually corroborated his evidence, as did her two sons, James and Allan—the bridegroom of the weekend in question. Another casually acquired gun appeared in Allan's evidence. "I got it in the Army. I bought it from a chap."

"Do you remember what kind of gun it was?"—"It was a .38 Luger."

When he came out of the Army, he put it on top of a wardrobe so that his mother would not see it. When he was hard up, he sold it for £2 to an Italian whom he knew as "Luge" (Luigi) or "Butch", the arrangement being that if he wanted it back he could have it at any time by repaying the £2.

Cross-examination failed to elicit any reason for Allan's possession of the Luger.

"Why did you buy it?"—"I was only eighteen at the time."

"What did you do with it while you had it?"—"I just left it where it was—put it by and never touched it."

He agreed that Tallis had been in the room where he kept the gun on top of the wardrobe.

He denied that there was any wild drinking at the wedding, where Tallis and James Bowes had provided the drinks, but agreed that the proceedings went on from 2 o'clock until 11, and even later. Everybody was in good form during the party. He himself had not touched whisky—he had had a sherry.

From the Bowes-Tallis menage, the scene now shifted to the Cairnbaan Hotel, two miles from Lochgilphead, where William Watt had spent his fishing holiday in September 1956. The first witness was Mrs Ruby Leitch, the proprietor's wife. She and her husband had known the Watts for eight years. William Watt, a keen fisherman, was a frequent visitor at the hotel, sometimes alone, sometimes with men friends and sometimes with his wife and daughter. The Leitches had also visited the Watts from time to time before the move to High Burnside.

One Sunday in September Watt arrived at the hotel, alone with his black Labrador. He said he had not been well and spent the first week very quietly. The fishing was not good. Mrs Leitch introduced him to some people called Bruce at Lochgilphead who had a stretch of fishing.

Watt went out in the afternoon of Sunday 16th September, but she did not know where. He returned about 7 p.m. Then he went out again about 8 to go to the Bruces' house to watch television, taking with him four bottles of beer, and a gill of whisky. She saw him again about 10.30 when he went into the bar on his return, and next about midnight, when he and two others came into the hotel's private room. He made a phone call about 10.45, but Mrs Leitch did not know to whom. He had telephoned his wife the previous Friday.

Mrs Leitch went to bed about 12.30 and fell asleep in about half an hour. Before she parted from him, Watt said he wanted to go out about 6 or 6.30 and do some fishing before breakfast, as the river was in good order. Mrs Leitch gave him the kitchen alarm clock.

Next morning she woke about 8.30 and heard a car coming up the drive. When she went downstairs, Watt had had his breakfast and gone. His car was normally kept in front of the hotel overnight.

About 11.20 a.m. she had a telephone call from a man calling himself a business acquaintance of Watt, but she disbelieved him when he had to ask what Watt's first name was. Ten minutes later, John Watt (William's brother) telephoned to say that he had just heard that Mrs Watt, her daughter and someone else had been found dead in bed.

Mrs Leitch sent the local taximan to the stretch where she knew Watt would be fishing, to ask him to come back to the hotel at once as there was an urgent telephone call. She then packed his bag as she knew he would have to return home at once.

About twenty minutes later Watt telephoned to ask what was the matter and Mrs Leitch told him to come to the hotel. He arrived in five or ten minutes. Mrs Leitch told him what had happened. At first he did not seem to grasp it, thinking that Mrs Leitch was referring to her own daughter, whose first name was the same as Mrs Watt's, "Marion". He then telephoned his own house and spoke to someone he called "the Super" and rushed upstairs. When he came down he was distraught. Soon afterwards he left in his own car, accompanied by Mr Bruce senior.

The hotel, said Mrs Leitch, was about 85 miles from Glasgow and the road by Loch Lomondside was very bad and full of twists. She and her husband usually took that route.

One evening Mrs Leitch had gone out with Watt in his car, coming back after dark. The lights were defective and went off and on for no apparent reason.

During the week before the murders, Watt spent only one

night away from the hotel. That was with the Bruces, with whom he was going fishing early the following morning.

In cross-examination by Mr Grieve, Mrs Leitch said that her husband could drive to Glasgow in about two and a quarter hours. If they wanted to get to the south side of the Clyde, they would have to go by Renfrew Ferry, but in fact they never went that way.

Mrs Watt had come to the hotel about four times with Mr Watt. Sometimes he came alone and sometimes with men friends.

Mr Grieve asked: "Sometimes with a lady or ladies and not Mrs Watt?"—"No."

"Never?"—"No."

"Were there ever ladies staying in the hotel who were friendly with Mr Watt when Mrs Watt was not there?"—"Yes."

In 1955, it appeared, a Mrs Milligan and her sister had been there, occupying a twin-bedded room, while Watt and a friend occupied a similar room.

When Watt left for Glasgow after receiving the news of his wife's and daughter's deaths, he drove the car himself.

"What sort of condition was Mr Watt in?"—"He was very upset."

"That is as high as you would put it?"—"He was distraught —he did not speak much."

"Were you able to form any impression of his state of mind?"—"Naturally I thought of him as a bereaved husband."

"Was he not extraordinarily composed for a man who had suffered the tragedy he had suffered?"—"I did not get any impression of that. I was upset myself at the news."

"You, being upset, might have assumed he was the same?" —"Yes, I put myself in his place."

Normally either Mrs Leitch or her husband locked the front door of the hotel at night. That Sunday she left her husband talking to Watt at that door when she went to bed. The back door was always available for anyone to get out of the hotel at night and Watt knew that.

Next morning, when she saw Watt's car, she assumed that he had been fishing.

When she went to bed, Watt was quite sober. He had never asked for an alarm clock before. Her husband could have called him when he got up about 7.30.

William Leitch, the hotel proprietor and an ex-policeman, said the Watts' relations were always very good. Watt had arrived by himself in his car, a maroon Vauxhall. He had his black Labrador with him. The witness did not see him very often during the day, as he was a general merchant and left the running of the hotel to his wife.

When he went to bed on the Sunday night the front door was locked, but the back door was left open for another guest, Thomson, who usually locked it. When the witness left the hotel about 7.45 the next morning, Watt's car was where he had left it the night before.

In cross-examination, he said that the top was frosted over. After corroborating generally his wife's evidence about Sunday, he said that Watt's dog went everywhere that he did.

George Laurie Thomson, the other guest at the hotel, left the hotel about 7.40 on Monday morning, but he could not remember whether Watt's car was there or not.

A waitress at the hotel, Katharine MacLean, who lived out, said that on Monday morning 17th September she left home about 8.5 to cycle to work. She saw Watt's car driving away. The windows were steamed up and Watt was leaning forward to clean them with his hand. They also seemed to be obscured on the outside, where she saw the marks of the windscreen wipers. It was a frosty morning.

She next saw him about 8.30, when he came into the dining-room for breakfast. There was nothing unusual about his appearance.

That evening about 6 o'clock she was in the kitchen when the alarm clock went off. It was quite a short ring and stopped by itself. She had taken the clock from his bedroom on his instructions when he left.

Donald McDonald said that Watt came in to his garage at Ardrishaig about 11 a.m. on Sunday 16th September for petrol. He returned about 1.30 p.m. and asked him to check over the lights. McDonald did so but found nothing wrong and it was arranged that the car would be brought in next day for a more thorough examination. About 12.45 next morning, he was passing the hotel and recognised Watt at a window.

Corroboration about the peculiar behaviour of the car lights came from George Bruce, the postman, who had been fishing with Watt on the night of Saturday 15th September. He and his father were both in the hotel when Watt received the news from High Burnside. He broke down and cried when he was told what had happened. The witness' father went with Watt in his car, as it was thought that he was not in a fit state to travel by himself.

Lawrence Dowdall, the Glasgow solicitor whose name was mentioned by Manuel shortly before his arrest, told the court he had been acting for Watt. He made certain investigations, during which he had received a letter dated 8th October. He read part of it. "I would like you to come and see me on Wednesday. The proposals I have outlined are to our mutual advantage, mainly due to the fact that I have some information for you concerning a recently acquired client of yours who has been described as an all-round athlete. Yours sincerely, P. Manuel."

A meeting took place and, after discussing certain preliminary matters, Dowdall asked "What else do you wish to see me about?" Manuel replied "Mr Watt."

He then said that Watt was innocent—"because I know the man who did it."

The witness asked Manuel why he did not go to the police but Manuel "indicated in a few sentences that he regarded the police with some disapproval".

Manuel had then told the following story: The night before the Watt murders, a man came to him, with a revolver in his possession, and asked Manuel to come on a housebreaking expedition to Burnside. Manuel refused. Next day he read in the papers of the murders. That night the man came back. He was "in the horrors". He told Manuel how he had broken into 18 Fennsbank Avenue and then gone down and broken into No 5, where he shot three women. He wanted Manuel to get rid of the gun and handed it to him. Either Manuel or the other man had

wrenched off the lanyard ring on the butt and thrown it out of
the window. The man also gave Manuel two rings, each of an
old-fashioned type, which he described.

Dowdall suggested that Manuel was pulling his leg and asked
for proof. Manuel described the position of some furniture in
the Watts' house and also the position of the door of what
he called the girl's bedroom, which was not flush with a
wall but in an angle between two walls. Dowdall arranged
to check this by a visit, with police permission, to the Watts'
house.

Another meeting was arranged, after Dowdall had found
that Manuel's information about the furniture and the door was
correct. Manuel then elaborated the story told to him by the
other man. He had, he said, broken a panel in the glass door
and got in that way. He went through the door on the left and
found two women in bed. One sat up and he shot her through
the head. The other sat up and he shot her, but as she was not
dead he put a second bullet through her head. As he left the
room, the girl came running out and he struck her on the chin
with his fist, knocking her out. He tied her hands behind her
back and laid her on the bed while he ransacked the house.
When he came back, he found that she had revived, so he shot
her through the head as well.

As Dowdall did not know about one of the women (Mrs
Brown) having been shot twice, he made inquiries and found
that this was true. A third meeting was then arranged.

At this meeting Manuel told him that the man to whom he
had referred had been in a house somewhere on the outskirts of
Glasgow before the murders with a woman on a housebreaking
expedition. There had been a quarrel. The gun had been fired
and a bullet had gone into a bed. [Remember, this was before
Mrs Platt discovered the bullet in the mattress in December
1957.]

Dowdall then said that he challenged Manuel with knowing
more than he had said. It was incredible that a murderer would
give Manuel "such unnecessary, piffling and fatuous" information about the position of furniture in the house, but Manuel
insisted that this was the case. He then offered to draw the

revolver used. The drawing corresponded to the Webley already produced in court.

Some time later he received another letter, dated 27th November 1957, giving the telephone number of the Manuels' house. The material part of the letter read: "I would like to see you on Saturday evening. The subject-matter of the interview you can put down to unfinished business concerning a party who was, to my certain knowledge, doubly unfortunate."

A further meeting was arranged in the Whitehall Restaurant, Glasgow, for 26th December 1957. At this meeting, Dowdall again urged Manuel to go to the police, but he refused. He said he wanted to see Watt. Dowdall arranged a meeting between the two men for the following night, but he was unable to attend. So far as he knew the two had never met before.

In cross-examination Mr Grieve suggested that at the earlier meetings, Dowdall had been acting as Manuel's solicitor, the imputation being that he was acting improperly in disclosing what had taken place. The witness agreed that, during the preliminaries, Manuel had been asking for advice, but contended that later, when the subject of the Watt murders came up, he was acting for Watt.

"Did it strike you that from the story which you have so graphically described Mr Manuel must have been there?"— "The thought did cross my mind. In fact, I said that to him. I said 'You were there'."

"When that thought crossed your mind, did it not also cross your mind that Mr Manuel should seek advice other than yours?"—"I told him to see the police. I thought they were the best people for him to see."

"Did you suggest he might consult some other solicitor?"— "No. I suggested he should go to the police."

"If my construction is correct, the information he gave you was highly confidential?"—"I did not regard it as confidential. I advised him to see the police about it."

"Did you go to the police yourself?"—"Yes, I went after the third occasion on which I spoke to him. Before that I had advised him to see the police and he again expressed disapproval of the proposal. I said 'What will you do if I go to the police?' and his answer was 'I shall deny that I said it.' "

In answer to further questions, Dowdall maintained that Manuel had described the house to him before he [Dowdall] had ever been in it. At no time did he mention the name of the gunman.

After the meeting in the Whitehall, he told Manuel that he did not propose to see him again until he wished to give information to the police.

"Was anything said about money?"—"On that occasion I said 'What is it you want to see Mr Watt for? Is it money you are after?' He said 'No, I don't want money.' He was quite frank about that."

"Did Mr Watt ever say to you whether he had given Manuel any money?"—"He did not."

An extraordinary story by any standards, and one which, standing as it did at first in isolation, many people found hard to believe. But as the trial went on, more and more the picture of Manuel was to emerge in brutal clarity as a man who had to talk, who had to keep himself in the limelight, a man whose stories were always full of circumstantial detail.

And on that sensational note the third day of the trial ended.

CHAPTER 6

THE TRIAL
—FOURTH DAY

WITNESS No 40 on the Crown list was William Watt. It is probably safe to say that no witness has ever been more eagerly awaited by spectators at any trial in Scotland. Husband, father and brother-in-law of three murder victims, he had himself been detained for over two months in connection with their deaths and then been released. He was now charged with the murders by the man in the dock.

As if this were not enough, his appearance had been delayed. At the time of the trial, he was suffering from the results of a serious car accident which had happened some months before, and had been attending the court daily on crutches, awaiting his call to the witness-box. On the third morning, about the same time as the advocate-depute suffered his temporary illness, Watt fell down some steps as he swung himself along and had to be taken to hospital. He was, however, able to attend to give his evidence on the fourth day, a big man with thinning hair, lying on a wheeled hospital couch in the well of the court.

He told the advocate-depute that he had been married in 1938 and that Vivienne had been born on Easter Sunday, 24th March 1940. After the birth, Mrs Watt's health deteriorated; latterly, after a heart operation, it had improved and, just before he went on holiday, she was better than she had been for a long time. The family moved to the house at Burnside in July 1956 and about the end of August Mrs Watt and Vivienne went for a week's holiday to Prestwick. A week later he himself went to the Cairnbaan Hotel, Lochgilphead. "I had been working very hard. I had just taken over another bakehouse and we were doing the place out. I was working about 14 to 16 hours a day and I took sciatica. I went to Cairnbaan."

While he was away he telephoned his wife every other night. He telephoned about 10.45 on Sunday night and she was then very happy about her sister staying with her.

On Sunday 16th September, he was out in the morning and went back to the hotel for lunch. In the afternoon he went to a garage, as he had had trouble with the lights of his car for several nights. They were "just blacking out". After dinner he went to the Bruces' house at Lochgilphead and returned to the hotel shortly after 10 o'clock. After telephoning his wife he was in the bar. He often helped there.

During his first week, he had very little fishing as the water in the river was low and he could not have his favourite stretch until the second week. He meant to get up, as he sometimes did, about 5.30 on Monday morning to fish some of the pools before breakfast and borrowed the kitchen alarm clock, which he set for that time. After cutting a corn to get relief, he went to bed about 1.45. Some blood got on the sheet.

Next morning, when he heard the alarm, he decided, as others have done, that he would have a little longer in bed. After a while, he looked at his watch and read the time as 6.40 when in fact it was 7.40, as he discovered when he went downstairs. He was too late to fish, but he went to the river to have a look at it, came back and had breakfast and then went out again. He had some difficulty with his car, as the windscreen was covered with frost.

Later a man came along in a car and told him to go back to the hotel as there was something wrong. He thought Mr Leitch must have had an accident and telephoned Mrs Leitch from a call box. She told him to come back. When he arrived she was "in a terrible state of nerves. . . . I put my arm around her, took her into the sitting-room and said 'Come on, now tell me what it is all about.' She turned to me and said 'No, you sit down.' I could not understand this, but she again told me to sit down. Then she told me that my family had been found dead in the house. I told her it must be ridiculous because I had spoken to

my wife last night. I said I would find out. I phoned one of my
places in Glasgow. It was then about a quarter to one and I
knew John [his brother] would be there. It was my secretary I
spoke to and she said they had gone to Burnside. I said 'What's
this ridiculous thing I hear about my family?' and she said . . ."

The witness broke down and sobbed and a doctor stood by
him. Eventually he recovered his self-control and explained
how he had then telephoned his house and spoken to a police
superintendent, who confirmed what he had been told. He
changed from his fishing clothes, got into the car with Mr Bruce
senior and drove off. After about three miles he realised he
could not drive to Glasgow, so he took the car to Lochgilphead
police station, where he was provided with a driver. He was met
at Alexandria police station by officers of the Lanarkshire
police and then went to Rutherglen police station.

Later he identified the three bodies in the city mortuary.

The only thing missing from the house was a watch belonging
to Mrs Watt, and that turned up later.

After investigations had been going on for some time, he was
asked to attend an identification parade, where he was picked
out by someone. He was then detained in Barlinnie for sixty-
seven days. He was later identified by a second man.

Lawrence Dowdall was his solicitor. On one of his visits to
Barlinnie, he asked questions about the layout of the house at
Fennsbank Avenue. He also mentioned a man called Manuel
and, about the middle of December 1957, a meeting was
arranged between himself and Manuel at the Whitehall Restaurant. A barman pointed out Manuel to him.

"I had heard so much about this man Manuel that I made up
my mind that something had to be done about this. So I went
over and said to Manuel 'Look here, there are two things I
want quite straight. If it is money you are after you can
forget it.' I was thinking of what I had learned earlier. I said
that if I thought he had anything to do with the Burnside incident I would not only lay hands on him, I would tear him to
pieces. Manuel sat bolt upright and said to me 'People don't
do that to Manuel.' "

Shortly after that they went and sat in a quiet spot in the

lounge bar of a public-house in Crown Street. Manuel spoke of Vivienne and took out a pocket-book. He then produced a photograph which the witness recognised, to his amazement, as one of Anne Kneilands. He tore it up and put the pieces in an ashtray.

"He told me that it was all a mistake about my house being broken into in Burnside. He told me that information had come to them from a fellow called Martin who was a relative of the Valentes. He said that if Martin was spoken to he would deny it, but he had given them information that the Valentes had a safe in the house with between £5,000 and £10,000 and that the safe was to be blown. They were to break into the house and everyone in the house had to be shot except one and that person would be forced to tell where the key of the safe was. Then that person was to be shot."

"You are talking about 'them' and 'they'. Did he tell you who 'they' were?"—"He did not at that time. But there were three people involved—Charles Tallis, Martin Hart and Mrs Bowes. He said they had come for him earlier that night to a hotel but he was not there and they carried on to Burnside. They had broken into the house at 18 Fennsbank Avenue. During the time they were there they came to see the Valente house and saw the young girl Valente. It was then they made up their minds that that was the Valente house.

"The young girl Valente was in my house that night. They returned to No 18 and remained there until the early hours and Charles Tallis broke through the glass door of my house. They went in, Manuel said, and shot my wife and sister dead. . . ."

For a second time the witness broke down and the progress of the trial was halted until he had recovered.

"They left that room, Manuel told me, and went to my daughter's room and Manuel said he was met by my daughter. He said he struck my daughter and tied her hands behind her back. When he had searched the house he came back and shot my daughter."

"You are using the word 'he'—with reference to whom?"—"Tallis."

"Then he told me about every item of furniture in my wife's

bedroom and sitting-room. He told me all this in detail—the colours, the inset display cabinet, the cabinet alongside it and the centre part I use as a cocktail cabinet, the three-piece suite, the standard lamp, a coffee table and the piano and where it was sitting and the photograph on top of it. Everything in detail he told me."

"Did he say where he got all the information?"—"From Tallis. Manuel told me 'There was no safe in your house.' That was not the case and I said 'Weren't you in the kitchenette?' The safe was lying quite open underneath the table in the kitchenette. Manuel said there was no safe in my house. It was then I said to him 'Now, look, you know far too much about this house not to have been there.' He said Tallis had told him."

[Mrs Collison's evidence had been that, when she arrived on Monday morning, all the interior doors were open *except that of the kitchenette*.]

Watt then charged Manuel with having got the gun from Scout O'Neil. He first denied this then said "I had several guns."

The advocate-depute asked if he had said anything about a bullet in a bed.

"Oh, yes. He said that Martin Hart, Tallis and Mrs Bowes had broken into a house at Bothwell. When they were in the house, Tallis caught Mrs Bowes and threw her into the bed and jumped in beside her. Mrs Bowes had pulled this gun and fired it at Tallis and it grazed his side. The bullet then went into the mattress or into the floor. . . . Manuel told me 'If that bullet is found there and that's the gun used at Burnside, it will prove conclusively that you had nothing whatever to do with the tragedy at Burnside, having been on holiday."

Manuel then said that Tallis had given him the gun and that he had thrown it into the Clyde.

All this conversation took place, more or less, in Jackson's Bar. They went to another public-house and waited for John Watt to finish work, when all three went to John's house. They stayed there until about 7 a.m., when Watt drove Manuel home to Birkenshaw.

A further meeting was arranged for the next evening. Nothing

F

very new took place, except that Dowdall did his best to persuade Manuel to go to the police or to the procurator-fiscal (the local representative of the Lord Advocate) and tell the story there. Manuel refused.

"Did you at any time give Manuel any money?"—"No."

"Did you see Manuel again after that second meeting?"—"No, never. I never spoke to him again."

"Do you know this man called Tallis?"—"I never saw Tallis in my life."

Examination-in-chief was over and Mr Grieve rose for probably the most difficult and important cross-examination of his career. A few questions about Mrs Watt's health led into a suggestion of motive.

"Were you always faithful to her?"—"No."

"Were you quite frequently unfaithful to your wife?"—"No, I was not."

"Several times then?"—"A few times, yes."

Questions about Watt's daily routine drew the admission that Mrs Collison did not see much of him and his wife together. Mr Grieve then turned to the Lochgilphead holiday. When he visited the garage on Sunday 16th September he had not been preparing for the long journey to Glasgow that night or the next morning.

"You said something in your evidence about cutting your corn?"—"That is quite right."

"Did you get blood on your finger from cutting your corn?"—"I don't think I did."

"Did you tell a police officer about that corn when you made a statement?"—"I told Dr Imrie."

"Didn't you tell Superintendent Hendry?"—"I may have done."

"What import did cutting a corn which bled have? Why did you mention it?"—"Because it was one of the things I did in the room that night."

"Did you think they might find some blood about your clothes?"—"It made no difference. It was on the foot of the bed and on my handkerchief—just very slight spotting."

The witness said that it took about two hours and ten minutes to drive from Lochgilphead to Glasgow, averaging 40 miles an hour. He never used Renfrew Ferry.

"Did you not cross the ferry on the morning of 17th September 1956?"—"I did not."

"Didn't you cross at 3 o'clock that morning?"—"That is a lot of nonsense."

"Weren't you in your car with your dog?"—"That is a lie."

"Weren't you subsequently identified by the ferryman Taylor?"—"That is true, but I can't understand it. I don't know how he identified me."

"Isn't it because you were there?"—"I was not there."

"Weren't you on your way to Burnside?"—"I was not on my way to Burnside. I went to bed at a quarter to two."

"Do you not remember going down Loch Lomondside on 17th September?"—"Impossible, I could not remember going down Loch Lomondside."

"Do you not remember drawing into the side?"—"No, nonsense."

"You were identified by another person?"—"I believe so."

The suggestion was made, and denied, that the lights had been giving trouble and that he had stopped the car to see about them.

"I must put it to you that you crossed the ferry at Renfrew about 3 o'clock on the morning of the 17th on your way to Burnside?"—"I did not. I was in bed."

"Thereafter you went into the house and shot your wife and ...?"—"I did not. I did nothing of the kind—my beautiful girls."

"Thereafter you went back to Cairnbaan and were there before 7 a.m.?"—"That's a lot of nonsense."

"Is that possible, Mr Watt?"—"It may be possible, but not for me."

"I further suggest that you broke the panel at the side of your door to make it look like ...?"—"That's a lot of nonsense. I was never near Burnside, Renfrew Ferry or Loch Lomondside that night."

The case for the defence against Watt had now been put in all its nakedness but no admission had been obtained. Mr

Grieve now turned to prepare for the pitifully few rags of evidence on which he intended to rely.

First Watt denied having met Tallis or having got a gun from him, but admitted having heard of him while he was in Barlinnie. He insisted that when the news of the murders was broken he was in a near state of collapse and that Bruce came with him to give him a helping hand.

When they got to Alexandria, they were met by Lanarkshire police officers, including Sergeant Mitchell. He did not ask for details, as he wanted to get home.

"Did Mitchell give you any sort of warning about not saying anything?"—"Not to my knowledge."

"Did you say something?"—"I wanted to speak to someone about it."

"Did you say something like 'Is it as bad as that? You don't think I did it'?"—"I don't remember."

"May you have said it?"—"I could have done. Yes."

"Didn't you say that because your conscience was guilty?" —"My conscience never has been guilty. Never once. I never did a wrong thing in my life."

"Did you say anything to Mitchell about who might have done these murders?"—"I was thinking about it. I remember speaking to Mitchell about a fellow there at night on a bicycle."

"Did you mention any name?"—"No."

"Don't you remember mentioning Ferrier to Mitchell?"—"I may have done."

The witness could not, however, remember telling Mitchell that there was a man called Ferrier who had a grudge against him.

After a few questions about his anxiety to get the insurance policies, which he explained by saying that the agent was pressing him about them, although there was little money involved, Mr Grieve turned to a passage in Mrs Collison's evidence.

"Did you say anything to Mrs Collison about believing you knew who had done this murder?"—"I believe I did. I think I said if it was who I thought, I knew who had done it."

"To whom were you referring?"—"Well, this will come as a

great, great shock to this person. I had given this thing very, very serious consideration and I came to the conclusion that it must be someone in the family. I knew that I had had nothing to do with it myself and I came to the conclusion that it must have been my brother-in-law. I never mentioned that all the way through, but that was what was in my mind."

He denied, however, that that was the first name that came to his mind. He had "thousands of names".

From Watt's reaction to Sergeant Mitchell's—

"Do you remember saying to Sergeant Mitchell that he thought he was coming back to pick up the man who committed the murders?"—"I could have said that, because Mitchell made it quite clear to me when he met me, not in any words, but by the way he looked at me and the way he treated me; it was quite obvious he considered I had something to do with it."

"What did Mitchell say to you in answer to your observation?"—"He said 'Not at all.' "

"Do you remember him saying 'I thought I was going to bring back a broken-hearted and bereaved man and I found a man with a smirk on his face and without a tear'?"—"That wasn't said that day, that was on the previous day, when we were alone in Fennsbank Avenue. . . ."

"Do you remember saying in reply 'I believe you are right, sergeant'?"—"That you are right about what?"

"That he had found a man with a smirk and without a tear?" —"Now you are talking a lot of nonsense. If he said that it is an absolute invention and quite like Mitchell too."

Evidence of another conversation followed, this time with the belatedly accused brother-in-law, George Brown.

"Did your brother-in-law not say that he thought his wife would get it first because she was a light sleeper?"—"No."

"Do you not remember saying to him 'George, Margaret did get it first'?"—"That's a lot of nonsense."

"Didn't you know that perfectly well . . ."—"I know perfectly well nothing."

". . . because you had been there?"—"What a profession!"

"Didn't you say that to your brother-in-law?"—"I didn't say that to my brother-in-law. That is a lie."

After a number of questions on some matters of less importance, the cross-examination turned to Watt's knowledge of
Manuel. The witness said that he did not meet Manuel for
about a year after his liberation from prison, but that he had
heard of him. "I heard a lot about Manuel when I was in
prison. I heard the type of madman he was while I was in prison."

"What was the purpose of your meeting Manuel?"—"I don't
know. I was asked to meet him. I was told Manuel wanted to
see me."

"Didn't you want to see Manuel?"—"No, I knew that if I
saw Manuel I was going after him because I had come to the
conclusion that Manuel was the man responsible for all my
troubles."

"If you had come to that conclusion, what were you doing
seeing Manuel?"—"Because there was nothing done about it
except what was done at the instance of my solicitor. I had gone
into the matter with the police over that year. I was at the police
incessantly about it, but only one officer would listen to me,
and he did listen intently."

"So instead of putting Manuel in the hands of the police,
you decided to meet him?"—"I put the matter in the hands of
the police. I spoke to Mr Hendry [then head of the Lanarkshire
CID] and I said to Mr Hendry 'Manuel is the man who did
this.' Mr Hendry said to me 'If there is anyone who knows
about Manuel, I know him.' That's where I spoke to the police
about it."

"When was that?"—"Oh, away back. It must have been
about May of last year, about then."

Questions about the meeting that began in the Whitehall
Restaurant and went to John Watt's house *via* Jackson's Bar
brought a burst of temper from the witness.

"Didn't you eventually admit to Manuel in Jackson's Bar
that you had committed these crimes?"—"Oh, Lord, no. Definitely not. But that does not surprise me in the least if it comes
from Manuel."

"Weren't you subsequently that evening trying to persuade
him to manufacture evidence, to name someone else, which
would clear you?"—"No."

Finally the witness said that he had information, from someone who had been in Barlinnie, that O'Neil had sold a gun to Manuel. He had given that information to the police in May or June 1957. He denied giving Manuel any money.

"Didn't you give Manuel £150 and say you wanted someone to be arrested for the murder of your wife?"—"I didn't require to bribe anyone. I am not in the least bit surprised about that, of course."

Re-examination was short. The total amount of insurance on his wife's life had been some £50 or £60. The man Ferrier whom he might have mentioned to Sergeant Mitchell was someone whom he had sacked and he might have had a grudge.

John Watt followed his brother into court. He described the family business as prosperous. William's family relationships were "very good". Then, after a reference to his telephone call to Lochgilphead, he was taken to the meeting in December 1957, where he had been impressed by Manuel's familiarity with the position of the furniture at 5 Fennsbank Avenue.

In cross-examination, he agreed that his brother and Manuel seemed to be on good terms when he met them.

"When my brother introduced Manuel to me, he said 'This is the Peter Manuel we have been hearing so much about.' They were quite friendly and he told me that he had been given a new slant on the Burnside killings."

"He did give your brother a new slant on the Burnside affair and your brother seemed quite pleased about that?"— "Yes."

The next few witnesses can be passed over shortly, as their evidence appears in the account of the crimes in the second chapter. After a surveyor had spoken to plans of the Mount Vernon area, Mr and Mrs Houston told of the thefts from their house on Christmas Day 1957. Mrs Elizabeth Hendrie identified the gloves which she and her husband had bought for Mr Houston as a Christmas present.

Next it was the turn of the Isabelle Cooke murder to occupy the attention of the Court. First the dead girl's parents told of their fruitless vigil and search and identified various articles of clothing. Her grandmother and an uncle also gave evidence.

Douglas Bryden described his lonely wait at the bus stop on a "dry, dark and windy night", and Mrs Gardiner told of the shout she heard about 7.30 p.m. on 28th December coming from the path that ran to Carrick Drive across the railway.

Then Thomas Docherty, like Manuel a labourer employed by the Scottish Gas Board, said he had been on a bus going into Glasgow about 6 p.m. on that Saturday. At Birkenshaw Manuel came to the upper deck and greeted him but, as there were no seats, turned and went down again. When the bus arrived at the terminus, Docherty got off but did not see Manuel. It was dark and the weather was very bad.

In cross-examination he denied that he was going to the dog-racing. He was going to visit a friend.

About 11.30 p.m. on 28th December, Donald Macfarlane, a 53-year-old special constable, was out exercising his dog. He described his route until he reached a railway bridge near the Zoo. There he heard a noise and stood on the bridge to watch. He saw a man stoop to get under the upper rail of a broken fence from the railway and go to the Hamilton road, with his right arm drawn up to hide his face. He did, however, get a good look at this man. There were street lamps on the bridge and near it and "there was, too, a full moon and it was brilliantly lit".

He identified Manuel quite positively.

In cross-examination Mr Leslie asked "You said it was a full moon that night. Would you be surprised that it was not full moon until a week later?"—"I am almost positive it was almost at the full. It wasn't very far off the full moon."

"Was it not a dry, dark, windy night?"—"No, no, it wasn't dark and dry because it had been wet prior to that."

He was sure the man he saw had been wearing a coat but no hat. He had been wearing a collar and tie, but the witness could not describe the tie.

Mr Leslie then took him over his route on the map. The witness, who wore spectacles, removed one pair and replaced them with another.

"The person you saw was going towards the Hamilton road across the bridge and away from you?"—"Correct."

Lord Cameron asked "How close was this man to you?"—
"Approximately fifteen feet."

"How long do you say you had him under such observation
that you could see his features?"—"He came out and halted,
saw me and came forward on to the roadway. He was never
nearer than fifteen feet. It was only for a few seconds."

After some evidence of the finding of certain articles connected with the Cooke case, the advocate-depute turned to the
final charges in the indictment, those relating to the Smarts. First
a constable spoke to plans of the Florence Street area in the
Gorbals, where the car had been found.

Alexander McBride, foreman joiner with W. & J. R.
Watson Ltd, described how he had been responsible for the
discovery of the murders on 6th January, when Mr Smart had
not returned to work after the New Year holiday. Then Stanley
Jackman, the Smarts' neighbour, told how he and his wife had
spent the evening of 31st December with the Smarts. He also
gave his evidence about the lights in the house in the early
hours of 1st January, and of the position of the curtains on the
different days of the following week.

The cashier at Mr Smart's office, Miss Mattie McDonald,
identified two cheques, one being Mr Smart's salary cheque.
She also identified seven new Commercial Bank £1 notes, which
were those remaining out of Mr Smart's repayment of his debt
after his visit to the bank on 31st December.

The evidence from the bank about the notes given to Mr
Smart was inconclusive. But 500 new £1 notes had been re-
quisitioned by the branch on 21st December and there was evidence that a cash payment had been made to Andrew Barclay
also on the morning of 31st December. Barclay gave evidence
on the next day that all the £1 notes issued to him were new
ones.

Finally on that day, Charles Jardin Freebairn, licensee of the
Noggin public-house in Uddingston, said that, among other
transactions, Mr Smart had been in on Hogmanay (31st December) and had bought two bottles of whisky, which he paid for
in "fresh" Commercial Bank notes.

CHAPTER 7

THE TRIAL—
FIFTH AND SIXTH DAYS

THE first witness on Friday 16th May was Victor Smart, brother of the murdered man. He saw his brother only some four or five times a year, the last time having been on 19th September, but he had spoken to him by telephone on 29th December. They then discussed arrangements for the New Year, when Peter said that, although their plans were a little unsettled, they would be going to Jedburgh, where their parents lived, on 2nd January.

The witness was in Jedburgh from 31st December until 2nd January. He was not greatly surprised by his brother's failure to arrive, because of the weather conditions. That night, on his return to Edinburgh, he telephoned Uddingston but got no reply. On the morning of 6th January he learned that his brother had not returned to work and that his car had been found damaged. On telephoning later to his brother's house, he found that the police were there. He went through to Uddingston and identified the three bodies.

Sergeant Frank Hogg of the Lanarkshire police told of McBride's inquiries on 6th January. He himself went to the Smarts' bungalow about 11 a.m. and got in by charging the back door with his shoulder. As far as he could see, he did no damage. He then described the scene as he found it, the man and woman lying dead in bed in one room and the boy in the other. He concluded that all three had been shot while sleeping soundly.

Friends, neighbours and the postman described the outward

90

appearance of the house and the position of the curtains in the front windows over the first few days of January.

Mrs Madge Dalton, who helped with the housework every Thursday morning, said she last did so on 26th December. Mrs Smart agreed that she should not come the following Thursday, which was in the holiday period. On the evening of 6th January police officers called on her and asked her to go to the Smarts' house. She looked round but could see no sign of anything having been stolen.

There was a Yale key lying on the draining-board of the sink and the witness recognised it as the key of the back door. She also noticed a half-open tin of salmon. She did not think Mrs Smart would have left it like that, but could not be sure.

After more evidence, which did not lead to any definite conclusion, about bank notes, George Gibson, a part-time taxi-driver, entered the box. He had been very busy with his taxi over the New Year period and about 5 a.m. on 1st January he was driving from the main road down Sheepburn Road. Some ten or twenty yards from the Smarts' house, he saw a motor-car coming up without lights. It was in the middle of the road but drew into its own side as Gibson approached. Gibson flashed his lights to attract the other driver's attention, but he paid no heed. There seemed to be two people in the other car, which was a small Austin like Mr Smart's. A heavy white vapour was coming from it, which suggested that the engine was cold and was being run on the choke.

Mrs Robina Graham, whose house overlooked the car park at the Ranco factory, not far from Birkenshaw, noticed three private saloon cars parked there on New Year's Day. At the time she thought this strange.

Francis Jack described a lift which he and another man had had from the driver of a grey two-door saloon car, which the witness thought was a Morris, on the morning of 2nd January. There was some difficulty in starting it and the driver remarked that it had been out all night. He identified a photograph of Mr Smart's car as the one in which he had been given his lift.

More dramatic evidence of a lift, this time in an Austin A 35, was given by Constable Robert Smith, who lived at Powburn

Toll, near the head of Sheepburn Road. At 8.10 a.m. on the 2nd January, he left home in uniform to take part in a search for clothing in the River Calder. A car was stopped at a road junction facing Glasgow. He went up to it and asked for a lift for about two and a half miles. He did not know the driver but was able to identify him later at a parade and in court as Peter Manuel. The car, which was a grey two-door model, was identical with one he had been shown at Glasgow police headquarters on 19th January.

Mr Leslie tried to throw doubt on the identification.

"Had you been discussing Manuel before the identification parade?"—"Well, he had been arrested."

"Answer the question. Had you been discussing Manuel?"—"Oh, yes."

"Had you seen photographs of him?"—"I had not."

"Had you his description?"—"I had heard it vaguely but did not recognise him from it."

"You were taking an interest in it, weren't you?"—"An interest in the case, naturally."

"In Manuel's description?"—"Oh, yes."

"A close interest?"—"Yes, a close interest."

"It was not difficult, was it, to pick him out at that identification parade on 18th January?"—"His description fits many others that I know well."

In answer to Lord Cameron the witness said that the purpose of the identification parade was for him to pick out the driver of a car from whom he had received a lift. This he had done.

After evidence had been given about the finding of the stolen car in Florence Street, Gorbals, Mrs Janet McMillan, who had been staying with her mother in Birkenshaw, said she went to get a bus about 9.5 a.m. on 2nd January. Peter Manuel was one of four men who got off a bus coming from Glasgow. "He wasn't as smartly dressed as he usually is. That's what drew my attention to him."

Donald Ross, a clerical officer in the National Assistance Board, proved that a man called Peter Manuel had received three payments in December 1957 and January 1958, and the manager of the Uddingston branch of the Bank of Scotland identified Manuel's passbook, the last entry in which was on 9th April 1956, when the balance was 2s 2d.

John Buchanan, who has a small green wooden kiosk at Birkenshaw, identified Manuel as a regular customer. He was the first customer on 1st January, about 10 a.m., when he bought cigarettes.

"Did you notice anything about his appearance?"—"He was very well groomed, I thought."

"More so than usual?"—"No, he usually was."

"Well, what I am asking is, was there anything unusual about him?"—"No, the unusual thing was that anyone at that time on New Year's morning should be so well groomed."

He was not sure of the last time that Manuel visited the shop. He always bought cigarettes, usually Capstan, but the last time it was five Woodbines. That was unusual. Manuel said he was short of money.

Cross-examination merely served to stress that the witness was uncertain about dates.

Walter Cameron said he saw Manuel on a bus going towards Glasgow between 10 and 11 a.m. on 1st January, but could not say where he got off.

The Crown now turned to proving Manuel's sudden accession of wealth on 1st January, the source being, by inference, Mr Smart's new notes. First his aunt Mrs Devina Greenan told of a party on New Year's Day to celebrate her daughter's engagement. Manuel arrived between 4 and 5 o'clock, went out about 8 and came back with a parcel about 9. He left about 11.20 p.m., but before doing so he gave her husband money to pay for a taxi for his mother. He also gave the witness a £1 note for the younger children. It was "all crumpled up and seemed to be soft."

Patrick Greenan, her husband, at first failed to identify Manuel in court until the accused leaned forward and went "Psst" to draw his attention. He too told of the engagement party. When Manuel returned after his brief absence he brought a dozen cans of lager beer. There was also whisky in the house, but the witness did not know who bought it. Manuel gave him a £1 note to pay for the taxi. "It was a British Linen Bank note, a blue note." It was ruffled up a bit and the witness straightened it out to make sure it was not a small £5 note.

His son, Peter, had also been at the party. He saw Manuel in the hall with five or seven £1 notes in his hand, but could not say what kind they were. He had heard that Manuel gave his sister £1 to mark her engagement and also £1 for his younger brothers. Manuel had three 20 packets of Capstan and a square bottle of whisky.

Other witnesses also spoke to Manuel's wealth at the party, where he had been displaying a handful of new notes and pointing out that the numbers ran in sequence. Their general impression was that they were blue notes, but no witness could identify the issuing bank. After the party, some of the younger guests went to a dance, where Manuel paid for the tickets. He had been trying to give money away at the party, without success.

Then Joseph Brannan, an unemployed miner, said that in December 1957 he and Manuel met at the Labour Exchange to draw benefit every Wednesday and Friday. One Wednesday about the middle of December Manuel, who had quite a quantity of money on him that day, said he had some arrangement to see someone about business in Glasgow. "I can't quite say whether it was the Gordon Club or not."

"Why do you think it might be the Gordon Club?"—"We had conversations and Peter seemed to be well known in the Gordon Club and had some business arrangements in the Gordon Club and was going there."

The witness spoke of visits with Manuel to cafés and public-houses and also to Manuel's house. He was then asked about an appointment to meet Manuel on the Saturday before Christmas.

"What was the purpose of meeting him in Birkenshaw?"—"We had some business but it never materialised, and we cancelled it. I had other business on and he left to go and see to his business."

"What was his business?"—"He said something about going round to do a snatch, what is commonly known as snatching a lady's handbag."

"What time of night would that be?"—"About 6.30 at night."

"Did he ask you to go with him?"—"He did."

"Is that what you meant when you say you had business arrangements that fell through?"—"I refused to go. On those conditions I refused to go."

Lord Cameron—"What conditions?"—"The conditions of snatching a bag, your honour."

[This evidence does not relate to any of the charges. The Isabelle Cooke case was on the Saturday after Christmas.]

On the Friday after Christmas, 27th December, they again met at the Labour Exchange, went to Pacitti's Café and then to Manuel's house and the Windmill Tavern in Birkenshaw.

"Did Manuel say anything to you about what he had been doing?"—"Yes, we had a conversation and in this he said he had done something out at Mount Vernon. Something about a housebreaking he had done there."

"Did he say anything about the house?"—"Yes, he said it was a minister's house."

"And did he say anything about the proceeds?"—"A small quantity of money and a camera."

On Hogmanay Brannan met Manuel and his father in the Royal Oak public-house. Manuel's father bought a round of beer and Brannan followed suit. Manuel's father then bought another round and laid down £1 for it. Manuel picked up the change and said "That's £1 I owe you." The witness got the impression that "Peter was financially embarrassed".

On New Year's Day, however, the picture was different. Manuel called at Brannan's house about 10.30 and gave each of the children two shillings. They then went to the Woodend Hotel, where Brannan ordered and paid for a round of drinks. While Brannan was in the toilet, Manuel ordered a second round. When Brannan came back, Manuel told him he had given the waiter a note, thinking it was a £1 note, but that the waiter had come back to report that it was a £5 note. "Peter was commenting on his honesty in coming back and telling him." Manuel then bought a refreshment for the proprietress and a friend.

: "Did you make any comment to Peter about his financial circumstances?"—"Yes, I asked him how he was fixed and he said he had had a bit of pay, you see. I thought he had got it from somewhere else, but according to Peter he said he had got it from the Gordon Club in Glasgow. He said he had to go in and see someone as he was getting payments through the Mr Watt business."

"Is that what Manuel told you?"—"It is exactly what he told me."

"You would be rather surprised having seen him borrowing money from his father on Hogmanay that he had a £5 note at midday the following day?"—"I was surprised when he wanted to give the kiddies two shillings each."

Both men then bought drinks, Manuel paying for them with new notes of a blue colour. Shown Commercial Bank notes, Brannan said that the notes in Manuel's hands looked like them.

On the Friday after New Year (3rd January), they met again at the Labour Exchange and went to the café. Manuel said he had been at a party at Mrs Greenan's.

"Did he say anything about a car?"—"He mentioned an Austin A 30 and said he did not think they went so fast. He said he had gone back to the Woodend Hotel to get a quantity of liquor to take back to the party."

"Did you take it that he had used the car to go from the Greenans' house to the hotel?"—"Peter made it quite clear that he did use it for that."

The two then left the café and went first to Manuel's house and then to the Woodend Hotel, where they drank beer and whisky. When they left, Manuel bought sausages and steak and they went to Brannan's house. After eating, they went out to the Royal Oak public-house, from which they moved on about 7.30 to the Old Mail Coach on Hamilton Road near the Zoo. There was entertainment in the form of singing and both men had a good drink, paying round for round. Before leaving, Manuel bought drinks for the two waitresses and also a half-bottle of brandy.

Next Wednesday, after their regular visits to the Labour

Exchange and the café, they boarded a bus in order to have a look at the policemen searching and the firemen pumping the River Calder. When they passed, Manuel remarked "that he thought it was a red herring they were looking for".

On Friday January 10th, Manuel said he was going into Glasgow on business. "He had to uplift some money at the Gordon Club."

"Did he say anything about going away?"—"It was suggested that we should both go down to London."

"What did you say to that?"—"It was impossible for me to go because I had a wife and two children to look after."

"Was any arrangement made about going to Glasgow?"—"Yes, but only if things went well for Peter. We would go and have a good night out. He was expecting to do well. I was to meet him at Birkenshaw on the Sunday, but when I got there his sister Theresa invited me into the house and I saw Peter. His nose was burst and his face was scarred at the side. He said that it was in an incident he had coming down the road when escorting a gentleman home."

"What was his financial position?"—"He had no money, but said he might ask Theresa for something and go to the hotel."

In cross-examination, Brannan confessed to difficulty in remembering dates. He was, however, sure that the evening in the Old Mail Coach was January 3rd. They had been there until 9.30, which was closing time.

"Were you drinking quite heavily?"—"No, Peter is quite a good conversationalist and when Peter is in conversation you can't drink." [If the specimens of Manuel's conversations recorded in the evidence at the trial are at all typical, they must have been fascinating, if a trifle onesided.]

Brannan had spent about 30s that night—not bad, one might think, for an unemployed man with a wife and two children to keep.

Mr Leslie then turned to Brannan's personal relations with Manuel.

"I suppose the evidence you have been giving gives you some pain, does it?"—"I don't think so."

G

"Are you friendly with Manuel?"—"I was."

"I am asking, are you friendly with Manuel?"—"I am not friendly with Manuel." [The same line of cross-examination as with Charles Tallis, and the same results.]

"Did you go about a great deal with him?"—"In the last six or seven weeks from December to January 1958."

"Were you in cars with him?"—"It depends on what you mean, sir. Private cars or tramcars?"

"Private?"—"No, never."

"Are you sure?"—"Sorry, yes, one car."

He explained to Lord Cameron that this private car was a taxi.

The witness was still attending the Labour Exchange every Wednesday and Friday, but was no longer in a financial position to spend much of his time in public-houses, although he wished he could. Manuel was to paint his picture later as a hanger-on, sponging on his more affluent friends, and there is perhaps a hint of that in his own evidence.

More evidence of Manuel's wealth on 1st January came from members of the Egan family, who assisted in the running of the Woodend Hotel, where their mother was licensee. On the night of the Greenan party, Manuel came in and bought drinks and cigarettes to the value of £8 17s 6d, which he paid in new £1 notes of the Commercial Bank. The witnesses thought he also had some £5 notes with him.

The honest barman, Thomas Mullen, told how he drew Manuel's attention to the fact that he had handed over a £5 note in mistake for a £1 note.

The source of Manuel's £5 notes was not revealed in the evidence.

This somewhat alcoholic chapter of evidence gave way to the story of another casual gun transaction in the Glasgow underworld. First, William Fullerton said that in 1952 he had been an occasional visitor at a pitch-and-toss gambling school run by a man Totten on the banks of the Clyde near Rutherglen. There were sometimes as many as two or three hundred in attendance. About May of that year, there was a fight, as a result of which Totten had been sentenced to four years' imprisonment. Before the fight, Totten had asked the witness to get him a weapon for protection—any kind of weapon.

By a stroke of luck, Fullerton was in a public-house one evening when a soldier approached him and asked if he had any use for a gun. It was a Beretta, loaded. Fullerton paid a deposit of £1 and reported to Totten, who gave him £6, £5 for the gun and £1 commission. He identified a Beretta shown him in court as similar to the one he had bought for Totten.

Cross-examining, Mr Leslie asked "Why did Totten come to you to get a gun?"—"Years ago I was a wee bit notorious."

"For your ability to get guns?"—"No, my ability to fight—no guns."

"How did you come to be approached to provide a gun?"—"I cannot answer that."

"Have you provided any other kind of gun for any other citizen of Glasgow?"—"No, sir."

Totten's account was a little different. According to him, in 1952 he had been a little worried about his safety, as a rival gang was trying to take over the pitch-and-toss school. "I was told they had a gun and they were going to set about me."

"What did you propose to do about that?"—"Nothing."

"Did you get a gun that year?"—"I was offered one by a man called Fullerton."

"How did he come to offer you the gun?"—"At a chance meeting."

He agreed that he had paid £5 for the gun and some ammunition. He kept it in a little bothy, or hut, near the school. On one or two occasions he fired it just before the start of operations. He was arrested after the fight and released on bail. While he was out, he collected the gun from the bothy, wrapped it in brown paper and put it in a wardrobe in his house. After he had been sent to Barlinnie to serve his sentence, he spoke about the gun to a fellow-prisoner, Lowe, who was soon to be released, and arranged with Lowe to go to the house and collect it.

Shown the Beretta in court, he said that it was not the gun—it was too big.

In cross-examination he said that he had no other gun—"not

to my knowledge". He had been shown one but told the man who had it to get rid of it, as it was too dangerous.

Mrs Mary Totten told how a man called for the brown paper parcel in her husband's wardrobe. Then Robert Joseph Lowe, who was now serving a term of imprisonment in Wandsworth Prison, gave his version of the transaction. While he had been in Barlinnie, Totten told him that he had two guns in the house and was anxious for his wife to get rid of them. "Being in a little bit of trouble"—this seems a routine explanation—"I asked him if he would arrange for me to go and collect them on liberation."

Totten wrote to his wife and gave Lowe the address. After his release, Lowe called on Mrs Totten. She "went upstairs and came down with two guns. I believe one was a Luger and one a Beretta. One gun was bare and one was in a holster."

"How do you remember this so clearly?"—"I can only accept the evidence of my own eyes."

"This was some years ago?"—"If it had been forty years ago I would still remember a woman handing me two guns."

Lowe took the guns and a cardboard box with twenty-five or thirty rounds of ammunition for the Beretta to Andrew Thomson's house in Florence Street, where he was then living, and put them in a drawer. They remained there until his next arrest about the end of April 1953. He came out of prison on 20th February 1954, but did not see either gun again until a policeman brought him one in Wandsworth and asked him to identify it. It was a Beretta, but he could not identify it as the one he had had.

He strongly denied to Mr Leslie that either of the guns was in a parcel.

Lowe's evidence ended the fifth day of the trial. Saturday 17th May opened with further stages in the history of the Beretta, the first witness being Andrew Thomson of Florence Street. By occupation he was a door-keeper at the Gordon Club.

He knew a man called Samuel Mackay, manager of the club, who some years earlier had been a lodger in his house for about a year. Lowe had also been a lodger for a year or more and there might have been a time when all three were there together.

When Lowe left the house, he left a small brown paper package behind and said "I will leave this up on the shelf. I will collect it some time or other."

Just before Christmas 1957, McKay told the witness at the Gordon Club that there was a man downstairs to see him. Thomson went down and McKay said "This is a Peter Manuel." Manuel said "I have a package to collect. Tony Lowe said he left it in your house on a shelf."

Thomson could not remember any package, so McKay offered to drive them over to the house to find out. When they reached Florence Street, Thomson went upstairs and found a package, which he brought down and handed to Manuel.

"Didn't you remember perfectly well that the article was in your house?"—"No, it slipped my mind."

The witness had been giving his evidence with considerable reluctance and almost inaudibly. Lord Cameron took up the questioning at this point.

"Which shelf was this package supposed to be on?"—"In the lobby."

"And I have to believe that it remained there for over four years?"—"Yes, sir."

"It must have been very dusty?"—"Yes, sir, it was. I never use the shelf."

"Thomson, you are here to do two things: first, tell the truth; second, to tell it clearly. You are not doing the second. I have some grave doubts if you are doing the first."

The witness did not benefit by the judicial rebuke. He did not think he would recognise Manuel again if he saw him, although he had been in the back of McKay's car with him. He peered through his glasses at the dock and said he was not sure if he saw him. Eventually he said he did not see anyone like him.

He admitted that there were drawers in his house, but he had never been present when Lowe put anything in them. They were kept for shirts.

The advocate-depute had refrained from asking what kind of a club the Gordon Club was, but Mr Leslie was more curious. The witness paused before answering, then shrugged his shoulders and said "Horse racing and all that." He was not a member; he only worked there. Apart from that, little positive evidence came out in cross-examination.

Another employee, Morris Dickov, first described the club as a bridge club but later admitted that it was a betting club. He remembered a man coming into the club about the end of 1957 and asking for McKay. McKay was out at the time and the man, whom he was able to identify as Manuel, left a telephone number for McKay to ring when he returned. He passed on the message and later heard McKay call the number. A woman's voice answered and it was obvious that Manuel was out. This took place about a week before Christmas.

He was followed by Samuel McKay. He agreed that he was employed at the Gordon Club and that it was a betting club. Eight days before Christmas he got a message that he was to telephone Manuel and did so. Manuel was out, but his mother answered the phone. McKay gave the number of the club and asked her to tell her son to call him back. The careful reader will remember that one of the articles found by the police when they searched the Manuels' house was a National Assistance form with the name "Mr McKay" and the club telephone number written on it, so it is clear that Mrs Manuel did what she was asked to do.

Next day, Thursday, he was going downstairs from the club when he met Manuel by chance. Manuel asked for Thomson. McKay told the story of the drive to Thomson's house and the production of the brown paper parcel. After that Thomson said he was going for a shave, and Manuel asked McKay to drive him to the corner of Buchanan Street and Argyle Street. On the way there Manuel opened the parcel and displayed a small gun and some bullets in a matchbox. Later McKay saw a picture of a Beretta in the *Daily Express* and recognised it as like the gun in the parcel.

The witness saw Manuel only once after that, between 6th and 10th January, when he came to the club and asked McKay for £150 because he wanted to go to England. McKay told him he was not going to get a halfpenny and ordered him downstairs.

"Did he say why he wanted the money at the time?"—"He said that he had got to get out of the road and get down to England."

"Have you ever, at any time, given Manuel any money?"—"Never in my life."

"Or arranged for Manuel to be given any money?"—"No."

Finally McKay identified the Beretta in court as like the gun he had seen in Manuel's hand.

Cross-examination gave the witness an opportunity for paying tribute to his own sang-froid. "Did you not nearly fall off the seat when you saw it [the gun]?"—"No."

"Are you in the habit of providing guns for people?"—"I have never provided guns for people."

"Are you in the habit of seeing people with guns?"—"No, but I have seen guns. I was in the Army."

"You were quite unconcerned?"—"Yes."

At the conversation about the £150 only he and Manuel were present. He never had the box of ammunition in his hands at all, but saw it while he was driving Manuel from Florence Street.

"It was the way he was fondling the gun and he put the gun in his pocket and took out the matchbox and pushed it right open. He took the two ends apart and I could see right away there were quite a few small bullets."

[In view of the evidence of the last three witnesses, it is not surprising that the Gordon Club was raided by the police on 31st May, the Saturday after the trial ended. On 2nd June McKay and Thomson were both fined £5 for assisting in the management of a betting house.]

William Martin, the licensee of the Old Mail Coach public-house, remembered several discussions in his bar about the Smart murders. At one of these a customer, whom he identified as Manuel, held forth at great length on the subject of firearms and particularly Berettas, which he described as very dangerous because of their recoil. He seemed knowledgeable about firearms. In cross-examination, he said that the conversation took place on 8th January. Also present were Joseph Brannan and David Cross, the pianist in the bar.

Evidence followed to suggest that Manuel was not familiar with the Smarts' house. The witness, Hugh McHugh, said he made an appointment with Manuel one Sunday to meet at Sheepburn Road but Manuel did not seem to know where Mr Smart's house was. He talked more of the traffic island at the top of the road. The purpose of this evidence was to discredit in advance some of Manuel's evidence about his relations with the Smart family and his extraordinary version of what happened in that house.

McHugh was, practically speaking, the last of the lay witnesses. He was followed into the witness-box by Professor Andrew Allison and other medical experts and then the police witnesses. Although Professor Allison's evidence began on Saturday morning, most of it was given when the court resumed on Monday, and it is more convenient to deal with it in the next chapter.

At this stage, the evidence may be summarised as follows:—

Charge 1 (Kneilands murder): Anne Kneilands was murdered on the evening of 2nd January 1956. Some of her belongings were missing. Manuel was working in the vicinity, though not on the day she was killed, and on 4th January he was seen with scratches on his face. According to Watt, Manuel was carrying a photograph of the murdered girl in December 1957.

Charge 2 (Platt housebreaking): The house was forcibly entered and articles stolen, including an electric razor of a special type. A bullet was fired into the mattress. Manuel knew about this bullet before either Mr or Mrs Platt did. He had claimed that Mrs Bowes had shot at Tallis.

Charge 3 (Martin housebreaking): Again, the house had been forced and articles stolen. Again Manuel blamed Mrs Bowes and Tallis, along with Martin Hart. According to Tallis, Manuel had two rings stolen from the house in his possession immediately after the crime.

Charge 4 (Watt murders): The house was entered in the same way as the Martins' house, probably on the same night. Three women were shot through the head at close range. There was no sign of a weapon. According to Manuel, the same gun was used as had fired the shot in the Platts' house. According to

Manuel again, the real object of the murder was the Valentes' house next door. Manuel had shown himself surprisingly familiar with the interior of the house, which he claimed had been described to him by the murderer—Charles Tallis. On the other hand, Manuel's case now was that William Watt had slipped away from his holiday at Lochgilphead to commit the crime.

Charge 5 (Houston housebreaking): The house had been forced and gloves and a camera stolen. They were found in Manuel's house. Manuel had admitted the crime in a conversation with Brannan.

Charge 6 (Cooke murder): Isabelle Cooke had disappeared and her body was still, on the evidence to date, undiscovered. The only evidence incriminating Manuel was a conversation with Brannan—the reference to a "red herring".

Charge 7 (Smart murders): The three victims were shot through the head at close range. No weapon was found. Mr Smart drew new Commercial Bank £1 notes on 31st December, but none were found in his house. Immediately before the New Year Manuel was apparently short of money. Just afterwards he was flaunting money which included new Commercial Bank £1 notes.

Charge 8 (Smart car theft): The car disappeared about the time of the murders and was found soon after in Glasgow. On 2nd January Manuel gave a lift to a police officer in a similar car going towards Glasgow. He came back by bus.

Other pieces of evidence, notably the acquisition by Manuel of two guns, one just before the Watt murders and the other just before the Smart murders, had not yet been linked up with these crimes: that was still to come.

CHAPTER 8

THE TRIAL—
MEDICAL EVIDENCE

IN some murder trials, all hinges on the medical and scientific evidence and virtually the whole interest lies in the close testing of rival theories. There was nothing of the kind in Manuel's case. Professor Allison was the first Crown expert. His examination-in-chief, spread over Saturday and Monday mornings, lasted for some four hours. Cross-examination took only ten minutes.

The professor first described the scene where Anne Kneilands' body had been found on 4th January 1956. It had cooled to a temperature of 50 degrees Fahrenheit and this, taken along with its appearance, was consistent with death having occurred two days earlier. There were twelve injuries in all on her body, four being on the skull, including a fracture $4\frac{1}{4}$ by $3\frac{5}{8}$ inches, with bone fragments driven into the brain. Death was due to a comminuted fracture of the skull and laceration of the brain. A piece of angle iron, which was produced, fitted one of the breaks in the surface, as the professor was able to demonstrate on the girl's skull in court, but he could not say definitely that that had been the weapon used.

The injuries to the rest of the body were minor—mere superficial abrasions which might have been caused by the body being dragged across the ground after death or, in the case of abrasions on the hands, from being pulled through a barbed-wire fence. There was no sign of sexual interference.

The witness identified various productions—articles of clothing, fragments of bone and a piece sawn off a tree stump at the scene of the crime. At first they thought this might have been casually connected with some of the injuries, but that theory was later discarded.

He next identified a report which he had made of an examination of the accused on 20th January 1958, but he was not asked to read it and its contents remain unknown.

Of the four wounds on the head, the fracture already described had caused death. It was impossible to say in what order the four blows had been struck.

Finally, the professor described the clothing of the body when it was found.

He was asked about the Watt murders and dealt first with the post-mortem examination which he had carried out with Dr Imrie. Mrs Brown's head bore two bullet wounds, one on the right side near the temple and the other under the right eye. From the blackening round both he concluded that each shot had been fired at close range, with the weapon touching or nearly touching the skin. Death was due to these wounds, the more serious damage having been done by the bullet which entered below the eye.

The entrance wound in Mrs Watt's head was at the right temple and the exit at the left side of the head. There was blackening in her case also. The cause of death was a bullet wound, fracture of the skull and laceration of the brain. There was some bruising on her left thigh.

In Vivienne's case, the bullet had passed from the left temple to a point above the right ear. The wound was surrounded by blackening characteristic of a shot at close range. She had bruises on her chin and lower jaw, minute bruises inside her mouth and above her eyebrow and there was also a small area of bruising at the entrance to the vagina. The cause of death was the same as for Mrs Brown and Mrs Watt.

He next described the surroundings in which the bodies were found. Inadvertently he referred to Mrs Brown as having been shot first, but explained that he could not say definitely. This might have been important in view of what, according to the defence, William Watt said to his brother-in-law: "George, Margaret did get it first."

In the room occupied by the older women, bedclothes and nightclothes bore bloodstains in the positions to be expected if the women had been shot where they were found. Mrs Brown's pyjama trousers had been torn, probably while she lay in bed, as they could not have been kept up in that condition. A slight tear in Mrs Watt's nightdress could have been caused by normal wear.

In Vivienne's room there was the disorder of which we have already heard. The bruise on her chin was consistent with having been caused by a heavy blow from a fist, sufficient to knock the girl out. Other bruises on her body and legs he associated with the damage to her clothing. There might have been a struggle. The damage to the brassiere might have been caused by a sudden pull, assuming that it was being worn at the time, but this was speculation.

Taken all in all, the room presented a confusing picture. "This makes one feel that some arrangement was carried out by someone, with what intention I do not know."

He concluded, from the unnatural and uncomfortable position in which her body was found, that the girl had not been asleep when she was shot. "She might have been knocked down, supposing she was sitting up or kneeling in bed. She might have been knocked down and her arm might have got behind her body. Again she might have been stunned after a blow and then picked up and put in bed in that position. But I cannot say with any assurance how she got in."

The professor was asked if he had considered the times at which the three women had died. The temperatures of Mrs Brown's and Mrs Watt's bodies were the same, some 10·6 degrees below normal. Assuming a fall of 1·5 degrees an hour, the deaths were placed seven hours before 1 p.m., the time of the examination, or 6 a.m. This was only an estimate and could not be taken as accurate. The room was warm and both women had an unusually large amount of bedclothing. These facts would tend to retard cooling, so that death might have taken place earlier. Vivienne's body temperature had fallen only 5·2 degrees, which would place her death about 9.30 a.m., or earlier. The degree of rigor mortis present in the three cases was consistent with the probable times suggested by the body temperatures.

The injuries to Mrs Brown and Mrs Watt made it a very reasonable assumption that death had been instantaneous. The damage to Vivienne's brain was in less vital areas and she might not have died so rapidly. His findings were consistent with all three having been shot about the same time.

After the Watts, Isabelle Cooke. The body was that of a well-developed girl with thick clay soil adhering to it. The only articles of clothing on the body were a cardigan, a suspender belt and a pair of nylon stockings, both torn. She had a bracelet on her left wrist and a ring on the ring finger of her right hand. There were five injuries, the first three being bruising on the forehead, the left eyelid and the left cheek.

"4.—A brassiere was tied tightly round the neck between the upper border of the larynx and the lower jaw. The knot was situated about midway between the point of the chin and the left angle of the jaw. When the brassiere was removed its pressure was found to have caused a deep depression encircling the neck.

"5.—A rolled head square was tied tightly round the face at the level of the mouth, the knot being pushed into the mouth. When the head square was removed a deep depression due to its pressure was found on the lower part of the face and on the sides and back of the neck.... Death was due to compression of the neck by a ligature and to the knot of a second ligature round the face entering the mouth and forcing the tongue backwards, thereby obstructing the air passages of the mouth and nose."

The bruises on the face might have been caused by the head knocking against the ground or by blows from a fist.

From a consideration of all factors involved, including the fact that the body had been found in a shallow grave in heavy soil in cold weather, "the state of the body was not inconsistent with death having occurred two or three weeks before we saw it. But I cannot be more definite than that."

In the Smart cases, death had been due in each case to a bullet wound through the head at short range. The appearance of Mrs Smart, whose body showed more signs of decomposition than those of her husband and son, might have indicated that she had been dead for a longer period. But, if there was other evidence that all had been shot about 1st January, there was nothing inconsistent with that in what he found.

All three bodies were lying in natural positions, with no signs of a struggle.

Finally, he was handed a black jacket and a pair of black trousers, which he said he had tested and on which he had found traces of blood. There was not enough to determine the source.

In cross-examination, he agreed that he could not assess the time of death accurately within hours in any of the cases. Mrs Watt had been suffering from a heart condition, but the cause of death was undoubtedly the bullet wound, which could not have been inflicted after death.

In the shooting cases, he had excluded suicide, although the wounds were all in positions appropriate to suicide. "But when a person shoots himself through the head he leaves the weapon behind. If it had been individual suicide in the six cases of shooting, then we would have expected to find six firearms lying around and there wasn't one." (Logically, two weapons would have been enough: but the argument still stands.)

He was unable to say whether Mrs Watt or Mrs Brown had been shot first or which had died first.

The impression which he had formed that there was something artificial about Vivienne's room was due to the articles that were scattered about. He had an idea that there might have been a struggle and that afterwards there had been some arrangement to try to disguise the fact.

It was not surprising to find that, whether Mr or Mrs Smart had been shot first, the other had apparently had no warning. The assailant's hand would have had only a very short distance to travel between the two shots.

Corroboration came, in the Kneilands, Watt and Smart cases, from Dr James Alexander Imrie, Chief Medical Officer of the city of Glasgow and, in the Cooke case, from Dr Walter Weir, consultant pathologist for Renfrew County.

CHAPTER 9

THE TRIAL—
INSPECTOR McNEILL

I F the medical evidence, now concluded, had been lacking in
the excitement of a forensic battle, the evidence of the detectives was to make up for that.

First came Detective-Inspector Robert McNeill of the Lanarkshire CID to be examined with the quiet, impersonal confi-
dentiality that often seems to exist between prosecuting counsel
and the police.

He was engaged in 1956 on the Kneilands and Watt murders
and the Martin housebreaking, but not the Platt case. In
December 1957 he took part in the investigations into Isabelle
Cooke's disappearance. On 6th January 1958, he was taken off
that case and assigned to the Smart murders.

Next day Detective-Superintendent Brown and Detective-
Inspector Goodall of the Glasgow CID arrived to assist in the
investigations.

After certain interviews with the manager of the Commercial
Bank, Parkhead Cross branch, a warrant was obtained from
the Sheriff on 13th January "to search for money, banknotes
and keys which we believed stolen from the house at 38 Sheepburn Road".

"What place did the warrant cover?"—"It covered the
dwelling-house at 32 Fourth Street, Birkenshaw, occupied by
Samuel Manuel, the father of the accused."

"Were you present when the warrant was executed?"—"I
was."

The witness described the impressive party—nine in all,

111

headed by Superintendent Brown—who descended on the Manuel house at 6.45 a.m. on 14th January. When he described how the superintendent asked the accused to dress himself and told him that he was being taken to Bellshill police station for an identification parade, the advocate-depute asked "What was your attitude to the accused at that stage?"

The witness hesitated for a moment and the advocate-depute followed up with "Was he suspected by you in any way?"

Mr Leslie was quickly on his feet, saying "I don't know what this is leading to, but . . ." He objected not so much to the form of the question as to the answer which might follow. Lord Cameron thought the question a proper one and allowed it.

In the circumstances the answer came as something of an anticlimax: "Our attitude was that we intended to take the accused to Bellshill police office for identification purposes." He added, however, with more effect, "And at that point, I recall, he said 'You can't take me, you haven't found anything yet.'"

"Can you say whether the search had taken place or not?" —"No, sir. The search had not taken place."

The inspector described the results of the search, after the accused had been taken to the police station by car about 7 a.m.

From Bellshill Manuel was taken to Hamilton, where an identification parade was held in the afternoon of Tuesday 14th January. After the parade, the witness saw Manuel in the CID room. Brown and Goodall were also present. "The accused asked Detective-Superintendent Brown what his father's position was—what had happened to his father. He was informed by Mr Brown that his father had been detained at Bellshill."

"Was he told for what reason?"—"I can't remember whether the charge was made known to the accused or not. I do recall that his father had been detained at the time. After he had been informed about his father's position, he indicated he wanted to talk about money. He was immediately cautioned by Mr Brown and reminded that we were making inquiries into charges of housebreaking and murder concerning three people. He then went on and made a statement regarding a man who had given him money."

"Was this man McKay?"—"It was."

"Was McKay known to any of the officers?"—"He was not known to me, but he was well known to the Glasgow officers."

McKay was later found and questioned and brought to Hamilton police office about 7.30 p.m. A further identification parade was held about 8.45. After the parade, the witness and Chief Inspector Muncie cautioned and charged the accused with the housebreaking at Mr Houston's house and the Smart murders. To the first he replied, "No, nothing" and to the second charge he made no reply at all.

After a night in the police office, Manuel was taken to the JP Court in Hamilton, where he was remanded in custody for four days and thereafter returned to the cells at headquarters about 10.15 a.m. About 12.30, the witness came back from making inquiries and was told that the accused wanted to see him. As he had some other matters to attend to, he did not go to the cells until about 2.50, when he was accompanied by Inspector Goodall.

"Did you say anything to him?"—"When I went into the cell I said to him that I understood he had made a request to see me. He agreed that was correct."

"Did he say anything further?"—"I said 'What is it about?' and he said 'It is important and it concerns unsolved crimes in Lanarkshire.' "

"What did you do then?"—"I cautioned him again as soon as he said that. I reminded him of his position, that he was on a grave charge—that of the murder of three people. I advised him the position was serious and to think before he said anything and told him that he could have the services of a solicitor."

"And what was his attitude to that?"—"His attitude to that was that he wanted matters cleared up. He asked also about his father, and I told him that his father had appeared at Airdrie that morning and had been remanded in custody for four days."

"Did you tell him what charge was against his father?"—"I told him his father had been charged with theft by housebreaking or alternatively reset [receiving]. He was considering, turning things over in his mind, when eventually he said to me 'Bring my father and mother here and I'll see them in your

H

presence and after that make a clean breast of it to them. You can take them away and then I'll clear up everything for you and I'll take you to where the girl Cooke is buried.' "

Mr Leslie was on his feet: "My lord, I do object to this line."

The jury and the witness retired while he developed his point. The evidence was incompetent, as it could not be said that any documents or statements by the accused were voluntary and spontaneous. He had been arrested between 6.30 and 7.30 a.m. and was thereafter in the hands of the Philistines, without any legal advice, until 3 p.m. the next day. His father had also been arrested and the accused was clearly concerned about him. He then referred to a document which began with a statement, which was clearly not that of the accused but of a police officer, and then extended to five or six pages of the utmost importance. He invited Lord Cameron to investigate, without the presence of the jury, the circumstances in which the statements had been made. Indeed, in view of the publicity which the trial was receiving, he suggested that the evidence might be taken in chambers.

The advocate-depute, while not accepting the suggestions made, agreed that the matter was serious and important.

The course now to be followed was a comparative novelty in Scottish procedure, having been laid down by the Scottish Court of Criminal Appeal in 1954. Evidence of the circumstances in which statements, challenged as improperly elicited, were made by persons accused or even suspected of crime, was to be taken by the Judge alone in the absence of the jury. If he considered the statements inadmissible, that would be the end of the matter. The jury on their return would hear nothing of it. But, if he considered the statements admissible and fairly taken, being truly voluntary and spontaneous, without pressure or inducement, and not prompted by questioning, then it would still be open to the prosecution and the defence to lead over again the evidence relating to the circumstances, in order that the jury could in their turn estimate what weight ought to be given to the statements themselves.

In this case, evidence was taken in the absence of the jury for three-quarters of an hour on the afternoon of Monday 19th

May, the whole of Tuesday and some two hours on the morning of Wednesday. On the advice of the presiding Judge, it was not reported in the press. The prosecution witnesses were Inspectors McNeill and Goodall, Superintendent Brown, Chief Inspector Muncie, Inspector Cleland, Sergeant Lyons and Constables Gordon and Wallace. For the defence, the accused himself and his mother and father entered the witness-box.

As the whole evidence was to be gone over again in the presence of the jury, it is unnecessary to deal with it here. It is enough to say that at 12.15 p.m. on Wednesday Lord Cameron repelled the objection, having come to the conclusion that the documents impugned had been written voluntarily and without any pressure.

"In these circumstances," he said, "I have come to the conclusion that no ground has been established for excluding the statements, to which objection has been taken, from the consideration of the jury. It will be for them to assess and determine what weight or value, if any, is to be ascribed to those productions and to any verbal statement which the accused may be proved to have made."

The jury returned and Inspector McNeill took up the story where he had left off. After Manuel had said "I'll take you to where the girl Cooke is buried," the inspector again warned him and advised him to have a solicitor, but he replied "I want to do this myself. I will write something out for you."

Goodall consulted Superintendent Brown by telephone and got permission to proceed. The accused was taken under guard to the detective-inspectors' room and provided with writing material. He wrote a document, read it over and said "This won't do, I'll write you another." He then wrote a second document.

The first document (production No 140) was dated January 15, 1958, and read: "To Detective-Inspector McNeill. I hereby promise to you personally that I am prepared to give information to you that will enable you to clear up a number of unsolved crimes which have occurred in the county of Lanarkshire in the past two years. This promise is given that I might release my father and my family from any obligations or loyalties they may feel on my behalf. I wish to see my parents and make a clean breast with them first. The crimes I refer to above are crimes of homicide. I further wish to stress that I volunteer this statement of my own free will without any duress or pressure of any description being brought to bear on me. Signed, Peter T. Manuel."

The second document (No 141) read: "To Detective-Inspector McNeill. I hereby freely and voluntarily give the following promise. I will lead information about the following specified crimes: 1. Anne Kneilands; 2. the Watt murders; 3. Isabelle Cooke; 3 (sic) the Smart murders; on condition that my father is released and allowed to see me with my mother. The information I refer to concerns me, Peter Thomas Manuel, and my part in the above-mentioned crimes. I will give complete and concise information on these crimes that will clear them up completely. Peter Manuel."

Both documents were witnessed by Inspectors McNeill and Goodall.

The advocate-depute asked "Did anything strike you about it when you read this document?"—"I felt obliged, on reading the second document, when I read the paragraph 'on condition that my father is released and allowed to see me with my mother', to say to the accused that I was not in a position to give him any undertaking whatever of any kind and that the matter would require to be referred to the procurator-fiscal at Hamilton."

"Did he appear to understand what he had been told?"—"In my opinion he did."

"What happened after that?"—"Following upon that, the accused said that he wanted to tell us now about the house at Sheepburn Road. We interjected again and we cautioned him and told him that if he was to say anything more we would require to take note of it."

Manuel then made a statement, which the inspector read from his notebook: "I did it about 6 o'clock on the morning of New Year's Day. I got in the kitchen window. I went into a bedroom and got £18 or £20 in new notes and four or five 10s notes in a wallet. It was in a jacket hanging on a chair in the man's room. I shot the man first and then the woman and I then shot the boy, but at first I thought it was a man in the bed. I then went into the living-room and had a handful of wee biscuits from a tray on a chiffonier, and I got about 18s from a red purse in the woman's handbag. I took the man's keys and then took the car. The car key was on a bunch on a ring and I put it in the Ranco car park and took it into Florence Street the next night. I left it there about 8 o'clock the next morning. I gave a policeman a lift on the way in. He is a young fellow who lives in Powburn. I never took those cigarettes I saw in the papers. I threw the gun in the Clyde and the keys in the Calder at the bridge. I think I threw the purse there too."

The procurator-fiscal was consulted and issued a temporary liberation warrant for Manuel senior, who was brought to meet his wife and son in the police office, at first in the presence of Brown, McNeill and Goodall. Brown explained the reason for the meeting and asked the accused to read out document No 140. Brown then left.

Manuel asked his father why he had not said he got the gloves and camera from him. His father shrugged his shoulders. "The accused then said to his parents that he found it very difficult to speak to them, that he couldn't speak freely to his mother. She said she knew this, that he kept things to himself, within himself. These are not her words exactly, but she asked him to tell her everything, to tell her the truth. He said then 'There is no future for me. I have done some terrible things. I killed the girl Kneilands at East Kilbride and I shot the three women in the house at Burnside.'

"He followed on, after saying that to his parents, that he intended to take Detective-Inspector Goodall and I out and show us where he had buried the girl Cooke. And again he said to them that he had left the house on New Year's morning about 5 o'clock after they had all gone to bed, that he had gone down to Sheepburn Road and that he had shot the three people in the house there."

He appeared subdued and repentant and genuinely wanting to get everything cleared up.

The accused's father was taken back to Barlinnie and his

mother to Birkenshaw. Peter Manuel himself was formally
lodged in Barlinnie about 11.30 p.m. He was taken out again
almost immediately on a temporary liberation warrant to go by
car to Baillieston House, as he had indicated that he would be
able to get his bearings from there.

A macabre cross-country trip followed, with Manuel handcuffed between Inspectors Goodall and McNeill, crossing fields
and ditches until a point where he warned them, in the dark,
to look out for a hole. He said "I dug that hole. I had her body
here but I was disturbed by a man and I had to take her away."
Near Baillieston Brickworks, in a heap of bricks beside the
path, he said "You'll find a shoe in there." Bending down, he un-
earthed a dancing shoe, which the witness recognised as similar
to those described to him by Mrs Cooke. Nearby, he uncovered
the fellow to it.

On went the strange procession until they reached a field
where Manuel seemed to get new bearings from a tree. He
walked a few paces into the field, stopped and said "This is the
field. It has been ploughed since I buried her." Another twenty
yards and he stopped again. This time he said "I think she is in
there. I think I am standing on her."

Other officers came up, spades were brought and digging
started. In the meantime, Manuel offered to take the two inspectors to find the girl's second walking shoe, the first having been
recovered from the river. When they returned, the body had
not been found and Manuel seemed anxious that it should be
found before he left.

About 2.15 a.m., the body was partially uncovered and
Manuel returned with his escort to Hamilton Police station.
Before leaving the field he said he would write out a full con-
fession and he repeated that promise in the car.

When they arrived Manuel was first returned to his cell and
Inspector Cleland, an officer who had had nothing to do with
any of the investigations, was roused from sleep to supervise
the writing. This was in accordance with official procedure.
Cleland arrived about 3 o'clock and he and Manuel were taken
to the CID typists' room, where there was an electric fire.
McNeill and Goodall went back to the field, returning about

6.30 when they were shown a statement written by the accused.

This was production No 142, a sinister document, which the witness read out to a hushed court, in which the only unconcerned person seemed to be the accused.

"I am at present in custody in county police headquarters, Hamilton, on a charge of murder. I have been informed that I am not obliged to say anything unless I wish to do so, but whatever I say will be taken down in writing and may be given in evidence. I have been informed that I am entitled to have the benefit of legal advice before making this statement. I wish to make a statement. Peter Manuel. 16/1/1958.

"I hereby confess that on the 1st of January 1956 I was the person responsible for killing Anne Kneilands. On the 17th of September 1956 I was responsible for killing Mrs Marion Watt and her sister, Mrs George Brown. Also her daughter Vivian. On the 28th of December 1957 I was responsible for killing Isabelle Cooke. On January the first 1958 I was responsible for killing Mr Peter Smart, his wife Doris and their son. I freely admit and acknowledge my guilt in the above-mentioned crimes and wish to write a statement concerning them.

"On the first of January 1956 I was in East Kilbride about 7 p.m. in the evening. At about 7.30 p.m. I was walking towards the Cross when I met a girl. She spoke to me and addressed me as Tommy. I told her my name was not Tommy and she said she thought she knew me. We got talking and she told me she had to meet someone, but she did not think they were turning up for the meeting. After a while I asked if she would like some tea or coffee. She assented and we went into the Willow Cafe.[1] I do not remember how long we were there but it was not long. When we came out, she said she was going home and I offered to see her home. She said she lived miles away and I would probably get lost if I took her home. I insisted and she said 'All right.' We walked along the road up to Maxwellton Road. From there we went along a curving country road that I cannot name.

[1] On the first day of the trial, the proprietor of the Willow Café gave evidence that the café had been closed from Saturday night 31st December 1955 until Wednesday morning 4th January 1956.

"About halfway along this road, I pulled her into a field gate. She struggled and ran away and I chased her across a field and over a ditch. When I caught up to her I dragged her into a wood. In the wood she started screaming and I hit her over the head with a piece of iron I picked up. After I had killed her I ran down a country lane that brought me out at the General's Bridge at the East Kilbride Road. I do not know where I flung the piece of iron. I then ran down to High Blantyre and along a road that brought me to Bardykes Road. I went along Bardykes Road and over the railway up to where I live. I got home about 10.15 p.m. I went up to East Kilbride from Hamilton about 6.30 p.m. in the evening.

"On the 16th of September 1956, I left the Woodend Hotel, Mossend, at 10 p.m. in the evening. I took two women into Glasgow. One named Jessie Findlay I dropped from a taxi at 283 High Street, Glasgow. The other one, who I only know as 'Babs', I took to Merchiston Street in North Carntyne. I left her there and took the taxi to Parkhead Cross. At the Cross I caught the bus to Birkenshaw. When I arrived home I met a man I knew and he took me in a car up to Burnside. He had another man and a woman with him. We broke into a house in Fennsbank Avenue, No 18. We were there some time and somebody went to bed. I do not remember much about this house. The car was left in a lane in a small wood bordering the East Kilbride Road. After a while I went scouting about looking at other houses. I found a house that looked empty and went back to No 18. Someone had brought the car around and put it in beside the house in front of the garage. I told them and they drove me up and I got out at the other house. The others did not like the look of it so they went back to the house at No 18.

"I broke into the house by breaking the front door panel which was made of glass. I then went in and opened a bedroom door. There were two people in the bed. I went into the other room and there was a girl in the bed. She woke up and sat up. I hit her on the chin and knocked her out. I tied her hands and went back to the other room. I shot the two people in this room and then heard someone making a noise in the other room. I went back in and the girl had got loose. We struggled around for a while and I flung her on the bed and shot her too.

"I then went back to No 18 and found them all asleep. We then took the car and they dropped me at Birkenshaw and they went on to Motherwell at about 5 a.m. on the 17th of September. I did not steal anything from the house at No 5 Fennsbank Avenue.

"That same day I went into Glasgow and flung the gun into the Clyde at the suspension bridge. I got the gun in a public-house in Glasgow called the Mercat Bar, which is at Glasgow Cross. I do not remember the date I got the gun. I got the gun as one of a pair I bought. The man who fixed it for me told me the two men who came into the pub were policemen. The other gun was taken by a man from Burnbank. I never found out what became of it.

"On the 28th of December 1957 I went to Mount Vernon about 7 p.m. going by bus from Birkenshaw to Mount Vernon. I walked up a road leading to the railway bridge that runs from Bothwell to Shettleston. Just over the bridge I met a girl walking. I grabbed her and dragged her into a field on the same side as Rylands riding school. I took her along the fields, following the line going in the Bothwell direction. I took her handbag and filled it with stones from the railway. Before going any farther I flung it in a pond in the middle of a field. I then made her go with me along towards the dog track. When we got near the dog track, she started to scream. I tore off her clothes and tied something around her neck and choked her. I then carried her up a lane into a field and dug a hole with a shovel.

"While I was digging a man passed along the lane on a bike, so I carried her again over a path beside a brickwork into another field. I dug a hole next to a part of the field that was ploughed and put her in it. I covered her up and went back the way I came. I went back to the road and got her shoes which had come off at the outset. I took these and her clothes and scattered them about. The clothes I flung in the River Calder at Broomhouse. The shoes I hid on the railway bank at the dog track. I went up the same path and came out at Ballieston. I walked along the Edinburgh Road and up Aitkenhead Road to

Birkenshaw, getting there about 12.30 a.m. The first hole I dug
I left as it was.

"On the morning of the first of January I left my home about
5.30 a.m. I went down a park path to the foot of Lucy Brae.
Crossing the road I went into Sheepburn Road and broke into
a bungalow. I went through the house and took a quantity of
bank notes from a wallet I found in a jacket in the front bedroom. There was about £20 to £25 in the wallet. I then shot the
man in the bed and next the woman. I then went into the next
room and shot the boy. I did not take anything from the house
except money. I got the gun from a man in Glasgow in a club,
the Gordon Club.

"I took a car from the garage and drove it up to the car park
at Ranco works. Later that day I took the gun into Glasgow
and threw it into the Clyde at Glasgow Green. The next day,
Thursday the 2nd, I saw the car was still in the car park, so I
drove it into Glasgow at about 8 o'clock in the morning and left
it in Florence Street in the south side. Then I caught a bus back
home.

"I got into the house through a window and left by the back
door. Peter Manuel."

The inspector paused, and there was silence, broken only by
the surprisingly quiet, disciplined departure of a number of the
press representatives.

After that, he went on, the accused was taken back to his cell
under observation. They all, including Manuel, had a cup of
tea. Soon afterwards Manuel said he wanted to point out the
position of the two guns he had used, and two cars left the
police station again. The witness and Chief Inspector Muncie
went with him in one car and Brown and Goodall went in the
other.

First Manuel identified an area near King's Bridge, which
crosses the Clyde between Ballater Street and King's Drive on
Glasgow Green, and said he had thrown the Beretta into the
river there. He then took his escort to the suspension bridge
between Clyde Street and Carlton Place, about a third of a mile
west of the High Court, and was able to point out the two bridge
supports between which he had dropped the Webley. [This exact

pinpointing explains why Diver Bell was able to find the Webley so quickly.]

The accused at last returned to Barlinnie. The witness next saw him on Saturday morning 18th January, when he appeared before the Sheriff in chambers. He was told there was to be another identification parade and replied, "You'd better dig up another two witnesses, for I gave two men a lift on the Thursday morning from Law Hospital to Carluke. I intended to dump the car at Lanark."

[One of these men was the witness Francis Jack, who gave evidence on the fifth day.]

After a second identification parade in the afternoon, the accused conducted the witness and Goodall round the East Kilbride area explaining and expanding his statement about the murder of Anne Kneilands. He had been told that his solicitor could accompany him, but he said he wanted to do it himself.

First they went to the General's Bridge between East Kilbride and High Blantyre. The accused pointed to the bank of the river and said, "I flung the bag down there. I flung the piece of angle iron and her knickers away farther down the burn, where it joins another burn beyond the big house. I used the knickers to wash the blood off my hands."

In East Kilbride, Manuel pointed out the route which he had taken from the Willow Café to the trees on the golf course. Building and road works had changed the scene quite a lot and he had a little difficulty in places. The spot he finally picked corresponded with Inspector McNeill's recollection. The accused seemed puzzled by the absence of a tree stump beside which he left the body. He then indicated the way he went home.

All statements and information by the accused in the course of the journey were entirely voluntary and he was not invited to say anything.

The inspector said he had organised a search for the keys missing from the Smarts' house. He identified a bunch as having been handed him by Inspector Watson, one of which fitted the back door and another the front. They had been found in the River Calder.

He had tested the time taken to walk from Fourth Street, Birkenshaw, to Sheepburn Road by two different routes. Each took about ten minutes at a fairly sharp walking pace. From the Ranco car park to Manuel's house took about seven minutes. The distance by road from Sheepburn Road to the car park was either six-tenths of a mile or two and a half miles, according to the route chosen.

He identified two pairs of gloves, one leather pair being rather shrunk. These had been traced to a firm in Ingram Street, Glasgow, who had provided him with a new pair of similar gloves. These were also produced. An invoice had been found in the Smarts' house.

Finally, the inspector gave Manuel's replies when cautioned and charged with the crimes for which he was now indicted, other than the Platt and Martin cases. The replies were as follows:—

Kneilands murder—"No, nothing."

Watt murders—"No, nothing."

Houston housebreaking—"Not guilty to that."

Isabelle Cooke murder—"Nothing to say."

Smart murders and car theft—"No, nothing."

Mr Leslie began his cross-examination at that point. The charges had been formally made after the tour of East Kilbride.

"You say he led you around the scene of the crime?"—"That is correct."

"And when he came back and was charged, his answer was "No, nothing'?"—"That is correct."

"That must have struck you as a fantastic change of front, didn't it?"—"I didn't regard it as a fantastic change of front. It is quite consistent with what I have known of the accused's nature."

"So that one moment he will give you a story and the next moment controvert it?"—"I would not say that. He had said what he wanted to say and would say no more."

[And that surely is the explanation of the laconic "No, nothing"—meaning that he had nothing more to say. Note that, when charged with the Houston housebreaking, to which he had not confessed, he replied, "Not guilty to that." It was the only direct answer he gave.]

Next the witness insisted that the police did not ask Manuel to go round the East Kilbride area or ask him any questions when they went. All was voluntary on his part.

"Was there complete silence on the part of the police?"—"We left him to give all the information he wanted to give."

"Without a single word from you?"—"We acknowledged his information."

They did not write their notes as they went along, the only strictly contemporaneous note being that about throwing the angle iron and knickers away at the General's Bridge.

From the East Kilbride tour, Mr Leslie turned to the statements—obviously the major obstacle which he had to overcome. His object was to show that they had been elicited unfairly, not by any third degree, but by questioning and by playing on his anxiety for his father. Counsel described what he called a "process of breakdown", in that statement 140 was a general statement, 141 a more particular one and 142 a very particular statement. "Can you account for that position in any way?"—"I am afraid that I cannot account for the accused's actions, sir."

The witness admitted that very extensive inquiries had been made into the charges, before Manuel made his statements, without much result—"in certain cases".

"Who was in 18 Fennsbank Avenue on the night of 16th September 1956—that is the finger-ring case? Can you tell us who was there?"—"According to the accused he was in it."

"And somebody else?"—"You mean his reference to other persons? We have failed to trace other persons, but we have interviewed persons."

"There were footprints in the garden?"—"There were."

"These were not brought home to the accused?"—"The footprints could not in themselves provide positive identification."

"Of anyone?"—"Of anyone, sir."

"You see, one man is charged with these crimes?"—"That is correct."

"And that one man is now so charged essentially because of admissions coming from himself, is that so?"—"I say he is charged through admissions which have now been supported by other evidence obtained."

"From him?"—"No, evidence of corroboration of statements he made."

Mr Leslie then took the witness again through the events connected with the execution of the search warrant and the arrest of Samuel Manuel. So far as he could remember, the accused was not told in respect of what articles his father was held.

When the search was made, the inspector was interested in the Kneilands, Watt and Cooke cases as well as the Smart case, although the last was the main reason for the search. The accused was taken for identification purposes only, no charge being at first made against him. Witnesses were found who spoke to his possession of money and he was given an opportunity to explain this. He said he got it from a man McKay, who had to do with the Gordon Club. When interviewed, McKay repeatedly denied that he had ever given Manuel money.

At this time the witness' personal opinion was that Manuel was closely associated with all the crimes with which he was now charged.

At the meeting of the accused with his parents, he was not allowed to see them alone. He did not ask for this and would not have been allowed to do so in any case, "because of the charges against him and the fact that it was his parents, with whom I have had previous dealings". If a solicitor had come to see and advise him, he would have been allowed to see him alone. But it would not have been advisable to make arrangements to let Manuel see his parents alone, even in some place where no escape could have taken place.

Mr Leslie turned to the accused's concern for his father. He drew the witness' attention to the condition which appeared in 141. The inspector said he had made his position quite clear that any release was a matter for the procurator-fiscal.

He described the accused's demeanour during the meeting with his parents: "I have seen accused on many occasions and at that time I would say he was repentant, sorry and anxious to get everything cleared up."

"Am I right to assume that he would be concerned about his father in connection with the Smart case?"—"He would be if he had reason to believe that any of the articles from the Smart bungalow were in his father's house."

At the beginning of the meeting, Brown had productions 140 and 141 and handed 140 to Manuel. "Mr Brown cautioned the accused again regarding his position. He again offered him legal aid and invited him to read production 140 to his parents as an explanation. It is my opinion that these actions were done by Mr Brown to convey to the accused's parents that this was all coming from Peter's own action and was all fair and above board from the police angle."

"He would be anxious to convey that?"—"He would be anxious. I know he is a very conscientious officer."

"Was there any prompting in the course of the reading of production 140?"—"There was nothing whatever said."

The inspector denied counsel's suggestion that the police knew the whereabouts of some of Isabelle Cooke's possessions before Manuel's midnight visit in handcuffs to the area. Everything, including the body, had been discovered only when Manuel led the way.

All the information he gave was entirely spontaneous.

"But he was in the hands of the police?"—"He was spontaneous in assistance, in tracing things, in pointing something out."

After a short re-examination, Lord Cameron asked a few questions to satisfy himself of the spontaneity of the statements.

The initial promise to "take you where the girl Cooke is buried" had been noted within ten minutes of its being made and there was no possibility that the witness was mistaken. Later he did in fact lead the police in the dark to the exact spot where she was buried.

With the words "Thank you, inspector, you have given your evidence very clearly", Lord Cameron dismissed him from the box and adjourned the trial to the next day. The critical moment had passed; but there was still sensation to come.

CHAPTER 10

"MANUEL, QC"

NEXT morning, 22nd May 1958, I travelled from Edinburgh with the three defence counsel on their way to the tenth day of the trial. They were, not unexpectedly, anxious about the evidence which had been admitted the day before. The jury, like everyone else in court, were obviously impressed by the detailed statements attributed to the accused, by the midnight visit to Isabelle Cooke's shallow grave at Mount Vernon and by the personally conducted tour of the East Kilbride area. Inspector McNeill had given his evidence clearly and well. How was all this to be circumvented?

Their anxiety was unnecessary. By lunchtime newspaper bills displayed three simple words that told of the newest sensation —"MANUEL SACKS COUNSEL."

Soon after 10 o'clock, Detective-Inspector Thomas Goodall of the Glasgow CID took his place in the witness-box. Before Lord Cameron could administer the oath, Manuel rose in the dock and said: "My Lord, before the examination of this witness begins, I would like an opportunity to confer with my counsel."

Lord Cameron looked inquiringly at Mr Leslie, who agreed that an adjournment was probably desirable, and the court rose.

Three-quarters of an hour of excited speculation followed. When the court resumed, Mr Leslie thanked the Judge for the adjournment and said: "I have to inform your Lordship that I am no longer in a position with my colleagues to continue with the case, Manuel being desirous of conducting the remainder of the trial. Unless I can be of any further service, I and my colleagues will accordingly withdraw."

"I take it," asked Lord Cameron, "that you have no further powers to act?"

"I have no powers."

Permission to withdraw was granted in the quiet words: "I am obliged to you and your colleagues for the services you have rendered."

Mr Leslie, Mr Grieve and Mr Morison bowed to the bench for the last time, then, in a silence broken only by the rustle of their gowns, left the court.

For some time Manuel had been critical of counsel's cross-examination of at least some of the Crown witnesses. Their difficult task was not made easier by the way in which their client's story had changed and was still changing. By the rules of evidence, they had to put to the adverse witnesses the version of the facts that the accused was going to give in the witness-box—and they could not be certain what that version would be in the end of the day. They had therefore a very delicate course to steer. They were bound to put to the Crown witnesses the main points at least in the defence case. Failure to do so would lay their client open to the suggestion that the case he put forward in his evidence was a last-minute attempt to explain away facts too ugly to be ignored. Similarly, if their client did not testify to specific points which they put, the inference would again be that he had changed his mind about where the truth lay. The presumption is that when counsel makes a specific suggestion of fact to a witness, he does so because he has information from his client or another witness to justify it. It would be improper to put a series of merely random suggestions without such foundation. So if his client does not give, or bring, evidence to that effect, the conclusion is obvious.

In such circumstances, discretion is a cardinal virtue. It always is in cross-examination, but in this kind of case supremely so. Mr Leslie and Mr Grieve, who shared the main burden of the defence, had been very careful to put, wherever possible, the bare minimum of general questions to foreshadow the defence

I

evidence without becoming too much involved in dangerous detail. There was no unnecessary hammering away at points on which the witnesses' answers were unfavourable—a favourite error of the unskilled advocate, which only underlines the damage done and can at times result in the witness recalling additional details that make his evidence more telling than before. Quiet acceptance of a hostile answer sometimes has the effect of suggesting that, after all, it is not so important as it might otherwise seem.

Manuel, however, could not or would not see this. He wanted everything put to the witnesses, heedless of the risks involved. He was convinced that he could do better than any counsel, however skilled and experienced. He had, as it happens, in October 1955 successfully defended himself before a Sheriff and jury at Airdrie on a charge of indecent assault. The success had gone to his head.

Accordingly, on 22nd May 1958, at the end of the surprise consultation with counsel, he told them he would dispense with their services and fight in his own way. He wrote the formal dismissal in Mr Leslie's notebook: "22nd May 1958. I hereby signify that having considered the case at this stage, I wish counsel to withdraw from case. P. Manuel."

The date is in Mr Leslie's writing. The rest is in Manuel's and the words are his.

It is probable that he decided on this course before the trial started and that it was all along a question of timing. The moment was well chosen. The only important question involving law was the admissibility of the statements: that point had gone against him. By dismissing his counsel suddenly and dramatically, he may have thought to distract the jury from that damning evidence. More important, he was assured of the sympathy which it is always natural to feel for the amateur taking on professionals, even at his own choice, and the court would surely extend to him the fairness—sometimes even more than that—which is always shown to a man conducting his own defence.

Whether calculated or not, the decision was made and Manuel stood alone as his only spokesman. His solicitors continued to act, but they could help only with advice; they could not address the court or examine witness on his behalf.

The trial restarted and Inspector Goodall began his evidence. In January 1958 he had been detailed with Superintendent Brown to assist the Lanarkshire CID in their investigations. As might be expected from McNeill's evidence, a great deal of what he said was corroborative and need not be repeated. There were, however, some matters on which he added something; and cross-examination, of course, took rather a different turn.

After describing the search at 32 Fourth Street, Goodall told the court what happened immediately after the first identification parade at Hamilton. He was present when Brown told Manuel that his father was detained, or was going to be detained on charges connected with property found in the house. He did not say what property. Manuel then referred to notes found in his possession and, after being cautioned, made a statement implicating Samuel McKay of the Gordon Club.

He said he met McKay in his car near St Enoch Square air terminal. "McKay gave me £50—six £5 notes and £20 new blue £1 notes. The £1 notes were new, and I remember that they had the figure 7 in the number. The numbers of the last three figures of two of the notes were something like 334 and 335 and I think they were numbered one after the other. I got the money from McKay for showing him Sheepburn Road district where he was going to break into a bookmaker's house."

After describing the making of the statements and the visits to Mount Vernon and East Kilbride, Goodall referred to two new points.

After Platt's report of a bullet in his mattress, the witness reopened investigation into the rather stale housebreaking at Bothwell and noticed in the list of missing articles an electric razor. This brought to his mind that he had seen, without thinking anything of it at the time, an electric razor in the room where Peter Manuel was sleeping when the search party arrived on 14th January. He took possession of that razor later, but did not notice whether there was a socket in the room which would fit the razor plug.

Second, Joseph Liddell [the witness who saw Manuel with a

revolver in a public-house just before the Watt murders] had
identified one of the police collection of firearms as similar to
the one he saw.

Examination in chief was over and Manuel rose for his first
cross-examination in this case. His questions were fluent and
well-phrased, with only one or two grammatical errors of the
"I seen" sort. His voice had the unfortunate glottal stop of the
urban Scot. His forensic manners were good.

From the outset, he made quite clear that his defence was
that he had been made the victim of a gigantic police plot, so
that the usual criticism of the amateur pleader, that he did not
put his case to the Crown witnesses, could not be made: this
was a technical improvement on his performance at Airdrie. On
the other hand he committed some serious errors in stressing
adverse points by a vainly repeated attempt to get a witness to
retract or minimise evidence already given.

He plunged into the thick of the battle and asked about the
search party of 14th January. "Before you came, had you any
knowledge that you might find gloves and a camera?"—"No
particular knowledge."

"Before you came to the house, did you know where Isabelle
Cooke's body was?"—"Isabelle Cooke's body? It is nonsense
to suggest that."

"That was not the main reason you came to the house—to
find Isabelle Cooke's body?"—"No, no, no."

Lord Cameron suggested that the question was ambiguous.
Manuel explained: " I am asking, my Lord, is it the case he
knew where Isabelle Cooke's body was, and possibly the case
that he knew where the camera and gloves were, and if that was
the main reason why the police came to the house."

The witness denied the suggestion. The main reason was their
suspicion that Manuel might have had money and keys coming
from the Smart house. He agreed that Joseph Brannan was at
one time connected with the notes. He, however, was not taken
into custody but merely attended an identification parade at the
invitation of the police.

A maladroit series of questions followed, letting in new evidence. "Is it not the practice when police are investigating a

crime in the suspect's home for the accused person, or the suspected person, to remain while the search is carried out?"—"In certain instances, yes; but not all the time."

The question was perfectly good, but the answer gave a warning rattle which Manuel ignored.

"Do you not consider that in the seriousness of the situation that existed here, regarding notes or possible notes that might have come from the Smart household, it was in everybody's interest that I should remain?"—"Yes, but I think it was obvious that if you remained in the house you were going to be a perfect nuisance."

"Was that obvious to all the policemen?"—"Yes. It was obvious to me."

"Was it obvious to Inspector McNeill?"—"I don't know."

"In what way was I going to be a nuisance?"—"You were cursing and started name-calling Mr Muncie and Mr McNeill and said that they were not going to search the house."

A small matter, perhaps, but likely to antagonise the jury as indicating a sense of guilt. More discreet questioning—perhaps a slight pause with a glance at the jury after the first question and answer quoted, then a quick switch to the next topic— might have left in their minds a feeling that the police had been perhaps a little unfair in whipping him off before the search began. But now it was explained, and unfavourably to the accused.

The inspector denied that Brown threatened to pin eight murders on Manuel.

After a few more questions, Manuel turned to the second search, when the razor was taken. The witness agreed that a bottle of champagne was also taken. The police had seen two empty whisky bottles at Sheepburn Road and they took the bottle of champagne "just in case". They had no evidence that any liquor had been stolen from the Smarts' house, nor did they search the Manuels' house for whisky.

All this, however, was trivial compared with the statements read to the jury the day before and still ringing in their ears. At last Manuel turned to the two preliminary ones. He did not challenge the authenticity of No 140, but accused the inspector of forging the signature to No 141, in which specific crimes were mentioned. The only admission he could get was that the signature had been written with the same pen as those of the witnesses.

Even these statements were of minor importance compared with the discovery of Isabelle Cooke's grave and the detailed final statement. Before facing these matters, Manuel shied off again to trivialities, then suggested that the police had used unfair pressure against him.

"Is it not a fact on that evening [14th January] between 5 o'clock and 7.30 you spent an hour and a half with me alone?" —"No."

"Do you not remember trying to get a confession from me?" —"No."

"Did you not say that unless I was prepared to make statements and confess, Superintendent Brown intended to charge my father with being involved in the Sheepburn Road murders?"—"That is nonsense."

"Did you not say that if I confessed to eight murders I would go down to history?"—"No."

"Did you not say during the course of that evening that there was one thing you had heard me say that had impressed you, that I had a real regard for my father?"—"I don't recollect that."

After questions about an interview with Brown, Manuel put his version of the Mount Vernon visit, namely that, before they started out, the police knew where the grave and the shoes were and that it was they who had taken him to "find" them.

"You said we went across all sorts of fields and saw a hole in a field. Had you ever seen that hole before?"—"I had never been in that field before."

"On leaving the field we went across a path that had bricks on it and we came to more bricks scattered around?"—"Yes."

"It is in fact a brickwork?"—"I think it is a dump for the brickwork, yes."

"And there were thousands of bricks?"—"Yes."

"And you contend that in the dark I just stopped and shoved aside a brick and pulled out a shoe?"—"You did."

"Just in the dark? Just like that?"—"You did."

"How did I pull the brick out of this hole?"—"You pulled it out with your hands."

"And picked up the shoe?"—"Yes."

"Why didn't you pick it up?"—"You picked it up."

"Why didn't you pick it up? You're the police officer?"—"You beat me to it."

"I couldn't beat you to it, I was handcuffed to you?"—"You reached down with the hand by which I was handcuffed to you and picked it up."

After similar questions about the other shoe, Manuel turned to the finding of the grave. The police did not take shovels with them and Manuel wanted to know why. "Is it your evidence that, having approximately ten hours' notice that you were going to search for a body, you arrived at the suspected locus of this body without a shovel or means of digging?"—"That is correct."

"Why?"—"We had grave doubts as to whether you were telling the truth. We did not realise that you were telling the truth until you found the shoe."

"You said that you thought I was showing genuine emotions and repentance. If that was your opinion, why didn't you believe me?"—"We still had grave doubts."

In answer to further questions, the witness described Manuel directing the digging operation.

There were no questions relating specifically to the final statement and only a few on the East Kilbride visit. Finally Manuel turned to Brannan's part in the identification parade. Goodall explained that he was brought along only because the police knew he was in Manuel's company when Manuel was spending money freely on and after New Year's Day, and he had to be there in case any of the witnesses got the two men confused. There was no suggestion in the minds of the police that Brannan was one of the two men in the car seen by Gibson coming up Sheepburn Road in the early morning of 1st January.

Detective-Superintendent Alexander Brown, Glasgow CID, in his turn mainly corroborated the evidence already given by McNeil and Goodall. At the end of his examination in chief he dealt with the finding of the two guns in the Clyde at or near the places indicated by Manuel.

Manuel's cross-examination began on this theme. The Beretta was not in good order, as the spring was missing from the magazine. Not being an expert, the witness could not say what effect this would have.

Brown denied that he knew where Isabelle Cooke's body was buried. He arrived on the scene only about 1.45 a.m., when digging was already in progress. He had been touring about the area in a car for some time before being attracted by the torches used by the officers as they dug. Like Goodall he had had doubts about the genuineness of Manuel's offer to find the grave. "Only after the body had been recovered did I make up my mind about you. I thought it was an escape attempt. The place was pitted with holes and ash-bings. It would have been very easy for you to pull two officers with you into a hole."

"Were there only two officers there?"—"No, there were three officers behind Inspectors Goodall and McNeill."

"If you were worried, Mr Brown, how did it transpire that these two officers took me along a railway line out of earshot?" —"They were warned before they left." [This refers to the finding of the second walking shoe, after digging started.]

"They were warned before they left about what?"—"About any escape attempt by yourself."

"And they were warned they must take the chance of being alone with me?"—"Yes." This answer must have pleased Manuel's self-esteem. Any gratitude he felt, however, was not reflected in his questions, for he continued to criticise the police investigation into the Cooke case until the witness retorted drily: "I was not going to conduct the investigation on the lines you would like."

Manuel went back to the search of his house. "Did you not consider it would have been a good idea that if this house was to be searched in connection with me I should have been present?"—"You would have been left in the house had you conducted yourself in a proper manner."

"What do you term a proper manner?"—"In the same way as your parents behaved."

"Is it not the fact that you had already intentions of taking me from that house as quickly as possible?"—"No."

"In what manner did I conduct myself improperly?"—"You became aggressive and told your father not to allow us to search the house."

Further questions emphasised the point. Manuel turned to an interview at Hamilton police station about 12.30 p.m. "Did you tell me that you were going to hang me for ten murders?" —"I could not tell you that."

"Did you question me about ten murders?"—"I did not."

"Did you threaten me in any way?"—"Never at any time."

"Did you threaten to arrest my father and charge him with being involved in the Smart murders?"—"I did not."

"Did you threaten to arrest my sister and did you inform me that you had found in her possession money and cigarettes that came from the Smart house?"—"I never said that."

"Did you threaten to arrest my mother in connection with a bottle of liquor you found in my house?"—"I did not do any of these things."

"Did you tell me, on the afternoon of 14th January, that unless I confessed to eight murders you would crucify my family?" Brown paused, as well he might, at this suggestion. Manuel broke in: "That is not a question that needs thinking about; you know if you did or you didn't?"—"I never used the word 'crucify' in my life."

There followed further complaints that Manuel had not been kept informed of all discoveries made in the house, but Brown's attitude was constant: "I preferred to keep that to myself, certainly not to tell you."

After some questions about McKay and the Gordon Club, Manuel turned to a key found in the Smarts' car. The witness could not say which door it fitted. Manuel suggested that it might be the key from the locking device on a bookmaker's betting clock, but Brown could not help him. The object was obviously to entangle McKay.

There was a characteristic switch back to 14th January, with Manuel alleging the use of pressure through his family and Brown stubbornly denying it. The further suggestion was made and denied that Brown refused to allow Manuel to see a solicitor. In fact, he said, he telephoned Lawrence Dowdall, who replied that he was acting for Manuel senior, but not for the son (not altogether surprising in view of what had happened). Another Glasgow solicitor, Dunlop, was also approached. At no time did Manuel ask him to get a lawyer.

The suggestion of forgery of Manuel's signature on the second written statement was repeated. Brown agreed that the first statement was signed "Peter T. Manuel" and the second "Peter Manuel". He denied, however, any similarity between either Manuel signature and the signature of either witness.

Finally, Manuel returned to what he obviously considered the most dangerous evidence, what he called the "midnight safari" to Mount Vernon. This only gave the witness an opportunity for reiterating that the police were utterly ignorant of where the body was until Manuel told them, and Manuel's last two questions seem almost to accept that.

"The body, so far as you are concerned, was not discovered before you came to my house on the morning of 14th January?" —"It certainly was not. It was recovered at the spot and at the time in your presence."

"So it follows that, if I took these police officers to find the body, that they couldn't possibly have known where the body was?"—"You were the person who knew where the body was."

The day's evidence ended with other police officers, each speaking to some detail of the investigations, but nothing new of any importance emerged either in examination-in-chief or cross-examination, except that the key which Brown failed to identify as coming from the locking device of a betting clock was shown to have fitted one of the doors of W. & J. R. Watson's office, of which Peter Smart had been manager.

CHAPTER 11

THE CROWN CASE CLOSED

WHEN the court met on Friday 23rd May, defence counsel's places, empty for most of Thursday, were occupied by Mr C. J. D. Shaw, QC, Dean of the Faculty of Advocates, and the Clerk of Faculty, Mr R. D. Ireland. When Lord Cameron entered, the Dean rose and stated that he attended in his official capacity.

"As your Lordship is aware, it is a cherished tradition of the Scottish Bar that any person facing capital charges is entitled to call on the Dean of Faculty or any senior member of the Bar for any help they may be able to give. It is only because I am assured in this case that the accused desires to defend himself that that rule cannot be applied. But, for the information of your Lordship and the ladies and gentlemen of the jury, and indeed of the public, I thought it fit to appear before your Lordship today to explain the position.

Lord Cameron, himself a former occupant of the proud position of Dean, the highest honour an advocate's professional brethren can bestow, was of course perfectly aware of the tradition. His own powers had often been used, and used brilliantly, in defence of such persons. He replied "I am grateful to you for coming here to make the position clear and to make it apparent that it is through no lack of available skill and advice— which will be freely available to him—that the present situation has arisen in which the accused is defending himself. I am happy to know that a tradition which has been cherished for so long in this country is still adhered to."

The Dean and the Clerk bowed to the Judge, who bowed back. They then left the court. An impressive little ceremony, newly devised to meet a novel situation, was over.

One man in court was not impressed. Manuel seemed impatient at the momentary diversion of the limelight from himself. As soon as the intruders left, he introduced his own sensation, by asking for the recall of two Crown witnesses, Inspector McNeill and William Watt. At the same time, he asked leave to add four witnesses to the defence list—Superintendent Myles Duncan, Lanarkshire Constabulary; Prison Officers Frank Critchlow and James Wilson; and David Knox.

Lord Cameron asked why he wanted the recall of the two Crown witnesses, pointing out that he could not allow unlimited further examination. Manuel said he had strongly objected at the time to the way counsel had conducted the cross-examination and he felt a little more might have been done. "The particular point with reference to Detective-Inspector McNeill is that there were several instances in the past two or three years in which this man has been actively engaged in investigating me in connection with certain crimes.

Lord Cameron asked, somewhat dubiously, "And do you think this is going to do you any good?"

"Yes, my Lord. Then in the matter of William Watt, there was mention made by Watt of two meetings he had with me. William Watt, in examination by the advocate-depute, made certain statements and allegations, and he covered statements I am alleged to have made to him only in part. During cross-examination by defence counsel, although defence counsel had available a written report concerning these two meetings, various subjects which could have been raised and properly put to the witness were not raised. I feel it is essential to the defence that I should be allowed to re-examine William Watt."

Lord Cameron—"You mean certain subjects discussed between you and William Watt which have a bearing on these charges?"—"Yes, my Lord. These points were not put."

"If I do accede to your request you will be limited to these points. I will not allow you to cover ground already covered.

You will be permitted to ask questions only on the specific matters to which you have referred."

The two prison officers, Manuel went on, were present at a visit to him in Barlinnie by Joseph Brannan. Knox was also present and he wanted all three to speak to a conversation that took place on that occasion. Superintendent Duncan had been in charge of the search for Isabelle Cooke's body and Manuel wanted to ask him about that.

In the circumstances, the advocate-depute suggested the re-call also of Joseph Brannan. The motions were granted.

The trial proceeded with the evidence of Inspector George Watson, who searched the River Calder for Isabelle Cooke's clothing. He identified certain articles found. On 2nd February he and other officers searched for a bunch of keys in a part of the river pointed out by Inspector McNeill, and the keys were found there.

On 9th January he made an inventory of the contents of the Smarts' house. In the course of his search he found a single glove.

Cross-examination was short and mainly directed to the suggestion that Inspector McNeill knew exactly where to look in the river for the keys. The witness insisted that the indication had been fairly general.

He could not remember, whether, in making his inventory at Sheepburn Road, he found any whisky bottles, empty or full.

The stream of police evidence was interrupted by three lay witnesses. First Mrs Margaret Whitfield, a friend of Mrs Smart, identified gloves shown her in court as similar to a pair bought by Mrs Smart on 2nd December, except for the fact that they had shrunk.

Robert Hamilton, Burntbroom Farm (on which Isabelle Cooke's body was buried), said that the ploughing of the field began on Friday 27th December, continued the next day and finished on Monday 30th December. The plough, he recalled, struck a stone on Saturday and ploughing started on Monday from the same spot. The hole was later found some two feet from the place where ploughing stopped on Saturday. He had noticed no disturbance. If the police had been digging in the field between the end of December and 16th January, he would probably have noticed.

In answer to Manuel, Hamilton thought at first that the place where the girl was found was ploughed on Monday, but he corrected himself, and said they had just gone past it, presumably on Saturday.

"If Isabelle Cooke's body was buried in your field on the 28th, it must necessarily have been buried in a part of your field that had already been ploughed?"—"Yes."

"And if a body is buried in a part of a field that has been ploughed, I think there would be some indication that the ground had been disturbed?"—"Yes. There would be more indication the other way."

"If somebody dug a grave and put a body in it I think he would have extreme difficulty in disguising the fact that the ground had been disturbed?"—"I am not an expert."

"Well, do you think in your experience as a farmer, especially a farmer familiar with ploughing, that you could bury a body and leave the field looking normal?"—"I would not like to say. There should be some disturbance."

Manuel left the point there—quite a good one and quite competently handled—and turned to Hamilton's movements on Monday evening, 30th December. He asked in particular whether he had to ask a man to move a car, parked without lights in a lane near the entrance to the field. Hamilton could not remember. "That," he said, "happens almost every night." The picture of a lovers' lane is irresistible.

The ploughman, Charles Hepburn, did not help much on the question whether the part of the field where the grave was had been ploughed on Saturday or Monday. His recollection was that "the hole had been dug on the edge of where I had finished ploughing on the Saturday".

Manuel suggested that a body in the unploughed part would have been brought to the surface by the plough. The witness would not commit himself. The plough had operated at a depth of nine inches. The grave, according to Brown's evidence earlier, was about two feet deep.

Chief Inspector James McLellan described the diver's finding of the Beretta in a brown paper parcel also containing two pairs of gloves, one leather and the other net. He identified the gloves and the gun. The depth of water at that point was twenty feet or more, with a swift tidal current. The water was fairly muddy.

Detective-Superintendent Henry Crawford told of the earlier finding of the Webley. On 3rd February he went with Brown to a point on the suspension bridge at Carlton Place, where he was shown a mark on the bridge. On 6th February a marker rope was lowered from the bridge at that point and a metal frame built for the diver to work in. He had to work blind because the water was so muddy. At low tide he could work without his helmet but had to put it on as the tide came in. After about half an hour's submersion, he came up with the Webley. There was a hole in the butt, presumably for the attachment at one time of a lanyard ring.

Diver David Bell corroborated. The Webley was only some three feet from the marker rope and the parapet of the bridge.

Detective-Sergeant George Sowter had studied firearms for twenty-four years and for more than sixteen had been engaged in their identification by the marks found on bullets and cartridges after firing. He had also studied the effect on human bodies of shots fired from different ranges.

On 17th September 1956 he was present at the post-mortem examination of the three Watt victims. The furthest distance from which any of the shots was fired was two inches. He carried out preliminary tests on a bullet which he was shown. The rifling marks proved that it had been fired from either a Webley and Scott revolver or a British services revolver No 2.

Later he went with Superintendent Maclean to 5 Fennsbank Avenue to carry out tests of the audibility of shots fired at close range from a similar revolver. Two officers were posted to listen in the house on each side of No 5, and it was arranged that shots should be fired at a certain time into a recovery box, the muzzle of the revolver being held about two inches from it. About twenty minutes early, Maclean told him to fire an extra shot in the back bedroom with the door shut. Then at the time arranged, six shots were fired; two in the front bedroom with the door open, two with it shut and one in the back bedroom with the door open and one with it shut. These six shots were fired within three minutes. Nobody heard the first, unexpected, shot; from the other six only a single indeterminate sound was heard. This confirmed Maclean's opinion that the sound of the shots would be muffled by the proximity of the muzzle to the victims' heads.

Sowter returned to the identification of bullets. In all he examined four bullets from the Watt house and could say, from a comparison of their markings, that all had been fired from the same gun. Examination of the bullet found in the Platts' mattress showed that it came from the same gun also.

The witness was handed the Webley revolver which had already figured in the evidence. When he first saw it, it had been damaged at the muzzle, the metal there being tapered inwards towards the bore. This could have been done by a heavy blow on something hard. He stripped and cleaned the gun, which was full of river sludge, and also opened up the barrel to allow a bullet to pass through. Four shots were then fired from it into a recovery box. One bullet, taken at random, was compared with the five bullets already tested. All bore the same markings, proving that they had all been fired from the same gun, the Webley recovered by Bell at the suspension bridge.

Sowter then dealt with the Smart bullets. Their appearance showed that they were all fired from a self-loading pistol: indeed, the extractor, injector and firing-pin marks on a cartridge case indicated that weapon to have been a 9 mm. Beretta, 1934 model. He was later shown a Beretta gun in a wet and muddy parcel and fired test shots from it after cleaning. Comparison of the detailed marks on the test bullets with the three from the Smart house proved that the Beretta recovered from the Clyde had been used in the Smart case. He had no doubt about that.

Finally he dealt with photographs taken in the Mount Vernon area, showing among other things the field where the grave was, the grave itself and the body.

Manuel began his cross-examination with some questions about the photographs and then turned to the Beretta. The witness said he loaded the gun by inserting individual cartridges

into the chamber through the ejection port, the reason being
that the magazine platform spring was missing when the gun
was found. Normally, in such a weapon, as each cartridge is
fired the empty case is ejected and the pressure of the spring
under the magazine platform brings the next round into position for loading. The normal capacity of the magazine was
seven rounds; with the spring missing it was eight; and with
both spring and platform missing ten rounds in all could be
carried.

"If you put eight bullets into that magazine at present, would
the gun work?"—"No, for the simple reason that, in order to
make this type of weapon work, there must be a cartridge in the
chamber. In order to make the gun work you can previously
load with one cartridge in the chamber and then put the magazine into its position in the butt. It will not go properly home
but it can be held there. If any person then pulled the trigger,
the cartridge in the chamber would fire, the cartridge case would
be extracted and ejected and the mechanism re-set and, because
of the pressure applied to the gun at the base of the magazine,
the cartridge would remain in position at the top of the magazine itself and be picked up by the breech block in the forward
travel of the slide. The cartridge would go into the chamber
mechanism and would remain set and ready to fire. A second
shot could then be fired."

The witness had been able, in ten tests, to fire two shots in
rapid succession in this way and once he could even have fired
a third.

"If someone intended to shoot three people with that gun in
that manner, they would have to be certain that they could load
the gun, fire the bullet and reload it within a second before any
person in the house could awake or raise the alarm?"—"All
I can say is that, in the tests, I fired on ten occasions two shots
in succession and that in other tests I was able to fire one shot,
reload and fire another shot, total time taken being seven
seconds."

The witness had told the advocate-depute that only one cartridge case was found where he would have expected to find
three. Manuel turned to this. When the police first examined the

K

floor, they found no cartridge cases and it was only after the bedclothes were disturbed that a single case came to light. This suggested that it had been among the bedclothes, which did not mean that the gun had been fired from inside the bed. The ejected cartridges did not take a constant course.

"Did you consider the possibility of someone in the bed firing that gun?"—"It was a possibility which was excluded by the attitude of the bodies in the bed."

"Is it not correct to say that it was a possibility that was excluded by the absence of any possible weapon?"—"Had any of the two persons in the bed fired the weapon, it would undoubtedly have been there afterwards. . . . Absence of the weapon was immediately indicative that it had been fired by some other person. The direction of entry of the wounds inflicted on the two persons concerned indicated to me that they would not be capable of any further action immediately the shot had been fired."

Manuel continued to press his suggestion that one of the persons in the bed might have shot the other and then himself but the sergeant would not agree. He did concede that the bedclothes must have been pulled up over Mrs Smart's head after she was shot. He also agreed that he never considered the possibility of the wounds having been inflicted by one of the people in the bed because of the absence of a gun. With that Manuel had to be content.

After lunch, Lord Cameron closely questioned the witness to make his expert testimony quite clear.

Finally he turned to put Manuel's case as it was beginning to emerge. The witness agreed that someone must have removed the two missing cartridge cases.

"With the condition of things as you found them, is it fair to say that some person must have adjusted the bedclothes in the case of Mr and Mrs Smart after they were shot?"—"I would say so."

"And that somebody could either have been the person who fired the shots or another party who might have come on the scene afterwards?"—"It is a possibility."

Simple questions and inevitable answers. But they laid a

better foundation for Manuel's own story than he had been able
to do for himself.

Sergeant Sowter was followed by Chief Superintendent
George Maclean of the Glasgow identification bureau—a most
distinguished scientific detective. First he dealt with fingerprints
in the Watt house. All had been satisfactorily identified except
one, found on a musical cherry brandy bottle. Comparison with
prints of all those named from time to time by Manuel as implicated in the Martin case, and indeed with those of Manuel
himself, brought no result. Similarly there was one un-
identified print in the Martin house, on the lintel of the kitchen
door.

The rest of his evidence in chief was devoted to corroborating
Sergeant Sowter's ballistic evidence.

In cross, Manuel first asked about photographs of the interior
of the Smart house, suggesting that they showed signs, in respect
of the number of glasses there, that some third party had been
in the house. The witness did not agree that any conclusion
could be drawn.

Turning to the fingerprint found in the Martin house, Manuel
asked if the witness had made a special study of fingerprints and
got the expected answer "Yes." Then, with a half smile, he asked
if he had made a special study of toeprints and, to his surprise,
got the same answer. The witness would not agree that the print
was even possibly a toeprint—Manuel's suggestion being that
Mrs Bowes got her feet wet and removed her shoes and stockings, thereafter stealing Miss Martin's nylons. Maclean did agree
that the print was a woman's, but "it was quite definitely a
finger". He went on to explain that "a person would require to be quite a bit of an acrobat to put his toeprints in that
position".

In answer to Lord Cameron, the witness was quite sure that
the Platt bullet and the four bullets from the Watt house were
fired from the same gun. He agreed, however, that he could
express no opinion about the identity of the hand that had fired
the gun.

That concluded the Crown case, with the important exception of the witnesses recalled at Manuel's request. First William

Watt was wheeled into court and took the oath in his loud booming voice.

The first matter raised was the meeting between Watt and Manuel in Jackson's Bar, where, according to Manuel, Watt confessed to the murders and then tried to persuade him to manufacture false evidence against some other persons. These two points had in fact been put shortly by Mr Grieve. Manuel put them at greater length but without useful results.

"Do you recall the subject under discussion between you and I when you outlined to me a plan whereby I might lead information to the procurator-fiscal with a view to having a man named Charles Tallis and a man named Hart arrested for the murder of your wife?"—"That is quite wrong."

"Do you remember a part of the discussion wherein you described how you had carefully planned for months to kill your wife?"—"That is atrocious and a lie."

"Do you remember a part of the discussion wherein you stated that so carefully had you laid your plans that they had even involved changing your address?"—"That is a lie."

"Do you remember offering to give me the biggest boost I have had if I pulled up my socks and played the game your way?"—"That is also a lie."

"Do you also remember describing to me how you could drive a car better than Stirling Moss?"—"That is also a lie."

"Do you remember that you said to me that when you shot your little girl it would have required very little to have turned the gun on yourself?"

Lord Cameron intervened. "Just answer the question 'Yes' or 'No', Mr Watt."

More quietly than he had been answering, the witness said "No."

Relentlessly Manuel went on. "Do you remember describing to me the manner in which you killed your wife?"—"I never did."

"Do you remember informing me that it was your intention at that time not to kill your daughter?"—"I never did."

"You made no attempt to kill your daughter?"—"I never said anything of the kind. That is a lot of nonsense."

Coming to the second meeting, at which Dowdall was present, Manuel referred to the story he had told of the house at Bothwell where the bullet had found its way into the mattress and asked, "Why did you not go to the police with this information about this house in Bothwell if you were anxious to prove your innocence?"—"That was left to Mr Dowdall, my solicitor."

"You were acting under solicitor's orders at that meeting with me?"— "I was."

"Did he consider that it was a good thing for you to take a man who might possibly have information and get him drunk?"—"Not at all."

"That was your decision?"—"That was my own decision."

For a moment there was silence. Manuel looked at the jury. Suddenly Watt realised what he had been almost hypnotised into saying and roared at his tormentor: "What was my decision? I never tried to get you drunk. I said we had a drink but I never tried to get you drunk."

With unaccustomed tact Manuel let it go at that and turned to ask questions about Scout O'Neil, who had given evidence in the early part of the trial about Manuel's purchase of a revolver shortly before the Watt murders. "This question I am going to put to you now, I would advise you to answer it as accurately as possible. Did you mention that between this man O'Neil and yourself there had been a financial transaction?"—"There was no financial transaction whatsoever. O'Neil never at any time received money from me except for a drink."

"Did he receive money for a drink?"—"One day I met him in the Gallowgate and he was in tatters. I gave him a suit and gave him £1 for a drink. That was the only occasion when O'Neil got money from me."

"Then you did on one occasion give money to O'Neil?"—"I have already explained that to the court."

It was probably wise of Manuel to stop there. But to say the least of it, this action of Watt's was a remarkable piece of generosity.

The examination drew to an end.

"Did you make a statement here that I told you there was no safe in your house?"—"That is quite correct."

"You also alleged that I described certain articles of furniture?"—"That is correct."

"Do you consider it feasible, if I killed your wife, that when I was in your house I would take a note in great detail of the furniture and miss the obvious fact that there was a safe in the house?"—"You must have taken a note of everything because you knew all about it."

"Did you mention to me the fact that you had deliberately removed your household from Muirhead with the intention of having all close associates of your wife cut off for the short period before you killed her?"—"That is a lot of nonsense. We came next door to one of our friends here."

"Did you mention that your only mistake had been using the Renfrew Ferry?"—"I never crossed the Renfrew Ferry and I can prove it now."

Manuel looked at the witness, then repeated "You can prove it now. Thank you, Mr Watt. That is all."

Joseph Brannan, Manuel's old drinking companion, re-entered the witness-box to be asked questions about his Barlinnie visit. Manuel's suggestion was that, asked whether he had told the police about a discussion of a snatch to be done in Mount Vernon and the burglary at the minister's house, Brannan had denied making such a statement and further promised that he would deny these matters if they were put to him in the witness-box. As we know, Brannan did just the opposite. In this second visit to the box he strongly denied Manuel's suggestion. "I told you that when I appeared in court I would tell the truth, the whole truth and nothing but the truth, as I stand here today and tell the truth."

When Inspector McNeill returned, Lord Cameron advised Manuel in his own interests to consider the form of his questions very carefully. At first the questioning was quiet and innocuous. The witness first dealt with a police visit to Manuel's house two days after the Watt murders, to search for a revolver which they had reason to believe he possessed. He did not examine Manuel's shoes on that occasion, as he had not had time to study casts of the footprint found in the garden of No 18 Fennsbank Avenue. He did examine a suit of clothes belonging to Manuel but there were no signs of bloodstains visible to the naked eye.

Gradually Lord Cameron's warning about care faded from Manuel's mind, if it had ever made any impression.

"I understand that in the investigation of a crime there is a process called elimination. Was I fully investigated and eliminated at the time of the Burnside murders?"—"I was not the officer in charge of the whole inquiry. I could only express an opinion."

"What opinion would you express?"—"I would say that in the initial stages I attached grave suspicion to you but not to the exclusion of all other persons. Subsequently, or in consequence of certain information which came into the hands of the police, our inquiries took another line. Again when that line had been expended certain of our inquiries returned in your direction."

"At the time William Watt was arrested, having investigated along other lines, you personally must have thought that you were arresting the man who had shot the three women at 5 Fennsbank Avenue?"—"I was acting under the orders of a superior officer who, having considered the information supplied by independent witnesses, had no other course than to apprehend the man whom that evidence pointed against."

"But did you believe at the time that you were arresting the man who had shot the three women?"—"It is not a part of my duty to give a personal opinion."

"Why did you say at the time of the Burnside murders that you thought I was connected with it?"—"Do you really want me to answer that, because it would not be in your own interests?"

The inspector's warning was lost on Manuel.

"You entertained an opinion regarding me where you now fail to entertain an opinion regarding William Watt?"

McNeill paused and gave as gentle an answer as he could in the circumstances. "The only reason which I can give is my previous knowledge of you."

The next few questions seemed to amount to a complaint by Manuel that he was not investigated by the police as soon as

Isabelle Cooke disappeared. McNeill explained that the police could move as the evidence pointed.

"Are you satisfied you did everything in your power as a policeman in satisfying yourself that you had arrested the correct man in connection with the disappearance of Isabelle Cooke?"—"Of that I am in no doubt whatsoever."

"Then there is no doubt in your mind that I killed Isabelle Cooke?"—"I have no doubt at all."

Finally, "Where did Isabelle Cooke die?"—"That would be conjecture on my part."

Some questions from Lord Cameron about the weather at the end of 1957 and the nature of the soil where Isabelle Cooke was buried led the inspector to estimate the time needed to dig the grave as three-quarters of an hour.

It is difficult to see what advantage Manuel hoped to win from the recall of the Crown witnesses. The only point of any value at all was Watt's admission that he had given a suit and £1 for a drink to the destitute O'Neil, and this was not very material. Against that, he had underlined some of the points previously made against him.

The Crown case was over. Lord Cameron asked Manuel whether he wanted to begin with his evidence at once or after an adjournment until next morning. Manuel asked for an adjournment and the court rose shortly after 4 o'clock—a shorter session than usual, but one not lacking in incident.

CHAPTER 12

THE DEFENCE CASE

MANUEL plunged into his impeachment of Watt for the Burnside murders with an attack on his Lochgilphead alibi.

In the early hours of 17th September 1956, Roderick Morrison, an engineering inspector, was driving north on Loch
Lomondside. Between Luss and Inverbeg a car approached at a
high speed, faster than he thought safe for that part of the road.
Morrison, who was momentarily blinded, put his foot on the
brake and dipped his own lights. The other car then vanished.
"I automatically went to the centre of the road and put my
lights on and I saw the car lying on the grass verge in beside
some trees. The lights were all out. I drew alongside it and
thought if by chance my lights had blinded this person the least
I could do was to go out and see if he was all right. I drew to a
stop alongside where he was lying. I opened the door to get out
and as I opened the door the car started up and headed south-
ward towards Glasgow."

"Did you notice anything about the occupant or occupants
of the car?"—"He was sitting smoking most of the time."

"Who was sitting?"—"A man. He had his hand out, level
with the dash and his other hand across his face. He never
altered his position from the time I saw him."

"Did you get a good look?"—"My mind was on him all the
time because I thought I had forced him off the road."

The witness later answered an appeal from the police for
anyone who was travelling in the area. At an identification parade he identified a man who gave his name as William Watt.
The time of the incident was about 2.30 a.m.

Watt was then wheeled into court to be identified as the man Morrison had seen on Loch Lomondside and at the parade.

In cross-examination the witness said that, when he stopped, his lights were shining down the road beyond the other car, which was in darkness. There were mist banks that night. The incident took less than forty seconds from the time he first saw the other car.

The identification parade was on 9th October. There had been quite a lot in the papers about the shooting of three women at Burnside, and photographs of Watt. At the parade, he asked all taking part to put their hands to their mouths as if smoking—because "it was a mannerism I wished to see, not the person himself". The witness demonstrated the manner of holding a cigarette he had observed in the driver of the other car.

"Haven't you seen many people smoking with a cigarette in a position like that?"—"Not in my society—possibly in others."

"Is that why you picked out Mr Watt?"—"I would say so."

"Was it just a question of this man being like the one you saw on Loch Lomondside?"—"I would say he closely resembled him."

In answer to Lord Cameron, Morrison said that when the two cars stopped alongside one another they were about twenty feet or more apart laterally. His driving window was open, the other man's shut. There was a beautiful moon.

Morrison's evidence reads very fairly. He was quite frank about his limited opportunity for seeing the other man and seemed anxious to be fair and not dogmatic. The next witness' evidence reads very differently and it is easy to understand why the Crown did not rely on it to try to break Watt's alibi.

John Taylor was on duty as ferryman at Renfrew Ferry on the night of 16th/17th September. He usually kept a note of the numbers of the cars passing over the Clyde after 1.30 a.m., but did not do so this night. Some time later the police came to him for information and he attended an identification parade, where he picked out William Watt.

"Were you also asked if you could identify a car?"—"Yes."

"Did you do so?"—"Yes, it was a red Wolseley." [Watt's car was a Vauxhall.]

"Are you sure it was a red Wolseley?"—"I did not notice at the time the proper colour of the car. There was a certain mark on the car which I could identify."

"Were you asked if there were any other occupants?"— "Yes. There was nothing in the car but a black Labrador."

Watt was once again wheeled in to be identified.

Taylor told the advocate-depute that he had identified the car by a scrape mark on the driver's side.

"Did you understand the car you picked out was a Wolseley?" —"Yes."

"Not a Vauxhall?"—"It was a Wolseley."

"And you saw the name Wolseley, did you?"—"It was a Wolseley, because I had to go round the front to open the gate and I had a good look at the front of the car."

Lord Cameron—"You heard the question?"—"Yes."

"What was it?" The witness did not answer and the shorthand writer read "And you saw the name Wolseley, did you?" —"Yes."

Lord Cameron—"You are quite sure about that?"—"Yes."

Further cross-examined, Taylor explained that he usually kept a note of the numbers of late cars because the police sometimes asked about stolen cars and this information was helpful. The incident occurred about 3 a.m., half an hour after the ferry had been hosed down.

He had no conversation with the man in the car beyond selling him his ticket as he sat there, but he spoke to the dog. The deck of the ferry was well lit and he could see the man distinctly. He agreed that the lights were good enough to give him a chance to see accurately what kind of a car it was.

He knew of the murders at Burnside, but had not seen the papers for some time before the identification parade, as he was decorating his living-room. He was quite sure that the man he saw on the ferry that night was Watt.

Manuel tried to repair the damage done by the witness' dogmatism about the car.

"Can you be absolutely certain at this stage that the car you saw that night was a Wolseley?"—"I think it was a Wolseley."

"Can you be certain? Was it a Wolseley you picked out in the police yard?"—"No, it was a Vauxhall, I am sorry."

"I do not think you heard the question properly?"—"Yes."

"That is why you answered Wolseley?"—"I couldn't hear the question properly."

"You are a little deaf in one ear?"—"Yes."

[A magnificent series of leading questions.]

Lord Cameron asked: "What colour was it?"—"To me it appeared just a dark car."

"Why did you say in your examination-in-chief that it was a red Wolseley?"—"I could not hear you properly."

"When you were being asked by Manuel, you said it was a red Wolseley car. Why did you say that?"—"I could not hear properly first time, sir."

Taylor was followed by William Mitchell, a retired detective-sergeant of Lanarkshire CID, who was one of the officers who met Watt at Alexandria on his return from Lochgilphead. At some stage he told Watt, "I think it is only right that you do not discuss this matter with me. You can discuss it with senior officers when we arrive."

"Did he make any reply?"—"He said 'Is it as bad as that? Do you think I did it?' or words to that effect."

On 20th September, he was in Watt's house. In the front room, Watt "placed his right hand on my left shoulder and said to me 'Sergeant, the day you came to Alexandria you thought you were coming up to bring back the man who committed those murders.' I said 'No, I went to Alexandria expecting to find a broken-hearted man, but I found a man with a smirk on his face and without a tear.' He replied 'I believe you're right.' I said 'I know I'm right.'"

"And when you did go to Alexandria is that, in fact, how you found Watt?"—"That is how I found him."

"He did not appear to be distraught and in a state of shock?"—"When Watt and the other officer came in, I thought they were police officers from the Dunbartonshire police."

Tests at the Cairnbaan Hotel showed that a car could be pushed from the front of the hotel without being heard from

Mrs Leitch's bedroom. On 3rd October, he and Sergeant Copeland drove from Lochgilphead to Rutherglen in two hours four minutes. The distance from Rutherglen police station to Fennsbank Avenue was about a mile and a quarter.

In cross-examination he said that this trial run did not go by Renfrew Ferry. They left Lochgilphead at 8 p.m. in the dark and drove for the 91 miles at an average speed of about 45 m.p.h.

He had not been surprised by Watt's reaction to his warning not to discuss the case with him.

"May I take it that you don't like Mr Watt?"—"I never met him in my life until I met him at Alexandria."

"May I take it that you don't like Mr Watt?"—"I have no reason to dislike him."

"Answer the question."—"I don't dislike him."

"Are you friendly with him?"—"I never met him until that day. I know nothing at all about him."

In re-examination, he said he visited Manuel's house with McNeill on 18th September 1956. Nothing was found to suggest that he was in any way implicated in the Fennsbank Avenue crimes.

Sergeant Peter Copeland corroborated Mitchell about the test run from Lochgilphead to Rutherglen. He used his own Ford Zephyr, which had a similar performance to a Vauxhall.

Watt's brother-in-law, George Brown, described a conversation with Watt during the weekend after the murders.

"Did you at any time communicate to Mr Watt that your wife was a light sleeper?"—"Yes."

"Did you give it as your opinion that if someone had broken into the house by smashing the front door then your wife would most probably have woken up?"—Before answering, the witness told Lord Cameron that Watt had been half-asleep with exhaustion, then answered "Yes."

"Did Mr Watt say something when you suggested that your wife would probably be shot first as she probably wakened first?"—"I volunteered it."

"And did Mr Watt reply to that?"—"He did suggest that

Margaret did get shot first, after a period of two or three minutes, after I had volunteered the suggestion."

"Were his words to this effect: 'George, Margaret did get it first'?"—"Yes."

The witness told the advocate-depute that at the time Watt was very sleepy. He had thought nothing of the remark until some hours afterwards.

Manuel next called James Hendry, until 28th December 1957 chief superintendent of the Lanarkshire CID and in charge of the Kneilands and Watt investigations. Asked about inquiries into Manuel's movements early in January 1956, he replied "You told me that on 2nd January, the day of the [Kneilands] murder, you had never left your house. On 3rd January you had gone to the pictures in Glasgow."

"Did I mention that at 7.30 on 2nd January there had been a new series on BBC television called 'I Was a Communist for the FBI'?"—"Yes."

"Did you check that and find it to be correct?"—"Yes. That, of course, could be got from the 'Radio Times'."

From some immaterial matters, Manuel turned to what was found at the scene of the murder, concentrating on the footprints. The only ones found were those of Anne Kneilands herself but it was possible that her pursuer took a different route. Manuel then asked why the girl had run into the wood and away from habitation, instead of towards Capelrig, where she had friends.

"I don't know the girl's mind. She was being chased for her life. I don't know what she was thinking at the time."

Manuel next tried to find out the witness' opinion on various matters connected with the Watt murders. These questions were, properly, disallowed by Lord Cameron.

For example, he told the witness not to answer the question "Were you confident when you arrested William Watt that you had arrested the man who shot his wife?"

He explained to Manuel: "I allowed you to ask Mr McNeill and other officers much which would normally be improper, because they had put forward a confession which you said was false, and I allowed you to put your questions. But what this witness thinks of any of the charges now standing is entirely irrelevant. That is for the jury at the end of the day. I will not allow you to ask that question."

Manuel made a few more attempts to ask further questions of the kind, but Lord Cameron had him under control and there was little further examination. Finally he turned to O'Neill's statement about the sale of the gun, and again tried to elicit the witness' opinion.

"Did you check his statement?"—"To the best of my ability."

"Did you find if it was a truthful statement or not?"

Again Lord Cameron pointed out that he was trying to ask the witness for his opinion, which was not a matter for the court. "You could ask him what steps he took to check the statement, but you cannot ask him whether he believed in the truth or falseness of the statement."

Manuel did not seem to understand. Lord Cameron phrased the question for him. "Did you obtain any statement which, on the face of it, appeared to confirm this story or not?"—"I could obtain no confirmation of his story other than by approaching the accused, and I was not able to do that."

The evidence ended tamely.

"But the statement was that O'Neil himself had personally sold me a gun?"—"Yes."

"Did he mention any amount of money?"—"No."

"And did he at a later date retract that story?"—"Not to me."

"Did you ask O'Neil why he made the statement?"—"I believe he said something about wanting to see justice done."

Superintendent Myles Duncan, Lanarkshire Constabulary, was in charge of the search for Isabelle Cook. All the policemen had searched conscientiously, but they could not turn over every little pile of bricks to find her shoes.

Two officers from Barlinnie Prison, Chief Officer Kinghorn and Assistant Chief Officer Kelly, were pressed by Manuel to say that he had been surprised when he was taken out immediately after being lodged on 15th January. They did not do so.

Prison Officers Critchlow and Wilson were asked about the

conversation in prison between Brannan and the accused, when, according to Manuel, Brannan had denied making any statement about Manuel's reference to a snatch at Mount Vernon and breaking into a minister's house there. Their evidence was to the effect that Brannan denied having signed any statement.

Further evidence about this conversation came from David Knox. He said that Brannan denied both the making and the signing of any statement and told Manuel that he had nothing to worry about. Brannan further said he would not acknowledge any statement in court.

It may be of interest to observe that on 16th June 1958, Knox was sentenced to eighteen months imprisonment at Airdrie Sheriff Court for his fourth conviction for housebreaking. One of the witnesses against him was Joseph Brannan.

Manuel's family then gave evidence in turn. First his mother, Mrs Bridget Manuel, told shortly of the search of 14th January. She telephoned Lawrence Dowdall next day to instruct him for Manuel senior. There was no question of his representing Peter.

On Wednesday evening a policeman called and asked her to go to Uddingston. A car took her to the police station and she was told to wait. "The next thing that happened was that your father came out handcuffed to a policeman. I spoke to him and he said 'Good evening.' It was dark in the car and I said 'Do you not know me?' He said 'Good God, have they got you too?' He asked me where we were going and I said I did not know."

They were then taken into a room in another building, where they saw Brown, Goodall and McNeill. Brown told them "you would be brought in to see us and you were going to read a statement".

Manuel was brought in but refused to read a statement until his father was released. McNeill said they could not release him without going before the Sheriff. Manuel then read a statement "about clearing up a few crimes and a few mysteries about things that had happened in Lanarkshire".

"Was there any mention in the statement about specific crimes?"—"No."

"After I had read this statement, what happened?"—"You

asked your father about his work. Mr McNeill said he would
see your father's job all right. Mr Goodall then said 'If anything
happens to your father's job in Uddingston, I will guarantee he
will get a job in Glasgow.' . . . You asked me if I was all right
and if everyone else was all right and said you didn't know how
these things happened or what made you do these things."

Manuel tried to persuade his mother to withdraw this ugly
piece of evidence. "Are you absolutely sure you heard me saying that?"—"I am not sure, Peter."

"Is it not a fact that you heard someone saying that?"—
"Wait a minute. . . . Mr Goodall said. . . . I'm not sure, Peter."

"Did you hear any of the two policemen making any statement?"—"Yes, Mr Goodall was saying 'Come on now, Peter,
speak up now, Peter, you know what you have to tell, Peter,
you know what you have to do, Peter."

"You heard him in effect urging me?"—"Oh, yes."

"Did they tell you at any time before that interview that I
had been charged with murder?"—"No."

Manuel then turned to the Watt murders. His mother said he
had not been out of the house on the afternoon of 17th September and Tallis did not visit the house on that day. [This was to
rebut Tallis' story of the hot rings.]

At that Manuel sat down. Lord Cameron reminded him that
he had asked no questions about his alibi for the Smart murders.
His mother's evidence was that he was in the house from midnight on. She went to bed about 4.45 a.m., Peter and James
volunteering to wash the dishes. When she rose at 8 o'clock she
wakened Peter, who was asleep in a bedchair.

In cross-examination she agreed that in September 1956 Tallis
was about the house quite a bit and she saw him from time to
time. Asked about the name and telephone number on the
National Assistance form, she confirmed, from her point of view,
the evidence already given by McKay.

At the meeting in the police office in Hamilton, she was quite
clear that the document read out bore no reference to specific
crimes. It referred only to unsolved crimes. And she agreed
again that her son said he did not know how these things happened or what made him do these things.

L

Shown the first two statements said to have been written by the accused, she said the first was in his handwriting, but thought the second was not. It was, however, very similar, although it had "gone off the line".

Re-examination caught Manuel in one of his fatal errors, emphasising hostile evidence by repetition. He asked why she thought he had said "I don't know why I do these things," and she replied "I am sure I heard you say it."

"Did you hear me saying it plainly and clearly or is it just an instance where you think you heard me saying it?"—"I heard it, Peter."

"You heard it?"—"Yes."

"Did any policeman suggest to you you might have heard me make that statement?"—"I was questioned by Mr Brown and during the questioning he said to me 'You have some questions to answer me about the Kneilands murder and I want the right answers from you.'"

"Did he or any other person examining you suggest to you that you heard me saying that I didn't know what made me do these things on that particular night?"—"I can't remember."

"If you can't remember the questioning that took place subsequently, how do you remember I said it that night?"—"I think you said it."

"That is what I am trying to get at. Is it a fact you think I said it or did I say it?"—"I don't know."

"Then can I put it like this—Did you definitely and plainly hear me saying 'I don't know what makes me do these things?'"—"Well, I heard you say it."

"You are quite sure no one tried to put that into your mind afterwards?"—"No."

Several times, had he been wiser, he could have stopped leaving at least a suggestion of doubt about the matter, but he pressed on, driving the point and its importance ever deeper into the minds of the jury.

Lord Cameron ended Mrs Manuel's ordeal with a few questions.

"Now, you told us you thought you heard him say 'I don't know what makes me do these things'?"—"Yes."

"Did you ask him any questions as to what he meant?"—"I didn't ask him any questions."

"Can you say whether you associated 'these things' with any of the unsolved crimes to which reference was made?"—"No, nothing like that entered my mind."

"As a mother, were you very upset and worried?"—"I had all my faculties."

"Did Peter appear to be in full possession of his?"—"I could not answer that, but he was not his usual self. I am talking about his appearance."

"Just tell us in what way you thought his appearance differed?"—"He had an old suit on. His hair was not as it usually is. The neck of his shirt was lying open and he had a big pair of boots on. I don't know whose they were."

"When he was living at home with you did he always appear to be in full possession of his faculties?"—"Yes."

The accused's father, Samuel Manuel, was of sterner stuff than his wife. After the Anne Kneilands murder, Peter was "severely questioned" several times; once there were nearly blows.

On Sunday 16th September 1956 Tallis called about 5 p.m. and asked for Peter, who was at the Woodend Hotel. He also asked if he could leave four sticks of gelignite in a coat. He mentioned he had a gun, but did not ask to leave that. The witness told him to take the gelignite away. When the police came two days later they were looking for a gun. McNeill came back and asked for a pair of Peter's shoes. "He told me that he knew you were innocent, and even what date Watt would be tried—6th January."

McNeill came back once again for more shoes and was told he would have to have a search warrant next time. This he got and on his next visit removed all Peter's clothes. The warrant was in connection with the Burnside murders but he could not be sure if it was also in connection with the murder of Anne Kneilands.

Lord Cameron—"How is it that you cannot recollect that? That would be the sort of thing that would stick in your mind?" —"I cannot remember."

The electric razor in the house came from Tallis about August 1956. Tallis offered to sell it for £2, but the witness refused to buy it and Tallis gave it to the accused.

Manuel then reached 31st December 1957. Father and son were in the Royal Oak public-house and Brannan was there for about twenty minutes. To get rid of him, Peter pretended to have no money, and Brannan left. Another two men joined them; one, who went out with Peter for a little, wore glasses and was greying at the temples, with a reddish face.

The witness went to bed about 3.30 on New Year's morning and was wakened by James about 5.45. He rose at 6.30 and went downstairs, when the accused said that he had wakened him. When he left for work the accused, he thought, was sleeping. He did not hear anyone leave the house that morning.

On 14th January, after the accused was taken away, the police searched the whole house and questioned him about a pair of gloves. No camera was mentioned at the time but he was later charged with the theft of the gloves and the camera. He had never been arrested before.

At the meeting next evening in Hamilton police office, the accused read a statement after refusing to do so. The police kept prompting him to do so all the time.

"Did you hear me make a statement that I did not know why I did these things?"—"You never made that statement at any time during my presence."

"Can you remember any of the suggestions these two policemen made?"—"I heard Inspector Goodall saying 'It will be all right. Now, Peter, we will see you all right. You won't even get a trial. We will see it all right.'"

"Did you hear Goodall saying I would get treatment?"—"I did hear him saying that. He said 'Now, Peter, you will be all right. You will get treatment.' I took it he meant you were insane or there was something wrong with you."

"Did you think there was something wrong with me that evening?"—"Yes, you were not your usual self. It may be silly but I felt you had drink or a drug on you. That was only what I felt that night."

"Would you say from what you know of me I was acting

spontaneously of my own free will?"—"Oh no, you were not acting on your own free will. Everything had to be dragged out of you. Your hair was all over your face and you looked very shabby and dirty. You looked as if you had had a good deal of pushing about."

The witness agreed with his wife that the statement the accused read out did not mention specific crimes. In fact, neither statement produced in court was the one he heard read.

In cross-examination the witness said the gloves were given him by Peter on Christmas Eve or the next day and agreed that he should have told the police so.

Lord Cameron—"Why did you not tell the truth to the police at the time?"—"I just couldn't give an answer to that question."

"Why not? Why can't you give a reason?"—"I was excited at the time."

"You are not excited now. What was the reason?"—"Well I had received a parcel from America and I thought the gloves might have come from there."

"Is that the best reason you can give?"—"I don't know why I said it at the time."

In answer to the advocate-depute, the witness painted a dramatic picture of the scene of the meeting at Hamilton. "When Peter was brought in there were well over twenty persons in the room."

"What were the names of the twenty persons?"—"I don't know their names. They were policemen. The room was packed. On the stair there must have been another twenty and when Peter was asked to read a statement there were another twenty in the room."

"What did you understand by unsolved crimes?"—"The police said they knew Peter and Tallis were doing a lot of jobs in Uddingston, but they could not prove it."

"Didn't you think it would be in connection with the murders?"—"No, because I knew Peter had not been out of the house."

"You were seriously concerned that Peter had been charged with the Smart murders, and when you heard a statement re-

ferring to unsolved crimes in Lanarkshire you took that to be
housebreakings in Uddingston?"—"Yes."

Later the witness agreed with the advocate-depute that Tallis'
request to leave gelignite in the house was rather an extraordinary one.

"Was there any conversation leading up to this matter?"—
"When we were talking he [Tallis] told me about being out in a
car with a lady the week before and the lady sticking a gun
into his side. That had happened the Sunday previous. I think he
said Peter was with him. He said that this lady stuck a gun into
his side, kidding like. She was the manageress of some dairy
round about Rutherglen." One cannot help remarking that, if
the Manuels are to be believed, Tallis had a genius for picking
dangerous girl-friends.

He and his wife had never liked Tallis, and "even Peter told
us that if he came to the house we weren't to let him in". On
the Sunday when he called for Peter, they told Tallis he was
at the Woodend Hotel to get him out of the house.

Lord Cameron—"Couldn't you have told him that you didn't
know where Peter was?"—"I would be telling a lie if I had
told him that."

The advocate-depute took up the story of the gun.

"When the police came to your house on 18th September
looking for a gun, did you mention that Tallis had been talking
about a gun?"—"No."

"Why?"—"I don't know."

"Didn't you think it was significant?"—"I didn't mention it
to the police at that time."

He told Lord Cameron that he realised he should have done
but he was "highly excited at the time".

At last he found a reason for not telling the police about
Tallis' gun. "I thought they had searched Tallis' place."

"Who told you that?"—"I saw the police and they said they
had been round a lot of people."

Further cross-examination left the witness' credibility a little
shaken but he stuck to the main features of his story. Re-
examining, the accused tried to make things easier.

"When the police questioned me on 18th September you

heard they were searching for a gun. Was it not that you thought it was not a judicial time to mention knowledge concerning guns?"—"I did think that."

"Is it that you were trying to cover up for me?"—"Yes."

"You thought if Tallis had a gun there was a possibility I got it?"—"Yes."

Lord Cameron—"Did you inform the police after 18th September 1956 that you had information that Tallis had acknowledged possession of a gun on Sunday 16th September?" —"No."

"So you never came across the appropriate time for telling the police?"—"I never told them."

After some questions about the camera Lord Cameron turned to the accused's demeanour at Hamilton.

"You said your son was not his usual self?"—"Yes, I did."

"You said he looked as though he was under the influence of drink or drugs?"—"Yes."

"Did he appear to have less than his full mental capacity at that time?"—"He wasn't the same person."

"I was interested in his mental condition?"—"I wouldn't say about his mental condition."

"About his mental capacity and possession of his faculties over the past two years, prior to January 1958, did you notice anything unusual or abnormal about him?"—"No, I did not."

"Are you quite sure?"—"Quite sure."

"Is there anything you can say or want to tell me about that? Now is the time."—"I never noticed anything."

And Samuel Manuel left the witness-box, having missed the only real, though slender, opportunity he had to give his son the chance to save his neck.

His daughter Theresa followed. She was a trained nurse, usually living away from home, but she was at home for Hogmanay. From 1.15 until 2.35 she was telephoning a friend. Peter was in the house when she went to bed at 4.35. A pair of gloves which had been in a drawer in the sideboard were no longer there after her brother's arrest. She also remembered a camera, which Peter gave her on the Sunday after Christmas 1957.

Lord Cameron asked her if, as a trained nurse, she had

noticed anything unusual about Peter during the past two years.
She replied "I would not say anything unusual. To me it was
his usual behaviour. I have always known him the same." This
answer shows that the witness was comparing Peter's recent
conduct with his previous conduct. It does not involve a comparison with a normal person, if such a person exists.

It must be remembered that (although this was before neither
Judge nor jury) of the two years before January 1958 Peter
Manuel spent fourteen months in prison. Opportunities for
observation were therefore somewhat limited.

James Manuel, the accused's brother, said that he and Peter
volunteered to wash up about 5.45 on New Year's morning. He
had looked at a clock and could definitely testify that Peter was in
the house until that time.

Robert McQuade had been in the Royal Oak with Manuel
on Hogmanay night. "You came over and asked if I had seen
any busies. Then you asked me if I would keep an edge up for
the busies as you had business to do. I says to you 'What's in
it?' and you says 'I'm going to sell this guy a shooter.' I says
'O.K. then' and went nearer the door."

He turned to the Judge and said: "Peter walked into the
toilet and this man followed him there. After five minutes he
came out. I went back to the table and a drink came over."

The other man was middle-aged and wore spectacles and a
hat. The witness had never seen him before. After the Sheepburn Road murders he saw photographs in the press of the
people who were killed.

"Did you see a photograph of Mr Peter Smart?"—"Yes."

"Was he anything like the man you saw that night?"—"It
was like him but I would not commit myself to saying it was
him."

"Did you see any photographs in the newspapers of Mr
Smart wearing a hat?"—"Yes."

"Was there any resemblance between the man you saw on
Hogmanay night and Mr Smart?"—"Yes, with the glasses and
that, going by newspaper photographs."

The witness told the advocate-depute he did not go to the
police about the incident, because "if I had gone to the busies

I would have been done for keeping the edge up when the gun was sold".

Lord Cameron—"Did you not think it was important to let the police know that a man unknown to you had acquired a gun on the night of Hogmanay?"—"I wanted to keep out of trouble."

"I didn't ask you that. Answer the question."—"It wasn't unusual. I didn't think it very important because I didn't think it had any connection with the Sheepburn Road incident."

"Did you ever inform the police authorities that you had been a witness of this transaction?"—"No."

"Didn't you get a drink as a reward for keeping your eyes open?"—"Yes."

"Didn't you know it was an improper and illegal transaction?"—"Yes."

The witness was dismissed sternly, almost contemptuously, from the witness-box.

CHAPTER 13

MANUEL'S STORY

ONE witness remained. Manuel rose in the dock and said, "My Lord, I intend to testify on my own behalf."

Lord Cameron invited him to go to the witness-box and the neat diminutive figure darted—there is no other word for it—across the court, dragging behind him the large constable who held his sleeve in token custody. After administering the oath, Lord Cameron offered his help and suggested that he should make a statement dealing with the charges in chronological order and separately with his alleged statements. Manuel followed this course. He spoke with a rapidity that had the shorthand writers in difficulty until the Judge asked him to slow down.

His evidence on the Kneilands case was short. He had been interviewed by the police and in particular Superintendent Hendry, who told him he had been identified by a bus-conductress as having been in East Kilbride on the evening of 2nd January 1956. Manuel advised an identification parade and after about half an hour Hendry went away. About 5 o'clock that evening, when he returned home, he found that his house had been searched and the police had taken away his clothing, shoes and some other things.

That evening Manuel once more told the police his movements over the New Year holiday. At work next day, he learned that another workman had been to the police and made a statement about marks on his face. "I had a few words with this fellow and he left East Kilbride and got a job in Uddingston."

Next day a newspaper reporter came and asked what the police interview had been about. Manuel told him that he was suspected of the murder. The reporter asked for a statement and a photograph to go on the front page the following day. He said "If you were in East Kilbride someone must have seen you and they will come forward and say they saw you in East Kilbride. If you were not in East Kilbride and nobody comes forward you will be in the clear." Manuel gave him a short interview and a photograph and both appeared the next day.

This evidence seems to refer to the *Scottish Daily Express* of Saturday 14th January 1956—exactly two years before his arrest.

About the end of July 1956, Charles Tallis was talking vaguely about being paid money to break into a house. Two weeks later Manuel was in the house where Tallis lived with Mrs Bowes. About midnight Tallis produced two guns, one an automatic and the other a Webley, both .38s. He asked Manuel for ammunition, as what he had would not fit. A week later, Tallis told him not to bother about the ammunition as he had got some. Later Manuel saw the ammunition in Tallis' house. The lanyard ring on the butt of the Webley was loose, so they banged it against an iron fixture in the fireplace until it came off.

Early in September, Tallis told him more about the offer of money to break into a house, £1,000 being mentioned. The house was to be messed about to make it look as though someone had been in for a considerable time. "I pointed out to him, 'Charlie, if I were offering £1,000 for some place to be broken into, it would be a place like Buckingham Palace and not an ordinary house. I don't understand the offer of money for just breaking into a house. It doesn't make sense.' "

Eventually he arranged to meet Tallis on the afternoon of Sunday 16th September, but Tallis did not turn up either then or at a later time he suggested by message. Manuel got home that night, without having met Tallis, about 1 a.m.

Next morning his father told him that Tallis had called the day before wanting to leave a parcel of explosives. About 10 or 10.30 a.m. Tallis came in. Manuel made him a cup of tea and after a little Tallis asked if he could get rid of two rings for him. He said they belonged to Mary Bowes. They went into Glasgow, but Manuel could not find the man he hoped to sell them to, so, after buying a bottle of whisky, they went to a cinema, where they stayed until 4.45. The film was "The Long Arm of the Law." They next went to the Double-Six public-house on the Broomielaw. About 5.30 Manuel went out to look for his contact but could not find him. He read in an evening paper that three people had been found dead in Burnside— believed to have been battered to death.

Back in the public-house he told Tallis he wanted no more to do with the rings and handed him the paper. Tallis said "These rings never came from Burnside." Manuel said "But you were telling me about a job that had been done last night and that you broke into a house and wrecked it for £1,000. Now three people have been killed in Fennsbank Avenue. I don't like it, Charlie, and there are your rings."

Next day eight or nine policemen came to his house to look for a gun. They did not search very thoroughly. Manuel was asked if he had a gun and said "No." McNeill then asked how he and Tallis were getting on and he replied "Not too bad."

Some time later by chance he found a ·38 revolver in a drawer. It had been fired and held five empty cartridges and one live round. He took it and "bunged it into the Clyde".

Next time he met Tallis he challenged him with having put the gun there. Tallis denied it but later promised to let him know about it. That night he told Manuel that "things had come unstuck" and that he had left the gun in Manuel's house.

Tallis told Manuel that for a couple of months he had been planning to go to Burnside and break into a house in Fennsbank Avenue. It had been arranged for the first week in September but something had gone wrong and it had been put back. The people were away that weekend and the house would be empty.

"Tallis said 'Mary and I broke into the house. She was drunk. A car came out of the house next door and Mary got a bit panicky and ran across the flower bed. I brought her back. We got into the house. After a while Mary went into a bedroom and got into a bed. She didn't undress or anything. Afterwards I lay down on the sofa. About 3 o'clock I looked up and down the road. I knew what we were looking for—the other man, who was later than I expected.' He told me that about 3.30 a.m. on 17th September he had met William Watt. Watt's car was parked in a sandpit or quarry near Fennsbank Avenue. He and Watt went to No 18 and talked for ten minutes, then Watt told him to break the front door as they left the house. He and Mrs Bowes left at 4 o'clock and went down the lane to where the car was parked.

"When they got down they found that Mary Bowes had left a handbag in the house. He took her back to the house and they went inside and took about half an hour to find the handbag. It turned out that she had had it in bed with her and it had worked its way to the bottom of the bed.

"Tallis said that prior to leaving the house Watt came back and asked if he could drive them into the city. Watt said to him 'Charlie, there is your gun back, get rid of it for me. I can't take the risk of taking the gun in the car.' Tallis said he would get rid of it. Then he told me that early on the Monday morning he found out that Mary Bowes had two rings. He said she had stolen them from the house. It was an odd sort of story. It didn't cover him leaving the gun in my house but I let it go at that."

However, next day Tallis told him that he had been told to put the gun in Manuel's house by the man who was concerned in the housebreaking.

Later Manuel was led to doubt Tallis' story. He got in touch with Dowdall, who seemed to know all about Tallis and asked Manuel to go to the procurator-fiscal. If he did not, Dowdall threatened to tell the police. He also said that if Watt went for trial, he would say that Manuel sold him the gun.

Manuel met the procurator-fiscal and told him that Dowdall wanted him to tell a fictitious story incriminating Tallis. The procurator-fiscal challenged Manuel with having sold Watt a gun, but Manuel said he had never met Watt. He then heard from a contact in the police that Dowdall was trying to persuade Hendry and other police officers that Manuel was guilty. He accused Dowdall of this, but was told "Tripe! You ought to know that these coppers are just looking for information."

There followed the meeting with Watt, first at the Whitehall Restaurant and then at Jackson's Bar. Watt invited him to come and meet his brother John and corroborate Watt in the story about Tallis. Manuel agreed to do so.

"Watt talked to his brother and said 'This is the fellow I have told you about. We have been hearing the wrong sort of story about him. He is not the kind of fellow you think he is. We are going to keep him here and have a talk.' Watt kept calling me 'Chief'. Everything he said to me he called me 'Chief'.

"The other man asked me what I knew about Burnside. I said 'It all depends, but I know one man who was at Burnside that night but I don't know what happened.' They kept the conversation going and we started talking about this story about Tallis and Hart. Watt said 'John, what happened was this. This man and Tallis went to break into the Valentes' house. They had a safe in their house and it was supposed to contain £5,000. These people went up there just to walk in and hold up these people and take the money. When they got there they looked in the window and saw the girl Valente sitting in this house and they thought it was her house. That was the time she was in my house.'

"They argued about this for a couple of hours and Watt kept turning to me and saying 'Isn't that correct?' and I, of course always said it was."

Much later, John asked Manuel to take his brother home. As he was living in Stirlingshire, Manuel refused to do so but said he would take him to Birkenshaw. "Watt was really gone, he was rolling all over the place."

They stopped the car and sat talking. Watt ran out of cigarettes and Manuel said he would get some from the house. He refused to take Watt in. "I told him that if I opened the door and told my mother I was bringing in Willie Watt she would have a fit." He brought out cigarettes and a jug of coffee and they sat until 8.30 a.m., talking about schemes for getting other people arrested.

Next day Manuel told Dowdall that Watt had confessed to the murders, his intention having been to kill his wife and leave his daughter tied up. He did not know of his sister-in-law's presence. Manuel advised Dowdall to have nothing more to do with him.

Dowdall suggested that if someone else was arrested Watt could sue the Crown for a large sum of damages for wrongful arrest and it would be worth Manuel's while to help. The sum of £5,000 was mentioned. Later Watt prompted Manuel with the story he was to tell and said he had two men, O'Neil and Hamilton, prepared to swear they sold the gun to Tallis. If Manuel did not co-operate, they would swear they sold the gun to him. They met only once after that, when Watt pressed £150 in £5 notes on him and urged him, as it was near Christmas, to buy some presents and have a good time.

Manuel then passed to the Platt case. He bought the razor from Charles Tallis some time between the end of June and the beginning of August 1956. He did not use it because he had no plug to fit and it did not cut close enough. Tallis told him he had got it from someone who worked at Phillips' factory.

The other things stolen from the Platts' house were of no interest to him.

He knew nothing of the bullet in the mattress. Dowdall told him about it, but he did not believe the story.

He thought it strange that the police should have handled the razor several times without realising that it was stolen, if that was the case. "One thing I am certain of. If I had known a gun used in a murder fired a bullet in the house the razor came from, and there was any possibility of that razor being tied up with it, it would never have been in my house. It is just a thing you would not do."

He did not break into 18 Fennsbank Avenue. "And if I had, I am sure I would not have had much interest in nylon stockings —they are objects which I do not wear." He knew Tallis had some project in hand there and assumed that the two rings he saw came from Fennsbank Avenue, either No 5 or 18.

"I know that in the early hours of 17th September I was not near Fennsbank Avenue. On the night of the 16th I was in the Woodend Hotel. I took a woman back to Glasgow and got the last bus home. After that I went to bed. This man Tallis came to my house the next morning. I cannot say much about 5 Fennsbank Avenue except that I did not shoot three women."

On 25th December 1957 he was at home watching television. He bought the camera and gloves in the Old Mail Coach Inn from three men he had seen there several times. Brannan was with him and saw the whole transaction.

On 28th December, when Isabelle Cooke was murdered, he was at a cinema in Glasgow.

He turned to the Smart murders. He had helped Mr and Mrs Smart to build the bungalow and was friendly with them. He often went to race meetings and boxing matches with Smart. Two or three days before Christmas 1957, Smart asked if Manuel could let him have a gun. Manuel said he had one but it was not up to much as it could only be loaded by pulling back the carriage and putting the bullet up the barrel.

Several meetings were arranged but Smart did not turn up. At last he came to the Royal Oak public-house on 31st December. Manuel saw McQuade and asked him to keep an eye open for the police. The public-house was just across the road from the police station and "on occasions like the New Year these policemen have a habit of nipping in and taking a walk round."

Manuel gave Smart the gun in the lavatory and asked for £10. Smart counted out £15 in new notes from his wallet, then took out the last of his money and handed that over too. Manuel thanked him and offered him a drink, but Smart declined.

That night there was a family get-together—not a party. His father went to bed about 3.30 and his mother and sister an hour later. When "the American" went, Manuel and his brother sat talking about him until 5.45 or 6, when Manuel said it was time for bed. He stayed down in the bedchair and James went upstairs. His father came down soon after, followed by his mother and James. "Everyone was getting ready to go to church. The place was like Central Station. Nobody could possibly sleep."

He made his sister a cup of coffee and went out for cigarettes for her, then took a bus to Glasgow and got papers. When he got back he went to see Brannan and they went to the Woodend until 8.30. After buying whisky, rum, sherry and beer, he went to the Greenans' engagement party. After a while he left and went back to the hotel for more drink, paying for it with the money he got from Smart. The party wound up at the dancing, which he thought ended about 3.30.

The night he met Peter Smart in the Royal Oak, Smart gave him the key to his house and asked him to go there on Friday to entertain a business friend, Brown. He explained that he had forgotten the appointment when he arranged his holiday. He could not get in touch with Brown, who was "on the go, or on the road, something like that". He promised to leave out a bottle of whisky for Mr Brown. About 4 or 4.30 on Thursday morning, Manuel was walking in Sheepburn Road and thought he would go in and sample the whisky. There were two half-full glasses on the mantelpiece, which he thought funny. He went into a bedroom and saw Mr and Mrs Smart, then tiptoed out again. In another bedroom he saw a boy. He could hear no sound. A cat ran in, all hunched up and in an awful state. Something made him go back to the Smarts' bedroom and switch on the lights. "When I put on the light I saw there was no need to look or listen in there, because Mr and Mrs Smart were lying dead, very dead." The bedclothes were down.

Manuel suddenly realised that his fingerprints would be all over the place. He found a pair of gloves, put them on and rubbed all over the house with an apron.

He re-entered the boy's bedroom and saw blood, then went back to the Smarts', where he saw that Mr Smart's hand was over a gun. He took the gun away and rubbed it. "I looked at the Smarts. They looked awfully bare, somehow. They looked cold. I don't know how to describe it. So I just took the bedclothes and put them over them. I thought 'I'll need to get rid of this gun because this is the gun I sold him.' "

The little cat was still running about. Manuel decided to feed it. There were two tins of cat meat, but he saw a tin of salmon and thought the cat might as well have it. So he opened it but the cat only messed about with it. It did, however, condescend to eat two pieces of meat from a dish of cold stew.

Manuel and the cat went out. He did not take the car. At home, he put the gun and the gloves he had taken from the

M

house, with a pair of his sister's gloves, into a parcel, went into
Glasgow and threw it in the Clyde. For the next three days he
read the papers and listened to the wireless for news of the
discovery of three bodies. There was no news, so he telephoned
Hamilton police headquarters and said "You'll see people dead
in a house in Sheepburn Road", hanging the phone up again
at once. Nobody, however, seemed to pay any attention, for
there was still no news. "On Monday afternoon my brother
James, who had been working down there, came in from work
and said 'There have been three people found dead in Sheepburn Road, the place is alive with policemen.' So I let it go at
that."

Two or three days later he and Samuel McKay visited a friend
in Barlinnie Prison. McKay told him the police were asking if
anyone had seen Manuel in Florence Street, where the car was
found. Manuel said he knew nothing about it. On Sunday a
waiter at the Woodend Hotel told him the police had been
asking about money spent by him.

On Tuesday he was in bed when the police arrived. Brown,
whom he did not know, introduced himself and asked if he had
spent any bank notes in the Woodend Hotel on 1st January.
Manuel admitted it and in answer to further questions said they
were new £1 notes. Brown told him to get up and dress as they
were taking him to Bellshill. There was no mention of an identification parade.

At 12.15 Brown came and asked about this money. Manuel
said nothing, but Brown insisted, saying that he knew it was a
mutual acquaintance who had given it to him. Manuel retorted
that acquaintances of policemen were not usually acquaintances
of his and Brown told him he was talking about McKay.
Manuel still refused to talk and Brown said "Then I am going
to charge you with murder." Manuel replied "Go ahead and
charge me with murder."

Ten minutes later he was taken into a police van. Brannan
was "slung into the van with me. He was screaming and throwing himself on the floor. He was in hysterics and was shouting
'Tell them I was not with you, tell them I was not in the car.'
I asked Brannan what the squeal was about. He said they were

trying to do him for the Sheepburn Road murders along with me."

The police view, according to this, was that Manuel and Brannan were the two men in the car seen by Gibson in Sheepburn Road. Manuel told Brannan that he was not in the car and so Brannan could not have been in it with him.

At an identification parade three witness picked him out as having spent new notes at the Woodend Hotel. Brown took him aside and said "That's you. You are identified as having Peter Smart's money and you gave no explanation. You are in trouble. What about McKay—are you going to tell us about McKay?"

Manuel said he could say nothing and asked for a lawyer. Brown said "You are getting no lawyer. I am the man in charge of this investigation and I am not a Lanarkshire policeman. You have got these people bamboozled, they can't get you. Well, you have run into your match this time and you are getting no lawyer."

Later that day Brown said "I have got you this time. I am going to pin eight murders on you. You murdered Anne Kneilands, that was the first one. You murdered the Watts, I know that. There was the little girl who disappeared in Coatbridge, Moira Anderson: you are responsible for that too. Then you murdered Isabelle Cooke and the Smarts. You are going to be held for all these murders and you are going to admit them."

Manuel replied "I don't think so, Mr Brown. It is usually regarded as a foolish thing to do, to admit murder, and I am admitting nothing. If you want to charge me, go ahead, that is your job, but I want a lawyer." Again Brown said "You are getting no lawyer."

He went on: "We know what happened. Watt paid you to shoot his wife. He paid you £5,000 and he paid you some more to get him sprung out of jail. You twisted that case up. You twisted that fellow Hendry round your little finger. You have been seen boozing with Watt in Glasgow."

Muncie then questioned Manuel for about an hour and a half, firing questions like a machine-gun.

About 6 p.m., after a break for tea, Goodall came and used

a new approach. "I know all about you, Peter. You are crazy. You definitely killed these people, but you did not know what you were doing. You just go up and down the country killing people and then forget about it and shut it out of your mind. You are balmy. But we can't understand your motive. You just kill people as a sort of hobby." He then said that Brown was a very determined man and would stop at nothing. "The only weapon he can use against you is your family and he knows you won't stand your family being messed about. My advice is that you deal with Mr Brown in the manner he requires. He is not a bad chap and he will do all he can for you. If you need treatment you will get it."

Manuel commented drily: "As far as I was concerned, I was getting all the treatment I needed."

Goodall did not seem to know very much about the Kneilands case: he even got the date wrong.

Finally Goodall urged him again to write a statement and said "It will stand you in good stead. You will go before a psychiatrist and you will be put away. There is no doubt about it—you are stone mad."

Later that evening, Brown confronted him with McKay. He said to McKay "You were in the car with Manuel." McKay said "That is a lot of lies." Brown repeated his accusation and McKay his denial, then Brown said "That is what Manuel said." McKay shouted "He is a liar."

From 8 to 10 p.m. there was a "massive" identification parade, after which Brown, Goodall and McNeill took up the questioning again. Brown told him to write a confession. "If you don't write this confession I am going to crucify your family because we found money in your sister's bedroom that came from the Smarts' house and in her room we found cigarettes that came from the Smarts' house. You have twenty-four hours and if you don't decide to write a statement confessing to those murders I am going to ruin your family. Your father has been arrested already."

After more threats and questioning, Manuel was charged with the Smart murders. His clothes were taken away and he was given a baggy suit and a pair of policeman's boots. Muncie arrived in his cell about midnight and stayed until 4.30 a.m., asking him about people who had sold him guns.

After a court appearance Manuel returned to the cells and heard that his father had been taken to Barlinnie. He asked to see McNeill, who came with Goodall about 2.30 p.m. Manuel asked whether, if he wrote a statement, his father would be released. McNeill explained that they could not guarantee this, but after consultation with Brown said that if he wrote a statement his father would be brought out of Barlinnie that evening.

Manuel wrote a statement, wording it carefully, but McNeill rejected it, again after consultation, as no good. McNeill then handed him a piece of paper with the words "(1) Anne Kneilands; (2) the Watts; (3) Isabelle Cooke; (4) the Smarts." Manuel wrote that as part of a second statement and added the condition of his father being released. After some demur McNeill accepted the second statement. Manuel, however, refused to sign it until he saw his father.

After another identification parade Manuel was brought back and told his parents were there. He "could hardly get up the stairs for policemen lined up against one side".

Manuel read the statement and after some discussion Goodall said "Go on, tell your mother all about it. Tell her about these murders."

Manuel replied "I am not going to tell her anything of the sort. I am not telling anybody I have murdered anybody."

Goodall then said "The trouble with Peter is that he's crackers. He does not know he is doing these things. He needs treatment, but if he writes a confession he won't go for trial, he'll be certified or something. He is the kind of fellow who can't talk to his own parents. He has it all bottled up and doesn't know he is doing these things."

Manuel was taken away. He again refused to write a statement in spite of the threat to involve his father in the murder charges. He was lodged in Barlinnie and taken out almost immediately. He asked what it was all about and was told that they were going to Baillieston to look for something. They went in a car, Inspector Scott sitting in front directing the driver. After leaving the car at a farm, they walked across a lawn and pasture land and over a hedge. They came to a ditch and jumped over it: Goodall fell in. At a hole in a field McNeill said "That is where you were going to bury Isabelle Cooke, isn't it?"

Goodall started kicking at a brick on a path near the brick-works but McNeill told him it was the wrong place and picked up a shoe, which Manuel did not recognise. He was told it was one of Isabelle Cooke's. Later Goodall picked up another shoe.

In another field Manuel was told he had buried the girl there. The police, however, were at a loss for some time as a stone had apparently been moved. After some digging a shovel broke. McNeill and Goodall took Manuel away to show him where they said he had thrown the girl's handbag. When Manuel denied all knowledge of it, McNeill said "There is only one thing we don't know. We don't know where she died. You are on the spot, you have written a statement. We have nothing to lose. We want to find the actual spot where you killed the girl. We want to see if there is anything lying about."

Back at the field men were digging trenches and cross-trenches. Another man was going over the ground with a mine-detector. McNeill said that he was looking for the Beretta.

At Hamilton, Goodall, who was numb with cold, went to get some tea. They sat until 3.30 a.m., when Goodall produced a written statement and urged Manuel to write one in the same terms. Manuel refused. Brown appeared and insisted on his writing at once. "If you don't I am having no more to do with you. I am going to walk right out of here and I don't care after that if you come to me on your hands and knees and write a dozen confessions. I am going to fix your family for that is the only thing that will make an impression on you."

At last Manuel agreed. He read the draft and made some criticisms, but was told not to worry. "There seemed to be a lot of stupid and idiotic things in it, like murdering people and burying them in parks."

Manuel wrote the statement in presence of Inspector Cleland and Brown took it away. Manuel then told him the story about the Smarts which he had already given in evidence. Brown asked him if he could show where the gun was and Manuel

took him and other officers to the Clyde and pointed out where
he had thrown both guns.

After another identification parade at 11 a.m., Goodall
brought him the second statement (141) for his signature but on
the advice of his solicitor, Mr Ferns, he refused to sign. He also
refused to take part in a further parade about 2 p.m. until he
was satisfied that there was someone watching in his interests.
Afterwards McNeill and Goodall took him to East Kilbride. He
showed them where the Gas Board hut had been and they
showed him the wood where the girl's body was found.

"That, ladies and gentlemen," said Manuel, "is what happened when I was arrested. This attitude the police had developed—I don't know where they got their ideas from—but
it was an odd way to conduct a murder investigation. I was
questioned repeatedly. I was threatened repeatedly. All sorts of
threats were put forward and the most cogent one and the one
I knew was the real one was that this man Brown would, unless
I wrote the confessions, ruin my family. These were his words.
There is no doubt in my mind. This is not the first time I have
been in company of policemen and at that time I was in the
hands of savage and ruthless people. They were determined to
make headway somehow and that was the way they chose. They
told me in no uncertain manner what they intended to do and
what they could do to my family. They said they would cripple
my family—that was said at one point. They said they would
ruin my sister. They kept on that way. That was why I wrote
these confessions—to keep my family out of this. By myself I
would still have been sitting there yet. If they had not done
that they would be there until they grew beards down to their
ankles. . . . My family is just an ordinary family—nice people.
I have given them a lot of trouble. I have given them a terrible
life but at no time would I tolerate getting them into trouble on
my account. I have never run them into trouble and I wouldn't
do it."

The force of this peroration was spoilt by Manuel going back
to deal with two minor points. First, the 'phone call from
McKay which his mother had noted was an invitation to go
to Barlinnie to see a man Morris, who was waiting trial for

sending a bomb through the post. Morris wanted them to give Fox, a prospective witness, "a real doing and land him in hospital so that he wouldn't be able to give evidence at the trial". Second, he had never bought a gun from O'Neil. "If ever I had any connection with guns the last person I would tell about them would be Scout O'Neil. In fact I may as well tell the Chief Constable of Glasgow as tell O'Neil."

And that was Manuel's story. Cross-examination was shorter but covered the main points efficiently. Mr Gillies put the defence case bluntly at the outset.

"Is your position that senior officers of Lanarkshire police and two senior officers from Glasgow have engaged in a criminal conspiracy to give evidence against you?" —"My position is that I told the truth. The three officers concerned are Brown, Goodall and McNeill."

"They compelled you to sign statements which you knew to be false?"—"They weren't false. They were ridiculous."

"They manufactured evidence to implicate you in the discovery of Isabelle Cooke's body?"—"There is no doubt they knew where the body was on the morning I was arrested."

"They led you there thirty-six hours later?"—"Yes, on Wednesday night, Thursday morning."

"There was a good deal of public anxiety about the disappearance of the girl. Do you suggest the police did nothing about it for forty-eight hours?"—"I can't answer for the police. I can only say they knew. It is my conviction they would have left the body for a week or a fortnight under the circumstances in order to get a conviction."

"In order to pin the murder on you?"—"Yes."

"If you agree on that, don't you agree that these police officers have been engaged in a criminal conspiracy to manufacture evidence against you?"—"Yes, I do."

Lord Cameron—"And they manufactured a conspiracy to have you murdered?"—"That is what it amounts to, my Lord."

He agreed that he had been working near where Anne Kneilands was found, that he made statements indicating considerable knowledge of the murders at Burnside, that he lived only about five minutes walk from the Smart house and about a mile and a half from Mount Vernon, that he disposed of a gun after the Watt murders and another after the Smart murders and that he had "scuff marks, not scratches" on his face about the time Anne Kneilands was murdered. He denied making any statements to Goodall and McNeill at East Kilbride.

He went to Dowdall with information about the Watt murders in order to ease his mind, as he did not want to see a possibly innocent man hanged. On the details of the conversations, Dowdall was a liar.

He never kept guns or stolen property in his house; he kept them elsewhere.

He did not shoot a cow on the Saturday before the Watt murders. What happened was that the witness Lafferty and his brother were stealing electric cable. The cable fell on the cow and electrocuted it.

The evidence of Hamilton and O'Neil had been bought by Watt.

In November 1956 he thought Watt might be innocent but "Mr Watt changed my mind. I found him a very arrogant and dangerous man determined to convict someone for shooting his wife. In fact in my opinion he is not quite right in the head."

"Why, when you found a gun in a table at your house, did you not take it to the police?"—"Are you kidding?" [To Manuel, with his long criminal record, the question must have seemed extraordinarily naïve.]

He denied making the drawing of a Webley that Dowdall had produced. Indeed he was very critical of the draughtsmanship and offered to draw a better one.

As for the Houston housebreaking, he bought the camera and gloves from tinkers in the Mail Coach. He had no suspicion that they were stolen.

The whole circumstances of the findings of Isabelle Cooke's grave pointed to foreknowledge on the part of the police. Brown could turn up in a field not directly accessible from the road. This showed he must have known where to come. The police failure to have spades with them proved that they expected just to have to pull back a few furrows, but they had to dig because their marker stone had been misplaced.

On 28th December he was at a cinema. Macfarlane could not possibly have seen Manuel where he claimed to have done. Manuel had laid gas mains there and knew it was impossible.

He got the Beretta he sold Smart in 1956, when he gave another gun for it. He did not steal Smart's car. The remark he made to Brannan about the speed of an A30 had no reference to that. Constable Smith, when he said he had a lift from Manuel, was committing perjury on the instructions of a superior.

The sale of the gun to Smart took place in a public-house "because that is the usual place for such transactions".

He took it that Smart had first shot his wife and son and then himself, but he did not know. He was only reporting what he saw.

The only things he took from the Smart house were the gun and the gloves. He also drank some whisky and opened the salmon for the cat. The money he had was the price of the gun. He did not interfere with the curtains in the house, only the front door, which he entered with the key given him by Smart. Unfortunately he had lost this.

He got rid of Brannan on Hogmanay not because he did not want to see him, but because Brannan was trying to get a bottle of whisky from him. "I had paid him enough. He had been running round with me for six weeks and it was costing me right, left and centre."

Mr Gillies turned to the statements. Manuel denied signing the second and suspected Goodall of forgery. He did, however, sign the other two. "I was seriously concerned about this man Brown and the threats he was making. He was like a lunatic."

It did not seem odd to him, in spite of the police anxiety to extract a confession, that when he sent for McNeill he took three hours to come. "If I had been in his shoes I would probably have said 'Let him roast for a couple of hours.'"

"The reason I confessed was because I was told by Brown that he would arrest my father and charge him with being involved in the Smart murders and that he would arrest my sister Theresa. He had been questioning her about cigarettes and money, and also my mother. He said he would ruin my family."

Again and again Mr Gillies pressed him on this vital point and again and again Manuel repeated his story of threats and conspiracy, becoming less and less likely with each repetition. He eventually said he signed the detailed statement (142) without reading the caution.

"Why did you sign it? Out of the goodness of your heart?" The answer was an apparently calculated outburst which was no more convincing than what had gone before. "It was because a rat of a man was going to ruin my father." A pause, then, spitting each word, "A real rat of a man."

A little later he bragged hotly "I am capable of looking after myself with any amount of police at any time—a dozen Browns, a dozen Goodalls, a dozen McNeills. On my own I can laugh at them."

Quietly Mr Gillies asked "If you can handle dozens of policemen in the way you mention there was no need to make a statement implicating yourself, was there?" Equally quietly Manuel answered "The statement, Mr Gillies, has been explained to you as carefully as I can explain it. I wrote it because my father was under a threat. If that cannot penetrate, I am sorry for you."

Cross-examination was nearly over. "Isn't the position this, that statement 142 is a true statement?"—"No, it is not a true statement. It is a silly statement."

"It fits in pretty well. . . ."—"It fits in with nothing."

"Let me finish the question. It fits in with a good deal of evidence led by the Crown during the past fortnight. Am I to understand that the bulk of the Crown evidence is perjured?"— "Yes, that is why it fits in with the statement."

During the cross-examination, quiet and unspectacular but none the less effective, the conspiracy had grown from a few police officers to the bulk of the Crown witnesses. The jury were being asked to swallow a great deal.

For thirty minutes Lord Cameron questioned Manuel about some points that had been overlooked. Manuel said he got £50 from McKay for the beating up of Fox in Morris' interests. He also had £150 from Watt and money from other, unnamed, sources, so that there was nothing strange in his being able to go round public-houses. He never drew National Assistance except to help Brannan.

Smart said he wanted the gun as there were prowlers about. Lord Cameron asked if there was anxiety in that part of Lanarkshire about unsolved crimes and Manuel proudly answered, "There was anxiety all right. There were about ten policemen watching my house every night."

He did not tell the police what he found in the Smarts' house, because they would not have believed him. Nor did he think they would believe McQuade, his only witness about the sale of the gun to Smart. That was why he threw the gun away. He did, however, tell the police after his arrest when he saw "things were getting a bit tied up".

He thought Constable Smith was mistaken about the lift in the car. "For one thing I would never give a policeman a lift."

"Even if he asked you?"—"He would never get the chance."

"Just answer the question."—"No." Manuel seemed subdued by the almost fatherly manner of the questions.

After dealing with the finding of Isabelle Cooke's shoes and Watt's confession and payment of £150, Lord Cameron turned to the letter Manuel had written Dowdall on 27th November 1957. "You say the subject-matter of the interview may be put down as 'unfinished business concerning a party who to my certain knowledge (and you underline 'certain') has been doubly unfortunate'. Who was the party?"—"That was me I was referring to."

"Yourself?"—"Yes. He had been representing me and had made statements to the police."

"You agreed with the advocate-depute that what you have said amounts to a conspiracy of a very grave criminal kind by three police officers?"—"Yes, my Lord."

"You have also said that you regard yourself as a match for most police officers but that the weapon used against you was the unfair one of pressure on your family?"—"Yes."

"Did it occur to you that if you were being made the victim of a grave conspiracy you could take that fact to higher authority?"—"I had no chance, my Lord, until I had written the statements."

"When you were put in touch with your legal adviser did you point it out?"—"I pointed it out to my solicitor and to my counsel the first time I saw him."

"Then this is not a last minute statement?"—"Oh no."

"And is the reason that you suggest they were doing this a desire to clear up certain grave crimes which were otherwise unsolved?"—"I don't know. I think they just made up their minds to do me. There is no doubt in my mind that McNeill has been gunning for me for years and would do anything to get me."

"You said that several times when you were in company with Inspector Goodall, in particular on the night of 15th January, he expressed the view that you were not wholly responsible for your actions?"—"Yes."

"And that you would receive treatment?"—"Yes."

"And that you didn't know what you were doing?"—"Yes."

"Was that put forward as an additional inducement to make you sign these statements?"—"No, it was not that."

"Have you anything to add to your evidence arising from the questions I have been asking?"—"No, my Lord. There is nothing else."

"Are you quite sure?"—"Yes."

Manuel left the box and once more darted across the court like an insect over the surface of a pond.

CHAPTER 14

THE SPEECHES

After a short adjournment the advocate-depute rose and first laid clearly and fairly before the jury the principles of law they should have in mind. "It is for the Crown, in criminal charges, to satisfy you beyond reasonable doubt that the accused is guilty of the offences with which he has been charged. There is in this case what is known as a special defence. In these special defences the accused has mentioned Charles Tallis with regard to a housebreaking and where the Watt murders are concerned he has named William Watt as the person responsible. It is for the accused to prove these special defences. If you think he has established them—if they even raise a slight doubt in your minds as to the proof of the Crown case—the accused must be given the benefit of that doubt.

"It seems to me that the simplest way to approach this case is by way of the statements made by the accused, because these statements are extensive in character and do perhaps provide the key to the whole case. But there is one thing, before you can accept any statement from an accused person, you must be satisfied that this statement is voluntary. It must be made of his own free will and not made under threats or coercion or anything else. But it is not sufficient to come to the conclusion that the statement is voluntary. A statement made by an accused person outwith the court is not sufficient to convict. There must be outside evidence to corroborate, so to speak, the accused. So if you accept in this case that the statements made by the accused were entirely voluntary in character, you must still go further and

190

look for evidence coming from an outside source which implicates the accused in the charges concerned.

"When you come to consider the evidence, you must consider it separately in the light of each charge."

There could hardly have been a fairer opening or one more favourable to the accused: every word could have been spoken by counsel for the defence. This is in accordance with the best traditions of Scottish—and indeed British—prosecutors.

From general principles, the advocate-depute turned to the statements. There was a direct conflict of evidence between the accused and the police. If they accepted the accused's version the statements were out.

From the beginning, when the accused asked his mother to send for Dowdall, he knew he might need a lawyer. He was frequently reminded of his rights by the police and warned that he need not make a statement but he insisted on doing so. It was clear that the police throughout had in the forefront of their minds the need for fairness to the accused.

In relation to the Kneilands murder the statement was a detailed one. It was corroborated by the medical evidence and by the discovery, just where the accused said he threw the weapon, of a piece of angle iron that fitted the wounds.

The charge was one of capital murder. The jury would convict as libelled if they thought the reason for the murder was an intention to steal the handbag. Otherwise they could convict only of ordinary murder.

The Platt and Martin housebreakings and the Watt murders were to some extent interwoven. Mr Gillies briefly reminded the jury of the circumstances of the Watt case, and then referred to the electric razor found in Manuel's house and the bullet in the mattress, which was linked with the bullets used to kill the Watts. The accused connected Tallis with the razor, but had not impeached him on the Platt charge as well as the Martin one.

Manuel had shown considerable knowledge of the facts of all three cases. There was evidence he had obtained a gun just before: admittedly the witnesses were "not of the highest moral character" but the jury would have to consider whether they had any reason to lie on this matter. He showed a gun to Liddell and told Lafferty the story of the cow. All this evidence pointed to Manuel as the possessor of the gun and exonerated Tallis.

The three cases were linked together by the mode of entry used in the Martin and the Watt cases and by the conditions of the Martin and the Platt houses. Manuel had a very good knowledge of what was going on in the district. He gave Dowdall information that was not publicly known. The gun was found where he threw it. All pointed conclusively to Manuel's guilt.

There was a special defence of impeachment against Watt. He had been arrested and charged and then released, no doubt after full investigation. He had no motive; there was evidence that he and his wife were an affectionate couple. The condition of his car on Monday morning showed there had been no high-speed run to Glasgow and back the night before.

Positive evidence against Watt was said to come from the two men who identified him on the road between Lochgilphead and Burnside. The time factor was against the ferryman, whose evidence was unsatisfactory in many ways. Morrison had no real opportunity of seeing the man in the other car on Loch Lomondside.

The gloves and camera stolen from Mr Houston were found in Manuel's house. According to Brannan, if the jury believed him, Manuel had admitted the crime. They had also to consider Manuel's own evidence and see which story they accepted.

For Isabelle Cooke's murder, he relied on Brannan's evidence about Manuel's reference to a snatch in Mount Vernon, though this involved altering the date put on that remark by Brannan. There was the identification of Manuel by Macfarlane, and there was Manuel's remark to Brannan about the "red herring", which could be explained only on the assumption that Manuel knew where the body was. This was in line with the police account that Manuel led them to the grave. Manuel's version, that the police took him there, was incredible. According to the farmer, there had been no undue police activity in the field before 15th January.

As in Anne Kneilands' case, the question of capital or non-capital murder depended on the object of the killing.

A feature common to the murders of the three girls was the interference with underclothing without sexual interference.

Finally there was the murder of the Smarts, who were last seen alive on 31st December, though one of them at least seemed to have been about until 2 a.m. The evidence against Manuel was the change in his financial position over the New Year and his possession of new blue £1 notes, which he explained as the proceeds of a rather unusual deal with Smart. There was a good amount of evidence about his acquisition of a Beretta, coming from people with prison records. It was for the jury to make up their minds but they should examine that evidence "in perhaps a fiercer light than you would put on the evidence of more honest citizens."

Gibson's evidence suggested a time for the theft of the car. Manuel had been talking about the speed of an A 30 soon after the theft. Constable Smith's lift and the time Manuel was seen getting off the bus coming back from Glasgow both tied up with the finding of the car in Florence street.

The defence was alibi. The evidence needed careful examination in view of the short time involved and the fact that the accused was sleeping, according to himself, downstairs while the rest of the family was upstairs.

Manuel's account of his transaction with Smart about the key of the house was hard to believe, bearing in mind the sort of man Smart was. Further the evidence about the newspapers and letters behind the front door disproved Manuel's story that he entered by that door on Thursday 2nd January.

In conclusion Mr Gillies said "If, after weighing up the evidence of both the Crown and the accused, you think Manuel's story is more likely, then it means that thirty Crown witnesses have given perjured evidence in this court. And that, I would suggest, is unlikely when you consider the witnesses. There were senior Lanarkshire police officers, senior Glasgow detectives, a well-known Glasgow solicitor, Mr Watt and all the others.

"That, ladies and gentlemen, concludes my case."

Manuel followed. His speech was a remarkable performance

N

in many ways, especially for the power he showed of picking up details from the evidence of many days earlier and fitting them together. But that was not enough. He had to convince the jury that he had made false confessions—not once but several times —out of genuine fear on behalf of his family. If he succeeded on that point, no matter what else was left, he had a good chance; if he failed there, he failed altogether.

He dealt with the charges in sequence. First, Anne Kneilands. Admittedly he was familiar with the locality: he had worked near it for some time. Admittedly too he had marks on his face after the New Year. He often had. The police must have been satisfied with his explanation at the time. There was no evidence that the marks were put there by Anne Kneilands. "It is always possible to examine the hands and nails of the girl to see if there are any traces of blood or skin under them. There has been no evidence of that." He denied all knowledge of the murder.

On his alleged confession he made an interesting psychological comment. "There was one thing that I kept in mind when I was writing these documents and it may strike you as being odd. At no stage in these writings is there a description of any of the people who have been killed—not one feature outlined, no colour of hair, nothing. There is no description of any person in this statement. It refers to people—just blank people. You, at this moment, have a case on your hands, but you don't know what Anne Kneilands looked like. The police have not told you what she looked like and the confessions do not tell you what she looked like. If they had been genuine they would have done."

This is an extraordinary criticism. Offhand I cannot recollect any statement by a murderer which described his victim. Indeed it is a common criticism by students of murder trials that the victim remains, after all the evidence, a shadowy figure in the background. Only in detective fiction does a murderer confess in such detail.

He denied all knowledge of the Platt case. The razor was in his house before the housebreaking. He did not impeach Tallis on this charge because he knew nothing about it until the indictment was served. He drew the jury's attention to the technical instruments taken from the house: whoever broke in must have been more interested in such things than in jewellery.

The third charge was the Martin case. There was a special defence of impeachment. "That means that I didn't do it and that Charles Tallis did."

Tallis claimed he "only got a brief swatch at" the rings but he described them in detail. He also claimed he read about them in an evening paper on 17th September, but Miss Martin said she did not know what was missing until 21st September. [This was, as Lord Cameron said, a shrewd point; but it was such a trifling detail.]

The theft of nylons pointed to a woman being concerned.

The Crown case was that whoever broke into 18 Fennsbank Avenue also broke into No 5 and shot the Watts. Therefore if there was reasonable doubt about Manuel's guilt at No 18, there was also reasonable doubt about the Watt murders. It was said that Watt had no motive. "It is obvious that I had even less."

He admitted giving Dowdall information about the Watt murders, but he said nothing about a house at Bothwell and gave no description of the Watt house. Dowdall claimed that he knew nothing about the layout of Watt's house until Manuel told him. "If that is correct, then all one can say is God help his future clients. . . . He has a client charged with the serious crime of shooting his wife, his daughter and sister-in-law. . . . I think if you take into account the calibre of Mr Dowdall as a very busy criminal lawyer, you can accept that there is no doubt that he questioned Watt closely on the layout of his house and would have a clear picture in his mind of what Watt's house was like. If he did not, then William Watt was in serious trouble."

The police actions at the time showed they were satisfied of Manuel's innocence.

Manuel drew attention to Watt's reaction to the news of the murders. Mrs Leitch and Bruce both said he was distraught and in a state of grief and shock. That is what one would expect. His mind would be "just a seething mass of pain, anguish and grief". But "while in that emotional state just before leaving the hotel he took time off to inform a servant that there was an alarm clock in his bedroom."

The witnesses who identified Watt on Loch Lomondside were not dug up by the defence: they were found by the police. Morrison's evidence was consistent with the evidence about the way the lights of Watt's car had been behaving during the week before. There was the ferryman's evidence about the dog. "I do not think there can be much doubt that William Watt, whatever his reason, was on the morning of 17th September away from the Cairnbaan Hotel."

He criticised O'Neil, Hamilton and Campbell, the witnesses to the purchase of the Webley revolver—no difficult task, but the ugly facts remained. But, he said, "If this O'Neil story contained one shred of truth, it would seem that William Watt was prepared to give money to a man who had sold a gun to kill Watt's wife and daughter." The statement that Watt gave O'Neil clothes and money was a very serious one: it explained why O'Neil went to the police with the story.

On the fifth charge, the Houston case, Manuel claimed he was at home that night. He knew the details of a television programme. He bought the camera and gloves at the Mail Coach Inn. He had a suspicion they might have been stolen, but just bought them for his father and sister. If he had suspected any possible connection with a murder, he would not have kept them in the house, as it was clear that he never knew when the police were liable to come to search it.

When Isabelle Cooke was murdered he was at a cinema. Macfarlane claimed he had heard a noise from the railway and then seen Manuel. This was impossible. All his shoes, as the jury could verify from four pairs in court, were soft-soled and made no noise. The place where Macfarlane said he saw him was invisible from the bridge. Macfarlane wore glasses and his eyesight was obviously not good. Further, he said there was a full moon, whereas Douglas Bryden and another witness said it was a dark, windy night.

The disposal of the clothing all over the place was strange. "I think I may assure you if I had killed Isabelle Cooke and taken the trouble to bury her body, I would have buried her clothing and everything connected with her, because if you bury a body the only reason for burying it is to conceal the crime, and to conceal the crime you have to bury everything connected with the body."

The evidence connecting him with the Smart case was "extremely slim". It consisted, originally, of the fact that he spent money in the Woodend Hotel on 1st January. The notes he spent were not produced. All that was said was that the notes in court were like them.

Proof of the theft of the car depended on the witnesses who claimed to have been given a lift but they contradicted one another. It was surprising that nobody had mentioned the car's outstanding feature—not unique but still a novelty—white-walled tyres.

He did not know how the Smarts died, but it was possible that there had been a suicide pact involving also the killing of the boy.

His failure to corroborate his story with the key was immaterial. If he had the key, the Crown would have said he stole it.

The advocate-depute had mentioned the papers and letters lying inside the front door when the police arrived. There was no delivery of either on 1st January, so there could have been nothing behind the door at 4 a.m. on Thursday 2nd January when he went in. [This was quite true, but it was a niggling point compared with the weight of the statements.]

It might seem odd to open the salmon for the cat. "But when you have entered a house and found three people lying dead, there is no accounting for what you may do—especially with a cat running round."

He denied taking the car. It would have been a stupid thing to do in the circumstances.

At last he came to the statements, and virtually repeated his evidence. "The thing I had in my head at that time was the threat, the diabolical threat, by Superintendent Brown to put my father in prison on the charge of being involved in the Smart murders. Brown was assisted in this by McNeill and Goodall. At that time, situated as I was, I had no doubt in my mind that this man would have carried out his threat. He was a savage and determined man and he knew he had to produce some kind of case. He threatened to arrest my mother and my sister."

He pointed out that only one word differed in the versions taken down by McNeill and Goodall of the long verbal statement they said he made about the Smart murders. That sort of thing just did not happen.

The police account of the Mount Vernon search was incredible. Mine-detectors were being used. It was obvious that whoever instructed the "search" knew the girl still had a bracelet on her wrist [this ingenious theory ignores the police explanation that they were looking for the Beretta].

How did Brown arrive on the scene so opportunely without previous knowledge? The official explanation was that he saw lights in a field. But all lights were put out whenever any noise was heard. The police naturally did not want outsiders interfering in what they were doing.

Inspector McNeill was able to point to the right part of the River Calder to search for Smart's keys. At the best, on McNeill's evidence, all Manuel said was, "I threw the keys into the river at the bridge." He did not say which end or which side but McNeill knew just where to go.

He returned from the statements to the money in his possession at the New Year. All Smart's money was in single notes; where did Manuel get the £5 notes he was said to have been spending as well? Another point. "I would have had to be a real idiot to have thrown new money about and walk into a place where I am well-known—I practically live in the place at weekends—and spend that money."

Once more he denied the genuineness of his confessions. "I can assure you I have never been the confessing type and have never been considered by the police to be the confessing type. I have never in my life been in a position where I have supplied a statement to the police. . . . Yet here we have a situation where they say that without pressure I just confessed on my own free will. You must realise that when I was in the hands of the police there must have been some powerful reason for me to write these statements. They don't produce the reason. I do." And out it came again, the old story of fear for his family, relying on the Carrollian logic that what I tell you three times is true.

At the end he came back again to the Watt case and claimed that he had given Watt the benefit of the doubt, which Watt would never give him. "If I had shot the Watts and seen another man arrested for it, it would seem silly to turn round and tell the man's solicitor that he might be innocent or furnish him with the information that might prove his innocence. On the other hand Tallis just sat and kept quiet. I would ask you to keep that in mind.

"There is no doubt that the only person who gave William Watt the benefit of the doubt at that time was me myself. I did it because I thought his lawyer should know, just in case there was any chance of his being innocent. I do not claim that I did it because I felt justice should be done. I simply did it to satisfy myself that there would be no flaw on my conscience.

"In finishing I can only say this. I have not murdered any of these people. I have got no reason to murder any of them. On the question you hear regarding Watt's lack of motive for murdering his wife, I can only say I have even less motive. She constituted no menace to my life.

"I would point out also that whoever went into William Watt's house, there can be no doubt he went in with the specific purpose of shooting the woman, or the women, in the house.

"Thank you, ladies and gentlemen."

And on that enigmatic note he sat down. His speech was an intellectual feat for a largely self-educated man, but that was not what was wanted. No reason or logic or feats of memory could help him. His task was to project to the jury a personality that would make his story seem at least possible and so destroy by doubt the intricate dovetailing of the Crown case.

And he failed even to hold their attention.

CHAPTER 15

THE CHARGE AND VERDICT

WHEN Manuel sat down and Lord Cameron leaned forward to give the jury his directions, the first quietly spoken words brought an immediate change in their attitude from apathy to alertness.

"For the past fourteen days you have been listening to evidence which has covered a catalogue of crime which in gravity is certainly without precedent in this country for very many years.

"There is one unusual feature which has been possibly unique in trials for murder in our courts in Scotland, in that the accused man elected, some distance through the trial, to conduct his own defence. That in itself means that, in considering your verdicts on the eight charges of the indictment, you must scrutinise the evidence with most particular and scrupulous care, because the accused by his voluntary action has deprived himself of the most distinguished forensic abilities and technical skill of the counsel who in the early stages of the trial appeared on his behalf. It means also that the accused is in the hands of the Court, yourselves and myself, and you must see that all points that can properly be made in favour of the accused are given due weight.

"I should add this: that from what we have heard in past days there is little doubt the accused has presented his own defence with a skill that is quite remarkable.

"You are fortunate also in respect that the case for the Crown has been conducted and presented by the advocate-depute and his assistant Mr Sutherland with a care and a skill and a fairness which is in accordance with the high traditions of the Crown Office in Scotland."

The indictment contained eight charges covering a period from January 1956 to January 1958—four charges of capital murder involving eight people, three charges of theft by house-breaking and one of theft of a motor-car. These were formidable enough, but the circumstances and the nature of the charges did not in any way affect the presumption of innocence which the accused in Scotland enjoyed, whatever his character or his demeanour or however grave or trivial the charges levelled against him.

After impressing on the jury that it was their verdict, not his, that was wanted on the facts, he went on: "You must decide this case only on the evidence which you have heard from that witness-box. You will discard, as I have no doubt you will, any feelings of prejudice or bias one way or the other which the narration of the evidence may have engendered in your minds and in particular you must refuse to allow your judgment to be clouded by any feeling of revulsion at the nature of the crimes which you are investigating. Innocent blood has been shed and young lives have been cut short in conditions of tragedy and horror, but neither you nor I are here as avengers of blood. You and I are here as ministers and servants of the law and, I hope, justice."

The Judge then repeated and elaborated the principles of law they had to keep in mind. The burden of proving the case beyond any reasonable doubt lay on the Crown throughout. It never shifted. Further, no charge could be established on the evidence of a single witness, no matter how credible that witness might be. Similarly, no charge could be held proved on admissions made by the accused, no matter how much they were believed, and no matter how often they were repeated. There must always be corroboration in the form of independent testimony, either direct or by way of facts and circumstances spoken to by other persons, which gave positive confirmation.

A good deal had been said, especially by the accused, on

the question of motive. It was not necessary for a prosecutor to prove motive, though it might be helpful to him. On the other hand he did have to prove criminal intention.

He referred briefly to the special defences, which he would deal with in their place. But there was one plea which they could not consider, that of insanity. The catalogue of crimes was so formidable, with so many curious features, that it might be very easy to infer that the person who committed them was not responsible for his actions. But no special defence of insanity had been intimated in the case and therefore it could not be considered.

"The law of Scotland has for long recognised, though other systems have not, that aberration or weakness of mind—mental unsoundness bordering on but not amounting to insanity—may, if established in a case of murder, reduce the quality of the crime from that of murder to that of culpable homicide. I have considered the question most carefully and in the present case, particularly in view of the nature of the charges and in view of the fact that the accused has deprived himself by his own action of the services of counsel and as I feel myself in some measure responsible for seeing that every point that can be put in his favour shall be put, I am not going to exclude that matter from your consideration; though I have little doubt as to what the result will be.

"I will direct you in law, and you must accept my direction, that, if you should come to the conclusion that the accused was responsible for more than one of the killings libelled, multiplication of killings is not by itself a fact or circumstance indicative or inferential of that aberration or weakness of mind, proof of which is essential before you can reach the conclusion that the quality of the crime should be reduced from murder to culpable homicide.

"It is not for the Crown to displace that proof in advance. The measure of the burden which rests on the accused is to satisfy you on evidence and on the balance of probabilities that his responsibility was diminished by reason of an established aberration or weakness of mind—I wish to emphasise the words 'established aberration or weakness of mind'—bordering on but not amounting to insanity, and with an element of mental disease at the root.

"Where can you find in the length and breadth of this case any evidence at all to warrant so merciful a conclusion? No doctor has been called to speak to the matter and in all the years of experience I have had I have never known of a case in which such a plea, when stated by counsel, was not supported by medical witnesses. Not one single witness has said he observed anything abnormal or unusual in the accused's conduct or manner at the times the crimes were committed. I especially asked his father, mother and sister if they had noticed anything abnormal and they replied 'No'. I did that on purpose that this matter should be as fully ventilated as it might be.

"In the past few days you have had a unique opportunity of judging for yourselves whether there is anything indicative of weakness or aberration of mind, and it is only with the greatest difficulty that I have come to the conclusion that I can leave this matter open to you in law. For my own part, I have had difficulty in seeing whether one scintilla of evidence can be found to warrant such a conclusion. A man may be very bad without being mad."

The jury were then directed to consider the evidence in relation to each charge separately. A conclusion of guilt on one charge must not affect their decision on other charges. Some of the evidence might have a bearing on more than one charge; but it had to be considered afresh in relation to each one. There were certain similarities in the circumstances of some of the charges, but it was dangerous to proceed by way of analogy and these apparent similarities and repetitions did not detract from the task of considering each charge separately. Finally, the jury had to reach their own decision and disregard any opinion expressed by any witness. "It is your verdict, not a police officer's verdict."

Next there was the question of the accused's statements and actings—actings which led to the discovery of the two guns, and, if the police were believed, of Isabelle Cooke's grave.

"I tell you as a matter of law that the statements and actings are evidence which you can take into account. But you must consider both the content of these statements and actings and the context in which they were made, emitted or performed. A suspect in the hands of the police is protected by the common law of Scotland from pressure or inducement imposed or offered to extract a confession or an admission. He is protected from cross-examination or interrogation with the same object in view.

"I have decided, after a full hearing, that these statements and actions should be laid before you. It is for you now to judge their weight, whether they were freely and voluntarily given. If you decide that they were made voluntarily and freely they are admissible as evidence. If you are not satisfied that they were freely and voluntarily made, wipe them out of consideration. On the other hand, if you do decide that they represent voluntary statements and are true, then they may lighten your task in reaching a clear conclusion on these grave crimes."

His Lordship referred to the statements said to have been made in the afternoon of 15th January, the meeting of the accused with his parents and the "trail that was to lead to the apparent discovery of Isabelle Cooke's body."

"Two questions arise at this stage. In the first place, was that action of Manuel's, in pursuance of the statement which it is alleged he made on that afternoon when McNeill first went to see him, volunteered without pressure; or was it the action of a man under extreme threat and pressure from the police having the truth extracted, but wrongfully extracted from him; or was it a ghastly farce in which the principal players were McNeill and Goodall, with other police officers in the background, plotting to take Manuel to where they knew the girl was buried? You have to decide that, not me."

It sometimes happened that the police erred in subjecting suspects to pressure and interrogation. But an excess of zeal to extract true information was one thing and a criminal conspiracy such as the accused had alleged to force a confession was another. If the accused's story was true, not only would the senior officers he attacked be unfit to hold their positions but they should be in the dock on a charge of conspiracy to murder. "You have got to weigh not only the content of these statements but their context; how they were obtained; whether they were freely and voluntarily given; or whether, on the contrary, as the accused maintains, they are the fruit of a careful, deliberate and indeed devilish conspiracy to provide a solution to unsolved crimes and to bring an innocent man into the dock on a charge of murder. There is no middle course and you must make up your minds."

The accused said he had no motive to make any statements and that he was not the confessing type. The Crown did not need to show motive, but perhaps the matter was not so motiveless as might appear. The Smarts were shot at the beginning of January, two at least, even on the accused's theory, having been murdered. Their bodies were discovered on 6th January. Eight days later there was the search of the accused's house. When he was asked to go to Bellshill, he was alleged to have said "You haven't found anything yet." ("One unfortunate word—yet," commented his Lordship.) The warrant referred specifically to articles believed stolen from the Smarts' house. At the police station, the accused was confronted with McKay; he was identified by Macfarlane; the Egans identified him as having had the Smart money on 1st January; he knew the Smarts had been shot with a gun which had been in his possession. "Would there not be ample motive for his realising that the game was up?" There might have been extreme pressure leading to the statements, but not pressure by the police, the pressure of events.

A decision on this vital question might help to solve others, such as the credibility of the police witnesses and of the accused himself and others, like his parents. His father in particular was an important witness in relation to other charges, such as the theft of the razor from the Platts' house and the alibi for the Smart murders.

Before coming to the individual charges, he restressed the need for independent corroboration: thus statements made by the accused to Watt or Dowdall could not corroborate the statements to the police, though they might have a very considerable bearing on the weight and credibility of these statements.

The first charge was that of the murder of Anne Kneilands. There could be no doubt that she had been brutally and savagely murdered. But that was not the question. Was there sufficient evidence to bring home guilt to the accused? After a review of the evidence, his Lordship came to the conclusion that, apart from the confessions, the evidence did not even create a suspicion against the accused. There was therefore no independent corroboration. In the circumstances, he directed them in law that, even if they believed the confession, there was insufficient evidence which could be regarded as positively incriminating evidence from an independent source. That being so, the Crown had failed to prove murder against the accused. "On my direction you will return a formal verdict of not guilty."

The charge of theft by housebreaking from the Platts' house at Bothwell was in itself a minor one but might have a bearing on a very much more serious charge. There were no footprints or fingerprints linking the accused with the house and the Crown relied on identification of the electric razor and of the bullet in the mattress. The bullet according to the experts was fired from the gun used in the Watt murders. According to Dowdall—"a very experienced man, a criminal lawyer of wide practice and high reputation"—Manuel had told him in 1956 about a housebreaking at Bothwell where a bullet was fired from the gun later used in the Watt case. He also told Watt the same story. How did he know? The bullet was not found by Mrs Platt until the end of 1957.

According to Manuel the story of the bullet was told him by Tallis—"the man whose name runs, not as a golden thread, but as a scarlet thread, through the case." Where did the razor in Manuel's house come from? Again Manuel said Tallis. In this he was supported by his mother and father—Mr Manuel, who had got into trouble for not being frank about the gloves. The jury had to decide which story to believe.

Next came the Martin charge and the first of the special defences, that impeaching Tallis and Mrs Bowes. "A special defence of any kind brings with it a burden of proof which lies on the shoulders of the person accused. The measure of that burden is different from and less than that which lies on the Crown. In order to satisfy you that the special defence has been made out, it is only necessary that the accused should demonstrate the truth of the defence on a balance of probability, which is a very much less onerous burden than to prove it beyond all reasonable doubt. If a special defence is made out, there is no question of guilt."

They should first consider the special defence. In evidence the accused said Tallis showed him the two rings. Against that there was his version of the Watt murder in statement 142, which referred to No 18 Fennsbank Avenue. Tallis and Mrs Bowes contradicted him, and it might not be likely that they would have chosen the wedding weekend for this housebreaking. If the jury believed Tallis and Mrs Bowes, there was an end of the special defence. But if they did not believe them, that did not mean that it was established. They still had to weigh the evidence of the accused. If they accepted this, the Crown could not overcome the presumption of innocence, and therefore could not prove the charge. Equally, this would be the case if the jury were left in such doubt that they could not say where the truth lay.

"What can the Crown rely on here? There is no fingerprint, no footprint, no stolen property identified as being in the accused's possession at his house. There is nothing, absolutely nothing beyond his own statement of association which I have just read to you. Where is the corroboration? So far as I can see, the only element on which the Crown can rely is the evidence of Miss Martin and of Tallis. Miss Martin described the rings in detail and Tallis described in detail what he says occurred on the 17th of September—the day following the Burnside murders."

He went on to consider and deal fully with the "very shrewd point" made by Manuel about the discrepancy between Tallis' story of what he read in the newspaper and Miss Martin's evidence about when she found the rings were missing.

There was also Dowdall's account of what Manuel told him. The jury might be left in doubt, but if they disbelieved Manuel and accepted his statement 142 and could find corroboration in Tallis, there was enough for conviction. They should, however, consider well whether it would be safe to convict. If they were left in reasonable doubt, they should acquit.

The fourth charge—the Watt murders—was in a different position from the Kneilands charge: murder by shooting was always capital murder. There was again a special defence and the onus was on the accused in this respect. It was a brutal and horrible crime and if Watt was guilty it would be even more brutal and horrible. But such things did happen. They had to consider, first, his demeanour when told the news, weighing the evidence of Mrs Leitch and Bruce against that of Sergeant Mitchell.

So far as time went, it was possible for Watt to have got from Lochgilphead to Glasgow and back again. He next reminded them of Morrison's evidence. He personally would have had grave difficulty in accepting an indentification on such a basis. Then there was Taylor, who identified both Watt and the dog. But he volunteered that the car was a Wolseley; if this was so it was not Watt's car. The jury had to make up their minds. It was significant, and in favour of the defence, that nobody had come forward to say that he had been on the ferry about that time with a black dog. But "mistakes of identification do take place and they have led in the past to very great miscarriage of justice."

If the jury accepted the evidence that Watt's car was covered with frost on Monday morning, that was against the view that he had been driving all night.

The matter did not end there. There was Manuel's story that Watt confessed to him and said he had given the gun "to whom? To Charles Tallis." This was possible—but what an extraordinary thing!

If on the balance of probability they held that the special defence was made out, that was an end of the charge and they would find the accused not guilty. Even if they believed his own evidence about Watt's confession, they should acquit.

But could they believe his evidence? There was the evidence of Lawrence Dowdall and John Watt about Manuel's apparent knowledge of the interior of William Watt's house. Again, Manuel seemed to have changed his mind about Watt's responsibility between 1956 and today.

Manuel had declared that he had no motive. There was,

however, a passage in Watt's evidence which might explain this, namely Manuel's story that Hart, Tallis and Mrs Bowes meant to break into the Valentes' house and were misled by seeing the girl Valente in Watt's house. "If that story about the girl Valente is true, you have a motive here. The motive was the cracking of a safe. The tragic mistake may have saved the Valentes from slaughter but it led to the deaths of Mrs Brown, Mrs Watt and Vivienne Watt."

[Lord Cameron did not mention that Mrs Valente had said that there was no safe in her house. It is, however possible that yet another mistake was involved in Manuel's story, as there are two householders named Valente in Fennsbank Avenue.]

If the jury did not accept the special defence, that did not mean that the opposite was the case. But the Crown evidence was formidable. The bullets which killed the women were fired from a Webley, which the accused admitted disposing of in the Clyde. If the evidence of O'Neil and Hamilton was accepted, he got it for a criminal purpose about nine days before these things happened. Could the jury accept that evidence? "One of your difficulties in this case is that so many of the witnesses are stained with some sort of crime."

There was no doubt that Watt took O'Neil to the police to make a statement; there was no doubt that he gave him £1 and a suit. "It may well be that O'Neil is of such a type that his evidence can be purchased for 6d, let alone £1 and a suit."

But they did not have to rely on that evidence alone. There was Liddell, to whom Manuel showed a gun in the Crook Inn; and there was Lafferty, to whom he told the story of the cow, which Manuel now suggested had been electrocuted. A cow did die that weekend. These witnesses might add support to the veracity, which might otherwise be doubted, of O'Neil and Hamilton.

If they accepted Manuel's confession and the Crown evidence there was sufficient corroboration. If they were satisfied on the special defence, they would acquit. They would also acquit if they were left in doubt. There was one qualification. If, having come to the view that the accused shot the women, they also found that there was evidence of mental disorder present

o

at the time of the shooting to reduce the crime from murder to culpable homicide, the verdict should be one of guilty of the lesser crime. "But I am bound to tell you that if it were my responsibility, which it is not, I cannot in my conscience see where that evidence lies."

Fifth, there was the theft from Mr Houston. The gloves and camera stolen from his house were found in Manuel's. "It is entirely a matter for you. If you accept Brannan, then there is evidence on which you can find Manuel guilty. If you are left in doubt about Brannan, there is not sufficient evidence to find Manuel guilty."

The sixth charge, that of murdering Isabelle Cooke, was uncomplicated by any special defence and the issue was the straightforward one whether the Crown had succeeded in proving the charge beyond reasonable doubt.

The foundation of the case was what the accused had said and written. If this was rejected, the whole case went. But if the statements were accepted as true and voluntary, the jury still had to find corroboration. In the first place, there was the evidence of Macfarlane, for what it was worth; they might think he had not much opportunity for accurate identification.

Much more formidable and damaging was the evidence, if believed, of the finding of the shoes. "Were they found as Inspector McNeill and Inspector Goodall say they were? Or were these shoes found by the police because they knew where they were and took the accused there for that purpose? If they were were found honestly, in the sense that the accused took the policemen there, then that is the very type of thing that is corroborative of a confession. It is one of the external circumstances in the confession which is supported by the finding in the presence of the police of one of the things which the guilty man must have put there.

"It does not end there. There is the finding of the body. You must have been struck by the almost picturesque and macabre story of the finding of the body, how they came along in the dark on that cold January night, the accused handcuffed to the two inspectors, how they came to the place, crossed a ditch, and how the accused takes his bearings by a particular tree, walks up the field and then stops and says 'I think she is here; I think I am standing on her.'

"It is for you to judge whether that is true or false. If it is false it is a falsehood which has been concocted with devilish artistry; if it is true then it is a damning piece of evidence in corroboration of the accused's admission because nobody but the guilty man knew where that wretched girl's body was buried. And don't forget the uncompleted grave of which the accused gave Inspector Goodall warning."

If they believed that evidence there was ample corroboration. But they must not forget the accused's evidence that he was at the pictures.

He reminded them of the question of diminished responsibility. He also reminded them that the charge was one of capital murder. If they believed Brannan's story about the snatch, there might be evidence on which they could hold that the intention was to steal the handbag; but "you may be well advised, if you come to the conclusion that the accused is guilty of murdering Isabelle Cooke, to refuse to take the further step of convicting him of capital murder. It is for you to say."

Finally, there were the Smart charges. There was no room for doubt that the Smarts were shot dead and, if shot dead by murder, that was capital murder. There was no doubt, on the expert evidence, that the gun used was a Beretta. On his own admission that gun was in the accused's possession until 31st December and it was thrown by him into the Clyde after the murders. There was no doubt either that he was in possession of new banknotes issued to Mr Smart. He did not admit this to the police when his house was searched, saying that the reason was that they would not have believed him. On his own admission, again, he was in the Smarts' house after the shootings. There was little doubt that the deaths took place on 1st or 2nd January.

There was a special defence of alibi. If they accepted the defence evidence on this, or if they were left in doubt, they must acquit. Proof of the alibi really depended on Samuel Manuel and James Manuel, up to 5.45 a.m.

The distance from Fourth Street to Sheepburn Road was

short and even a small error in estimating time would throw the alibi out. They had therefore to consider the evidence very carefully. But even if they rejected the corroborative evidence, if they believed the accused's story, they would acquit.

Manuel's story about the sale of the gun to Smart was extraordinary, but it was possible. One party to the transaction was dead and could not corroborate it. "The witness McQuade, whose appearance and demeanour may be a very ample certificate of his character, was employed for the price of a drink to scout against the unwanted attention of police officers."

One thing led to another and Smart gave Manuel the keys of his house "to enable Manuel to act as what? Host to a business acquaintance who was to have an important meeting with Smart on Friday, whose movements were such that he could not be contacted and whose name was the not uncommon one of Brown."

It was for the jury to consider. If they believed the accused's denial that he was there at the time of the shootings they would acquit.

In support of the story about Mr Brown, Manuel could point to the evidence of the Leonards that they saw a light on the Friday night. But did that square with the presence of the papers and letters behind the door on Monday morning?

If they rejected Manuel's story, they still had to consider whether the Crown had proved the case. First, there were two statements by Manuel, the verbal one and No 142, both detailed. If the verbal statement was not made as recorded then McNeill was guilty of more than perjury.

Was there corroboration? There was the evidence about the pistol—Manuel's apparent familiarity with the weapon, its finding in the Clyde and the evidence from the Gordon Club witnesses about its acquisition. The accused admitted an association with McKay "for the purpose of engaging the accused to attack a certain gentleman who might give evidence in a trial in which another gentleman was involved, so that injuries would be caused which would keep him in hospital for a considerable time."

There was the accused's possession of Smart's money. There

was the car, found where Manuel said he left it. There was the lift to Constable Smith and there was Manuel's reference to Brannan about the speed of an A 30.

If they believed that, there was sufficient corroboration. Against this, the accused said that when he went to the house, the family were all dead and there was a gun in Smart's hand. There was a point in his favour there, for the main reason for excluding suicide was the absence of a gun and Manuel's story explained this. It opened the door to speculation and meant a double murder and a suicide for no apparent reason. As in all the charges, they must give the accused the benefit of any reasonable doubt.

He would not detain them long over the theft of the Smart car. They had the evidence of Brannan and Constable Smith.

Once more he stressed that the burden of proof lay on the Crown. The burden of proving a special defence was less than that lying on the Crown and, even though a special defence was rejected, there might still be enough to cast doubt on the Crown case. But "if the evidence on any of these charges, however grave, leaves no room for reasonable doubt, then your duty in accordance with your oath is to bring in a proper verdict, however grave or serious the consequences may be".

On the first charge they would return a verdict of not guilty. On all other charges, their verdict might be guilty, not guilty or not proven. All could be unanimous or by a majority. On the charges of murder by shooting a verdict of guilty would be guilty of capital murder or, technically, of culpable homicide. On the sixth charge, if they found that the accused killed Isabelle Cooke, the verdict might be guilty of capital murder, murder or culpable homicide. If they accepted the special defences, they would find the accused not guilty and if they had reasonable doubt the verdict would be not proven.

"Members of the jury, I have no doubt that as you have followed the evidence over these past many days with anxious care you will decide this case with courage and resolution and not shrink from the consequences of your verdict in accordance with your duty, if you see your duty lies in a certain direction. I must ask you now to retire to consider your verdict."

The jury retired at 2.24 p.m. and returned at 4.45. Their verdict was, as directed, "not guilty" on the Kneilands case but "guilty" on all other charges, except for the Houston housebreaking, where they found the charge "not proven". In the case of Isabelle Cooke, they convicted the accused of murder only. In all cases, the verdict was unanimous except in the Martin case where there was a majority verdict.

The advocate-depute having moved for sentence on the murder charges only, Lord Cameron pronounced the death sentence sombrely but clearly: "Peter Thomas Anthony Manuel, in respect of the verdict of guilty of capital murder and of murder done on a different occasion, the sentence of this court is that you be taken from this place to the prison of Barlinnie, Glasgow, therein to be detained until the 19th day of June next and upon that day, in the said prison of Barlinnie, Glasgow, and between the hours of eight and ten o'clock, you suffer death by hanging; which is pronounced for doom."

With the last words the black tricorn hat was swept up for a moment to rest on the Judge's wig. Some women moaned. Manuel was taken from the dock to the cells below.

Turning to the jury, Lord Cameron thanked them for their careful and discriminating discharge of their onerous public duty. In view of the length of the case, he would give instructions that they should be released for life from further liability for jury service. Then with a word of thanks to the magistrates of the city, to which Bailie James Bias replied, he left the bench.

His first murder trial as a Judge was over. It is hard to conceive of a more difficult initiation; and hard also to imagine the task better done. Throughout the whole trial he was firmly in control and he controlled it in the great Scottish tradition of fairnesss. When the accused dismissed his counsel, Lord Cameron unhesitatingly shouldered the additional burden which that placed on his shoulders and Manuel, in a sense, had the great criminal experience of Sir John Cameron, QC, Dean of the Faculty of Advocates, at his service. He and the Scottish legal system were alike fortunate in that fact.

CHAPTER 16

THE APPEAL

BEFORE the date was fixed for his execution Manuel appealed against his conviction and won a temporary respite. For a while there was speculation whether he would conduct his appeal himself or once more have the assistance of counsel. Finally it was announced that the Dean of Faculty had nominated Mr R. H. McDonald, QC, who took silk in 1957 after a busy eleven years at the junior bar. Mr A. M. Morison, who had been junior at the trial, was junior at the appeal also.

The grounds stated were six in number:—(1) That the alleged confessions, both written and verbal, should not have been admitted as evidence; (2) that there was misdirection as to the burden of proof in relation to all the special defences; (3) that the verdict in respect of the third charge (the Martin case) was contrary to the evidence; (4) that the jury were misdirected on the subject of motive in respect of the fourth charge (the Watt murders) in reliance on the uncorroborated evidence of William Watt; (5) that there was unfairness in reviewing the evidence of the witnesses Taylor and Morrison, adduced for the pannel (accused) in support of the special defence to the fourth charge; and (6) that there was misdirection in classifying, in respect of the sixth charge (the Cooke murder), the finding of the shoes and body as independent evidence sufficient to corroborate the alleged confession.

The first ground was obviously the most important. If it succeeded, certainly none of the murder convictions, capital or otherwise, could stand. The second, if upheld, would result in

Manuel's avoiding the death sentence, as both convictions of capital murder were on charges involving special defences. The rest were of minor importance. Even if all were upheld, there would still stand the conviction of the capital murders of the Smart family.

The court which heard the appeal consisted of Lord Justice-General Clyde, Lord Carmont, the senior Scottish Judge, and Lord Sorn. The Crown was represented by the Lord Advocate (Mr W. R. Milligan), QC, Mr Gillies and Mr Sutherland, and the appellant, as already stated, by Mr McDonald and Mr Morison.

When the court assembled on Tuesday 24th June, the public seats and those reserved for members of professional bodies were packed. One seat was empty, that in the dock, where all eyes had expected to see the already legendary Peter Manuel. Mr McDonald told the court he had advised his client that it would not be in his own interests to be present. He submitted that it was competent to hear the appeal in his absence. The court agreed; and a great deal of the public interest at once evaporated.

Mr McDonald began by briefly recounting the history of the case—the indictment, the special defences, the trial, the verdict and sentence. The minor grounds of appeal, for example that relating to the Martin case, had been included because they might have a bearing on the more important grounds. It was in any case open to a convicted person to have a conviction quashed, if unwarranted, even though no sentence had been imposed. After summarising the grounds of appeal he said he would leave the first ground until the end, arguing the other five in order.

First he contended that, by overemphasis, Lord Cameron might have persuaded the jury that an accused person had to prove his special defence to win an acquittal. In support of this he quoted passages from the charge to the jury and complained that it had not been expressly put to them that an accused person might be acquitted, even though he had not established his special defence. In some cases, as in the Smart alibi, the charge gave too much prominence to the special defence.

The Martin verdict was contrary to the evidence. The Judge

had almost directed the jury that there was insufficient evidence to convict. The only possible corroboration was the evidence of Charles Tallis, and that could not stand. Further passages from the charge were read to show this.

When he came to the fourth ground, Lord Clyde asked in some bewilderment what it meant. Mr McDonald seems to have shared this difficulty. He said that the grounds of appeal had been framed before he came into the case and he would explain what his understanding of it was. This was that it referred to Watt's evidence about the girl Valente having been seen at Watt's window and having thus misled the murderer into believing that Watt's house was the Valente house where lay the safe with the £5,000. This had been, on the Judge's part, an excursion into the realms of speculation as to motive. If the court thought that he had speculated to an excessive extent that would be a reason for quashing the conviction.

Lord Cameron had dealt at some length with the identification of Watt by Morrison and Taylor and stressed the peril of mistaken identification. While that in itself might not be particularly open to criticism, the Judge had not been nearly so careful in dealing with the alleged identification of Manuel by Macfarlane, whose evidence he just said the jury could take "for what it was worth". It was unfair to devote several pages to criticism of the defence witnesses and only half a dozen lines to Macfarlane. Lord Cameron had been more than stringent in his comments on Morrison and Taylor and shown a lack of impartiality.

The finding of the shoes and Isabelle Cooke's body, as described by the police, did not amount to independent corroboration of Manuel's statements. They were simply part of his actions and no more than an extension or repetition of the statements.

On the main ground of appeal, the admissibility of the statements, counsel submitted that no statement was admissible which was elicited from a person detained by the police under suspicion if there was any form of inducement causing the statement to be made. Evidence about such a statement must make it quite clear to the Court that there was no room even for doubt on the question of inducement. If there was room for doubt, the statement must be excluded.

In this case there had been inducement; at the worst for his argument there was room for doubt. Mr McDonald outlined the history of the statements which, he claimed, bore internal evidence of some kind of bargain. It was significant that the terms of the bargain they suggested were carried out, when Manuel's father was brought to see the appellant and was later released.

Where grave crimes were concerned, the police should be very cautious even if a suspect seemed anxious to make a statement. It would be better if no such statements were made except before a neutral person such as a magistrate.

If inducement had once been used no number of formal warnings could remedy the situation.

The test was always fairness to the accused. In determining whether any statement passed that test, regard must be had to the nature and gravity of the charge, the mental and physical capacity of the prisoner, the time and place of the statement, and the persons present, whether or not the prisoner was legally represented and whether or not he had any access to the outside world. During the critical period in this case, apart from the brief visit from his parents, the appellant saw no one but the police. He knew his father had been arrested but he did not know exactly on what charges.

McNeill's evidence showed quite clearly that Manuel, though arrested at first on a comparatively trivial charge, was under suspicion for all the murders for which he was eventually tried. He was kept under very close observation, every movement as he lay asleep being recorded. The Court might well think that this was part of a deliberate breaking-down process.

The police had exceeded all the bounds of fairness. It was very significant that this out-of-character remorse should have visited him only at a time when he was in custody and without access to the outside world.

"These considerations paint a picture which leads one to the conclusion that the statements were not made voluntarily or they at least leave the matter open to grave doubt. Having regard to the fact that the case, as the trial Judge described it, was unusual and indeed unique, the police should have taken steps to see that no statement was taken unless before a neutral person such as a magistrate. If your Lordships were with me on this submission in relation to ground of appeal No 1, it would result in the conviction being quashed in respect of every charge except possibly the theft from Douglas Drive, Bothwell."

After a brief conference on the bench, Lord Clyde did not find it necessary to call on the Lord Advocate to reply, but at once delivered judgment dismissing the appeal. In recognition of Mr McDonald's "conspicuously clear and cogent speech" and of the service which he had so faithfully performed, Lord Clyde did not merely give the conclusion which the court had reached on each ground of appeal but dealt with the arguments submitted in support of each. In this he followed the order in which counsel had dealt with them.

The trial Judge, in dealing separately with each of the special defences, pointed out quite clearly how limited a burden of proof lay on the accused; he had gone further and stressed each time that, even if the special defence failed, the Crown could not succeed unless their evidence satisfied the jury beyond reasonable doubt of the guilt of the accused. "We are quite satisfied that there is no substance whatever in this ground of appeal."

On the appeal in the Martin case, it was true that there was some difficulty in reconciling Tallis' evidence with that of Miss Martin. But this was placed very fairly before the jury by the Judge and, though the evidence was thin, there was enough to warrant the jury finding the charge proved.

On the question of a possible motive for the Watt murders, the court saw nothing wrong in the Judge putting the evidence before the jury. He had properly left to the jury the task of deciding what inference to draw from that evidence.

Again, the trial Judge had been amply warranted in drawing the attention of the jury to the vagueness of the evidence about the identification of Watt by two defence witnesses. A Judge had more experience than they had and there was nothing wrong in his laying that experience before them as long as he made it clear, as Lord Cameron did, that they and not he were the final judges on this question.

The Court rejected the submission that the finding of Isabelle Cooke's shoes and her body were so interconnected and interdependent with the statements as to afford no independent corroboration. A passage from Alison's Criminal Law might have been written with this case in mind: "If a person is apprehended on a charge of theft and he tells the officer who seized him that if he will go to such a place and look under such a bush he will find the stolen goods, or if he is charged with murder and he says he threw the bloody weapon into such a pool in such a river and it is searched for and found, without doubt these are such strong confirmations of the truth of the confession as renders it of itself sufficient, if the *corpus* is established *aliunde*, to convict the prisoner." The presiding Judge's charge in this respect therefore was perfectly proper and correct.

On the first and most important ground of appeal, Lord Clyde said: "The law of Scotland goes further than many other legal systems in protecting a person who is detained by the police from any risk of being driven or cajoled or trapped into admissions of guilt, even though this might complicate the quite legitimate detection of crime by the authorities. So anxious is our law to secure that such persons get fair play under our system of criminal administration and so firmly rooted in our law is the principle that no man is bound to incriminate himself. But, although this is all true, there is nothing to prevent a man who is detained by the police or who has been charged with a crime from making a voluntary statement to the police if he chooses to do so. It is perfectly proper that such a statement, if made, should be proved in evidence to the jury as one of the factors for them to consider in deciding whether a crime has been committed. But the test is always whether that statement was fairly obtained. To be a voluntary statement which can be proved before a jury, that statement must have been freely given, not in response to pressure or inducement and not elicited by cross-examination other than by what is directed simply to elucidating what has been said."

In several past cases the difficulty arose in regard to the fairness of questions put by the police. But here no questions were put and the argument was that the statements were inadmissible as having been obtained by inducement, in that the appellant had been promised that if he made them his father would be freed from the charge or charges hanging over him. In deciding the question the presiding Judge followed the course laid down in the case of Chalmers and the propriety of so doing was not and could not be challenged.

The appellant and his family had given evidence on this. But their picture had been so extravagant that the Judge had had no hesitation in rejecting it. He had seen and heard these witnesses and an appellate court could not differ from his conclusion. The appellant had therefore to rely on the police evidence to make out his complaint. But each of the officers emphatically denied any pressure or inducement. It was further clear that they could not make a bargain such as was suggested, as the appellant's father was out of police control and in the hands of the procurator-fiscal, an independent authority.

It was clear that on each occasion the initiative came from the appellant and not from the police, who warned him each time of the inadvisability of making a statement and of the dangers involved. They quite definitely discouraged him from making a statement and went out of their way to try to get a solicitor for him.

"The appellant was thirty-two years of age. He was in good health and, on the evidence, in full possession of his faculties. The evidence to which we have listened on this question of the circumstances surrounding the confessions has satisfied us that he was fully and rationally aware of what he was doing and deliberately made up his own mind to unburden his soul of the dark deeds which he narrated with such convincing detail in statement 142. We can find no evidence of any inducement, far less threat or pressure, from the police. On the contrary, their conduct in this difficult and anxious episode is a model of propriety and fairness.

"It may be that the appellant confessed to his crimes because he was afraid his father might otherwise be implicated in them, but this is no evidence of inducement by the police to make a confession. At the best for the appellant, it shows that he may have been induced to make the statements by a feeling of remorse for what he had done and the desire on his own not to implicate others in the crimes which he had committed. In these circumstances the evidence led before the presiding Judge amply justified the course which he took in allowing the confession evidence to go before the jury and this first ground of appeal accordingly fails."

In conclusion, Lord Clyde emphasised that all material facts relating to the different issues were fairly put before the jury for their consideration and that no advantage of any kind had been taken of the apellant's decision in the course of the trial to conduct his own defence.

The court fixed Friday 11th July as the date for execution of the death sentence already passed. There was no reprieve and Manuel's life ended at one minute past eight on that morning.

CHAPTER 17

SOME PROBLEMS

THE result of the trial and of the appeal was, on the whole, greeted soberly by the Scottish press, a very proper pride in the conduct of the trial mingling with disquiet about some of the facts that had emerged in its course. Two years had elapsed between the murder of Anne Kneilands and Manuel's arrest. Was police organisation adequate, in the light of modern techniques, to prevent multiple murders? To put it bluntly, assuming that Manuel did kill Anne Kneilands, had the lives of the Watts, the Smarts and Isabelle Cooke been lost because of inefficient investigation?

Secondly the trial revealed in Glasgow, as probably in all large cities, a sinister underworld, where crime was regarded as normal business and where guns passed from hand to hand in public-houses with a casualness that in some ways was more alarming than a regular trade in such weapons would have been. This world had been perhaps suspected by some but undreamed of by most of the respectable citizens; but none could now be blind to the truth.

Then there was the problem of Peter Manuel himself. What sort of a man was he? Were there others in our midst? What could be done to prevent a successor indulging in the same kind of terrorism? Had his earlier criminal career been treated too leniently—or too severely?

These are all grave problems which need a far fuller treatment than can be given here. But a book of this type would lose most of its point if no attempt were made to put forward some suggestions for the consideration of the general public.

First, the police problem. In the second sentence of the book I described the investigation as "patient". Patience is doubtless a virtue but excess of it may become a vice. Was the police investigation into the Anne Kneilands murder too patient?

Some criticisms can easily be made. One was made by Manuel himself in his closing speech to the jury: "It is always possible to examine the hands and nails of the girl to see if there are traces of blood or skin under them. There has been no evidence of that." There were signs that the girl had fought for her life. In such cases, nails are a common weapon and it seems an obvious thing to take scrapings from under them. Such examination may prove negative; if so no harm has been done. But it may provide specimens of skin and tissue and possibly fabric for laboratory investigation. These are perhaps unlikely in themselves to give a lead towards a suspect; but once other evidence has been obtained sufficient to justify police action and an individual comes under serious suspicion, they may prove invaluable pieces of legal evidence for the trial.

According to James Hendry, who was at the time head of the Lanarkshire CID, writing in the *Glasgow Evening Citizen* on 3rd July 1958, Manuel came very soon under suspicion because of his working in the district, his previous record, the scratches on his face and his unusually subdued behaviour after the New Year holiday. It is not impossible, and one can put it no higher, that scrapings from the dead girl's nails might have provided another link between her and Manuel.

There is another curious gap in the evidence. Whoever killed Anne Kneilands must have had his clothing stained with blood from the savage battering the girl's head received. Now Manuel's clothing was taken away from his house on 12th January 1956 for examination but there was no evidence at the trial of the result of any test. Similarly there was at least a possibility that the killer of the Watts and the Smarts might have got some blood on his clothes. There was evidence that Manuel's clothing was removed in November 1956 and again on 14th January 1958 but no evidence of any tests having been made.

It is, however, clear from the list of productions which was, in accordance with Scots practice, appended to the indictment, that there were several reports by Professor Allison and Dr Imrie which were not spoken to by these witnesses at the trial. These cannot be made public, but it is not beyond conjecture that they may have referred to examination of Manuel's clothing on these occasions. Indeed such a surmise is even probable.

If that is so, the further surmise may be made that the tests on each occasion proved negative. Such a result would not prove innocence as there was ample time, for example, to destroy clothing between 2nd January 1956 (Anne Kneilands' murder) and 14th January 1956. One might have expected a negative result to have been disclosed in the fair way in which the Crown brought out the negative fingerprint evidence from the Martins' and the Watts' houses. But it must be kept in mind that the evidence in fact led was voluminous enough without introducing purely neutral evidence. It should also be remembered that, when Professor Allison and Dr Imrie were giving evidence, Manuel was still represented by counsel, who, of course, had access to these reports and could have put them to the witnesses if they thought fit; on the other hand, when the fingerprint expert was in the witness-box, Manuel was conducting his own defence. The difference in dealing with the medical reports and the fingerprint evidence, on this view, would be an example of the way in which the Crown refused to take advantage of the accused's decision to dispense with the services of counsel.

In a trenchant report on the case, John Gordon Westland, formerly chief superintendent of the City of Aberdeen CID, cites as an axiom of crime investigation that "it is impossible for the criminal to approach the scene of the crime, commit the crime and depart, without leaving some traces of his passing". He then poses the question "Why is there undetected crime?" and answers it: "Because the investigators are not yet for various reasons efficient enough to find the traces and deduce from them facts beyond reasonable doubt, which will solve the mystery and bring the criminal to book."

That inefficiency may be either blameworthy or blameless. If techniques have not yet been evolved for detecting certain

P

traces, that may be inefficiency but blame can hardly be attached to the investigators. But where recognised techniques are not used, some explanation and improvement are called for.

Westland's report states that the Scottish detective training school functions at present only for four weeks in each year, catering only for a few officers at a time. He comments, "This is ridiculous." It is hard to disagree. True, academic training never made a detective and there is no substitute for hard practical experience; but the modern detective has to have some knowledge of a wide range of subjects—at least enough to know how the specialist experts work, how to use their services, what questions to ask them and how to provide the necessary raw material for their investigations.

A suggestion for improving the present police organisation which has been made by Westland and others is that there should be a central Scottish CID, perhaps on the lines of the FBI in the United States. This is a controversial matter. "Regionalisation" is a dirty word to many police officers, who believe that the whole work of the police is better done locally, co-operating with neighbouring forces in emergencies. There is force in both arguments and certainly local knowledge is essential. A centralised body could not have the personal knowledge of and familiarity with local characters and conditions which a local force possesses. But local forces cannot maintain the specialist services that exist, for example, in Glasgow. While the larger forces are always ready to give assistance, some of the smaller forces seem at times reluctant, because of jealousy or mistaken local pride, to call on them. If a central reserve were set up to provide the highly skilled auxiliaries needed in most local forces, local patriotism would be less offended by the presence of strangers. A rule might be established that the central CID (or even, in the existing organisation, a larger force like Glasgow or Edinburgh) should automatically be called in where murder and perhaps other grave crimes were concerned and such a rule also might help to avoid the feeling that a confession of failure was somehow involved in the use of outside assistance.

If a central CID were set up, it could usefully be linked with a more continuously working detective college and also with the universities, who would have to provide, as they do at present, their distinguished scientific evidence.

It seems clear from the evidence that in the end Manuel owed his conviction to his own statements. Detectives must, of course, pay attention to such statements. But they are an uncertain foundation on which to build a case, in view of the jealousy with which the law protects suspects and accused persons. There have been a number of cases where convictions have either not been obtained, or, if obtained, quashed on appeal, because the Crown has relied too much on statements that did not satisfy the stringent tests laid down by Scots law. In a case in 1954, the late Lord Justice-General Cooper, who had often expressed uneasiness about the practice of relying largely on voluntary statements, suggested revival of the system that prevailed before the Criminal Evidence Act of 1898 allowed an accused person to testify on his own account, namely that such statements should be made before a magistrate or a Sheriff. The suggestion was repeated by Mr McDonald in his argument on the appeal. There is a lot to be said for this and it would come near to providing the required assurance that the accused has made his statement quite voluntarily and in full awareness of his rights. It would not altogether prevent the making of a statement induced by promises or threats; but it would give more assurance than the present system. I do not wish to suggest that statements now are wrongly elicited as matter of routine. But in some cases there are grave doubts.

These are not questions to be settled lightly. They require considerable thought and study.

Next, there was the problem of the Glasgow underworld. It is not a problem, as revealed at the trial, of gangsterdom. None of the criminals who appeared in the witness-box seemed the kind to make good gangsters in any proper sense of the word, Manuel himself perhaps least of all. The organisation which is implied in the word "gang" calls for certain virtues of loyalty and discipline which these people, fortunately for society, lack. It was reported after the trial in several papers that, at various stages of his life, Manuel tried to break into the organised large-

scale crime in London but failed. He was a bad security risk.
He talked too much.

The Glasgow problem is rather that of a sizable shifting and
shiftless population, which does not consider any other way of
life. It is not in the main a question of poverty or even inability
to earn a living in a normal way, but a disinclination to work.

There is nothing glamorous or spectacular about the inhabi-
tants of this world. In their earlier years some—but only some
—affect a certain smartness (or oversmartness) in their appearance and have a certain intelligence. But this lasts very few of
them beyond their early thirties. Even Manuel, whose neatness
and intelligence impressed those who saw him in court (and it
was not just an act put on for the occasion), showed signs after
his conviction of physical and mental degeneration. This may
have been an attempt to sham mental illness or even, as has
been suggested, to induce it in order to escape hanging. But it
is more probable that an inevitable process had been acceler-
ated by his realising that his career had come to its end. Two
photographs in George Blake's *Trials of Patrick Carraher* in
the Notable British Trials series, one showing Carraher at the
age of thirty-two and the other at forty, reveal the physical
collapse brought on by a life of imprisonment interrupted by
short hard drinking bouts.

The causes of crime have not yet been properly investigated
in this country. But to a large extent they seem to be a matter of
environment, of social example both in the home and among
neighbours. Some districts seem to breed criminals, others do
not. This is not just a question of old and new houses, of con-
gested slum areas contrasted with more spacious modern housing districts, for some of the latter have already records that
compare with the worst of the old. It may even be that some
of the new housing areas encourage criminality by destroying
the sense of belonging to a community which exists in a district
that has grown up gradually over many years to be a distinctive
unit and, in the real sense, a neighbourhood.

Basically the problem is not one for the courts. It is a social
problem. The courts can deal only with the misfits, potential
or confirmed, who cannot or will not find a settled place in our

society. What is needed is some way of fitting them into society before their criminal careers start.

Finally there is the individual problem of Manuel himself. After his trial accounts of his short life story appeared in several newspapers in more or less lurid detail. The general picture is clear.

He was born in Manhattan on 15th March 1927. In 1932 the family returned to Scotland, which they had left in search of prosperity and security, and settled in Motherwell. In 1937 they moved to Coventry. In October 1939, Peter Manuel was put on probation for twelve months for breaking into and stealing from a cycle dealer's shop near his home. Five weeks later he appeared before the same juvenile court for housebreaking and was sent to an approved school. He escaped and there followed a monotonous series, at intervals of only a few months, of an offence (usually housebreaking and theft), apprehension, return to an approved school, escape, offence, return. On one occasion he was guilty of a vicious assault with a hammer in addition to his usual theft. In all he was returned to an approved school eleven times by the end of 1942.

Just before Christmas 1942 he escaped again. This time he attacked the wife of a school employee, robbed her and indecently assaulted her. He was eventually caught; he had been hiding in the school chapel behind the backcloth of a Nativity scene for over a week, coming out at nights to forage for food and, on one occasion, to steal a suitcase belonging to a visitor to the school. In March 1943 he was sent to Borstal.

On his release in 1945 he rejoined his family in Scotland, where they had returned after being bombed out of Coventry in 1941. Soon he went to Blackpool, where he found easy money and a society not unlike that of Graham Greene's *Brighton Rock*. In August 1945 he was acquitted on a charge of burglary there.

Soon after his return to Scotland once again he was sent to prison, in March 1946, for one year on fifteen charges of housebreaking: this was at the age of nineteen. While he was serving this sentence, he was convicted in the High Court in Glasgow on a charge of rape and sentenced to eight years imprisonment.

He was one of the youngest prisoners ever sent to Peterhead. In spite of violent conduct, he won remission and was released in the summer of 1953.

Not long afterwards he met a girl from Carluke and became engaged to her. A revealing story is told about him at this time. He bought an expensive engagement ring, then took it back on some pretext and substituted a much cheaper one for it. That was bad enough, but it might have been the act of a merely stupid young man. But Manuel boasted publicly of his trick.

The engagement was broken off after the girl received an anonymous letter, which some say came from Manuel himself, painting a lurid picture of his past, partly true, partly fictitious. On the day that had been arranged for the wedding, he appeared in Airdrie Sheriff Court to defend himself successfully on a charge of indecent assault.

Anne Kneilands was murdered on 2nd January 1956 and the Watt family on 17th September 1956.

On 2nd October 1956, Manuel was sentenced to eighteen months imprisonment for housebreaking at Hamilton. He was thus, by a coincidence too strange for invention, in Barlinnie prison at the same time as William Watt, who had been arrested on 27th September.

Manuel was released on 30th November 1957. On 8th December Sydney Dunn, a Newcastle taxidriver, was found shot through the head and with his throat cut, near his deserted taxi on the moors at Edmondbyers on the border of County Durham. On 28th July 1958, after Manuel's execution, a coroner's inquest found that he had murdered Dunn.

Isabelle Cooke was murdered on 28th December and the Smarts on 1st January 1958.

In addition to these nine murders, it was reported in the *Sunday Pictorial* that shortly before his execution Manuel confessed to three more: Helen Carlin ("Red Helen"), a prostitute found strangled in Pimlico in September 1954, Anne Steele a fifty-five-year-old spinster battered to death in Glasgow on 11th January 1956, and Ellen Petrie ("English Nellie"), who was stabbed in Glasgow on 15th June 1956.

It is an appalling record for a man of thirty-one. But it is typical (except perhaps in degree) of the aggressive psychopath and there is little doubt that that is the appropriate label to hang on Manuel. It does not, however, explain matters. The causes of such a condition are as yet largely unknown and it is not yet possible to treat psychopaths, except the very young, with any real hope of success. They are the victims not so much of a disease as a deformity; they are born lacking any social or moral sense.

Before his trial, Manuel was examined by doctors, including eminent psychiatrists and neurologists, on behalf of the Crown and presumably found sane and fit to plead. The defence also had him examined, with a view to putting forward a special defence of insanity, but could not find support. They also considered putting forward a case of diminished responsibility, as explained to the jury by Lord Cameron, but were dissuaded from doing so by their client who told them, with genuine laughter, that he "wanted nae mair o' that insanity business". It may be said that a plea of diminished responsibility, based on his being a psychopath, would not have availed him. It was put forward in 1946, in the case of Patrick Carraher, when Lord Justice-General Normand observed, "Much of the evidence given by the medical witnesses is, to my mind, descriptive rather of a typical criminal than of a person of the quality of one whom the law has hitherto regarded as being possessed of diminished responsibility." This case, of course, relates only to the Scots common law. In England, the doctrine of diminished responsibility was introduced by the Homicide Act of 1957. By section 2(1), a killer is to have the quality of the crime reduced to manslaughter if he was "suffering from such abnormality of mind (whether arising from a condition of arrested or retarded development of mind or any inherent cause or induced by disease or injury) as substantially impaired his mental responsibility for his acts and omissions in doing or being a party to the killing". In the case of John Francis Spriggs in 1958, the Court of Criminal Appeal held that it was sufficient direction to a jury for the presiding judge simply to lay the words of the statute before them and that it was not for him to define or re-define the definition given by Parliament. Further, it was not for him to attempt to draw nice distinctions between intellect and emotion. It is therefore possible that in England a psychopath might be held by a jury to be of diminished responsibility because of "abnormality of mind . . . arising from . . . any inherent cause", although the Attorney-General assured the House of Commons that one purpose of the retention of the death penalty in section 6 of the Act for persons who had been convicted of murder done on a different occasion was to punish the multiple murderer, like Haigh and Christie. It is therefore a possible result of the attempt in section 2(1) to equate the English and Scots law that English law is now less draconian than Scots where it was formerly more so.

Not all psychopaths become criminals; indeed many geniuses, reformers, successful business men have something of the same kind in their make-up that urges them roughshod over all who seem to stand in their way. But where the condition is allied with criminal tendencies, his complete lack of self-control and regard for the rights of others makes the psychopath an extremely dangerous criminal, and an unpredictable one. Most criminals tend to stick to their own trade, picking pockets, safe-blowing or whatever it may be. The psychopathic criminal is not so inclined to specialise.

There is, however, one feature of such criminals which often, as it did with Manuel, leads to their downfall. They are, even more than other criminals, vain of their exploits and are for ever boasting about them. They must always be the centre of attraction. If nobody knows about their crimes, they lose their savour. That is why they often talk. In the nineties, Thomas Neill Cream, chosen by Miss Tennyson Jesse in her *Murder and Its Motives* as typical of the murderer driven by a power lust, was a victim of this characteristic when he wrote letters to prominent London citizens accusing them of the murders of the prostitutes whom he had killed. In one instance, that of Matilda Clover, none but Cream knew she had been poisoned, for the death certificate bore that death was due to *delirium tremens* and syncope. In the present century, Neville Heath showed the same trait when he wrote to Scotland Yard after the murder of Mrs Margery Gardner, saying that he had the whip with

which she had been beaten and that he would send it to the
police. Incidentally, Manuel showed other points in common
with Heath. Both had the habit of displaying medals and claiming service to which they were not entitled. Both had sexual
perversions: Heath was a sadist, Manuel possibly a sadist and
almost certainly a fetichist.

Peter Manuel belongs quite clearly to the psychopaths. Not
only in the statements to the police that were produced at his
trial but in his conversations with Lawrence Dowdall and
William Watt he behaved characteristically. The same behaviour can be found in his previous history. Sometimes he
claimed knowledge of or responsibility for crimes with which
he had nothing to do. He claimed (to the police) that he was
concerned in a £40,000 bullion raid at London Airport in September 1954 and that he was the brains behind a bank robbery
that cleared £55,000 in Glasgow in 1955. He also claimed inside
knowledge of the disappearance of Burgess and Maclean. And
these are only examples of the lengths to which he was driven by
his vanity, which would not suffer others to enjoy the limelight
while he remained in obscurity.

It has been suggested that the police eventually used this
feature of his character to catch him. In the earlier cases, he
had been a prominent suspect and he may well have been grati-
fied by the attention paid to him. Further, frequent questioning
may have given him hints as to the amount of information
which the police already had and the way in which their minds
were working. The suggestion is that when the Glasgow CID
were called in, Superintendent Brown decided to leave Manuel
alone for a week. This annoyed him and kept him on edge. The
psychopath is not a contemplative type and is far happier in
actively pitting his often considerable wits against the police.
Some confirmation for this view may come from Manuel's examination of Inspector McNeill, when he almost complained
that he had not been investigated immediately after the disappearance of Isabelle Cooke. Then without warning Brown
pounced in the early hours of 14th January. The sudden altera-
tion of stresses may have driven Manuel into speech. Sooner or
later, however, he would probably have talked to some one else

—even a police officer—disclosing things that only a guilty man could know. But this might have taken some time and other lives might have been lost in the interval.

It is likely that Manuel realised the tactics used to catch him; he may even have accorded them in his twisted mind some grudging admiration. He told the advocate-depute in cross-examination that he was not surprised when McNeill did not answer his summons for some three hours: "If I had been in his shoes, I would probably have said 'Let him roast for a couple of hours.' "

Manuel's reading was extensive, his favourite subjects being the lives of the more notorious American gangsters: the boy from Manhattan hankered to occupy the same niche in the hall of disfame. But one wonders if he ever thought of British criminals, and in particular of Frederick Field, when he made his statements. Field confessed in 1933 to the murder of Nora Upchurch, who was found strangled in an empty building in October 1931. At his trial the prosecution relied almost entirely on that confession but Field withdrew it and pleaded not guilty. He was acquitted. In 1936 he confessed to another murder, that of Beatrice Sutton. He again withdrew the confession but this time there was more evidence against him and he was convicted and hanged. Did Manuel think of the first and forget the second trial? Or did he simply, like so many of his kind, think he could get away with it?

There is no doubt that Manuel did think he was too clever for the police, especially those of Lanarkshire. This is apparent throughout a series of six articles contributed by ex-Superintendent Hendry to the *Glasgow Evening Citizen* during the week beginning 30th June 1958. It is equally apparent in Manuel's conduct of the trial—particularly in his calling Mr Hendry as a defence witness. It is apparent in the words he put into the mouth of Superintendent Brown when he came to give his own evidence: "You have got these people bamboozled. You twisted that fellow Hendry round your little finger." (It is probable that many of the remarks attributed by Manuel to the police merely represented what he thought of himself.)

His amused tolerance of Hendry is in sharp contrast with the vindictiveness with which he referred throughout to Brown and Goodall, particularly the former, to whom he knew quite well his conviction was largely due. He tried once to make Goodall ridiculous; that was when, in describing the trip to Mount Vernon, he referred to the crossing of the ditch and said, after a slight pause to draw attention to it, "Goodall fell in."

This ridicule of those he felt responsible for his position was apparent throughout his evidence. Brown raved like a lunatic. Brannan was a sponger and a chicken-hearted squealer, hysterical with fear at the thought of being associated with the Smart case. Watt did not seem right in the head. Dowdall was incompetent—"God help his future clients." These are a few examples of the same approach. The aggressive psychopath wants to hurt. He does not care how much he hurts or whom he hurts, so long as he hurts or destroys. That may also explain why William Watt was recalled to give evidence at the end of the Crown case.

Could Manuel's psychopathy and its probable development have been recognised and halted at an earlier stage? In some legal systems provision is made for a very full psychiatric examination of some criminals. This may last for several weeks and as a result there is considerably more material available than there is in Britain to assist in the final decision of the court. In some American states, for example, it is obligatory to have such an inquiry before sentence in all cases of felony. It is at least possible that, had such a system of thorough examination been in use in England at the end of Manuel's approved school career, or in Scotland when he was convicted of rape in 1946, his condition would have been ascertained and its probable development foreseen.

Diagnosis and prognosis, however, are one thing; treatment is another. The practical question to be answered is, supposing a successful diagnosis and prognosis had been made, could the natural downward progress have been halted? Could the later crimes have been prevented? This seems in the highest degree doubtful, although successes have been claimed in Sweden, where ten psychopaths were convicted of murder between 1930 and 1945, seven of whom were released by 1953. For many years there has been no example in Sweden of a murderer once released repeating his crime. But even in Sweden it does not seem that their methods prevent non-homicidal recidivism, which is, as in all countries, a far greater problem numerically. It may well be that these psychopathic murderers are too few in number to permit of any safe inferences being drawn: after all, the multiple murderer is comparatively rare in any country, although it must be admitted, that of all killers, the psychopath is the type most likely to repeat his crime.

It seems to be a general characteristic of psychopaths that they do not learn from experience, so that reformative treatment is usually lost on them and they are not deterred by harsher punishment. All that can be done with any certainty is to try to prevent them from committing further crimes and to protect society against them. The death sentence is one method of doing this: but this cannot prevent the first murder or, under the Homicide Act of 1957, the first two murders, unless the first is itself a capital murder, as being done in furtherance of theft, or by shooting or an explosion, or in the course of resisting arrest or escaping from custody, or on the person of a police officer or prison officer. What we are seeking is some method whereby, if Manuel's probable development had been foreseen before murder was committed, it could have been halted and even the first murder prevented. The only course seems to keep such a person detained, either in prison or a special institution, for the term of his natural life or to impose a sentence of indeterminate duration, which would be subject to review by the Court with suitable expert advice or by some other body, probably after a minimum period, in the event of the psychopath being cured. And quite obviously, for the protection of society, that cure would have to be beyond doubt. Such treatment might seem more savage than present-day methods, as it could involve life or indeterminate sentences for comparatively trivial offences: not all offences committed by psychopaths are serious, and we are now dealing with psychopaths who have not yet committed murder.

In the present state of psychiatric knowledge, it is probable that indeterminate sentences would in most cases involve detention for life. The alternatives therefore seem to be the death penalty, if the psychopath is allowed to go on until he commits capital murder, or detention or imprisonment for life, if he commits non-capital murder or some lesser crime. It is primarily a problem for the psychiatrist to resolve this dilemma, which means for the courts a choice between two policies of seeming despair. There may be a gleam of hope in some exceptional cases on record in America, where psychopathic or "mad dog" killers have reformed even in the unhelpful atmosphere of prison. One, quoted in Playfair and Sington's *The Offenders,* is Joseph Redenbaugh, who was sentenced in 1917, at the age of nineteen, to imprisonment for life for one murder and thirty years imprisonment, to follow that sentence, for another. This was in Minnesota, a state where the death penalty for murder has been abolished. He is still in prison and two applications for parole have been turned down. But he seems to be one of the rare men on whom prison has had a genuinely reforming effect: it may be that he was not so completely psychopathic as his career would give one to believe.

Another, but more fortunate, example is Nathan Leopold who, at the age of nineteen, pleaded guilty in 1924 to the kidnapping and murder, along with his eighteen-year-old friend Richard Loeb, of fourteen-year-old Bobby Franks in Chicago. All three were sons of millionaires. The murder, which has been described as "foul, savage, senseless, barbaric, indefensible, motiveless, contemptible", was committed primarily for the sake of the thrill it gave its two depraved perpetrators. They were fortunate in escaping the death sentence, which was within the court's discretion on both charges, kidnapping and murder. Instead they received sentences of imprisonment for life for kidnapping and ninety-nine years for murder. Richard Loeb was murdered in prison in 1936. Nathan Leopold was paroled in February 1958, a reformed character. Cases such as his and Redenbaugh's, where reform was achieved in spite of rather than because of prison life, raise sharply the question whether an increase in the use of psychiatric treatment could cure the potential murderer and thereby prevent murder.

There are difficulties. The general feeling of society is against such a reform and there would probably be a great outcry against "letting criminals off" and complaints about the expense involved. It would be expensive, of course. Psychiatric treatment would have to be available at all stages and in all methods of dealing with offenders—at the stage of probation, in the approved schools, in Borstal, as well as in prison and in special institutions. But every offender cured of his criminal tendencies is a positive gain to the community. Crime costs us high enough already in every way; and orthodox methods of punishment in prison are expensive methods, both for their intrinsic cost and for the fact that prison life—indeed institutional life generally, as in Borstals—seems to act as a training-ground for new crime. Probation, approved schools and Borstal training had no reformative or deterrent effect on Manuel; neither had prison or the fear of the death penalty. It is at least worth considering whether a new approach is now called for.

The case of Peter Manuel is unique not for any single feature, except perhaps the dismissal of counsel in the course of the trial —and even that was to be repeated on 3rd June 1958 by an eighteen-year-old youth, David Dennis, at his trial for capital murder at Lincoln Assizes. What makes it truly unique and important is the way in which it gathers together in one trial features that have made celebrated many other trials. It is just because Manuel is so typical of one kind of murderer—perhaps a little larger than life, but still typical—that he poses so sharply and so challengingly the problems which he does.

POSTSCRIPT

My thanks are due to the Lord Justice-General, Lord Clyde, and to Lord Cameron, who read over in MS the chapters dealing with the appeal and the charge respectively. I was also greatly helped by Mr Harald Leslie, QC, Mr R. H. McDonald, QC, and Mr Gordon Gillies (now also QC, and Sheriff-Substitute at Lanark).

The Justiciary Office, Edinburgh, have been unfailingly helpful.

I should make it clear that this book is the story of a trial; it does not claim to tell the story of the crimes with which that trial was concerned. That fuller story will not be written for many years, if indeed it is ever possible to find out anything like the whole truth.

Even as an account of a trial, the book is necessarily incomplete. The trial lasted for sixteen days and the appeal proceedings for another two. During those eighteen days, Judges, counsel and witnesses spoke some 700,000 words—about eight times the length of this volume. I hope, however, that my summary is a fair one. I have tried to give the words of the principal actors as much as possible.

J. G. W.

December 1958